The Keyword Series

Keywords Science

Lydia Radford
Ruth Davies

Peppermint Publications Limited

Published by Peppermint Publications Limited
6 Chestnut Road
Cimla
Neath
SA11 3PB.

ISBN 0-9545097-2-2

Introduction
During a History exam, a student was having difficulty answering a particular question. The question paper asked, 'What primary sources of evidence explain the events of 1066?' Unfortunately the pupil didn't understand the keywords 'primary sources of evidence'. Although the student knew all about the Battle of Hastings and the events of 1066, she found it difficult to answer the question. If she had been familiar with the keywords she would have been able to answer the question with ease. How frustrating for both pupil and teacher. Teachers are so busy teaching the syllabus that many perceive time taken specifically teaching the reading, understanding and spelling of keywords to be a waste of valuable time. However, a little time spent teaching keywords will greatly improve teaching and learning and exam results. The Keyword Series will help you to effortlessly teach the reading, understanding and spelling of keywords.

Why are keywords important?
Why do pupils fail? Pupils often fail because they don't have access to subjects. This is sometimes due to their reading ability in that subject and/or understanding of the vocabulary used. The more access a student has to a subject the better his/her performance will be. Therefore it is imperative that students are able to read, understand and spell keywords in that subject. An extensive vocabulary provides students with the tools they need to communicate effectively, when writing and speaking. Their ability to read and understand the keywords in a subject greatly enhances their ability to succeed.

Link with National Curriculum
All keywords have been carefully selected in line with National Curriculum requirements. They have been divided into two categories:

Subject Specific Keywords – These words permeate the whole of the subject. For example 'evidence' in History. They need to be fully understood by students as quickly as possible and are vitally important as they provide the key vocabulary on which the whole subject hangs.

Topic Specific Keywords – These words generally only occur when studying a particular topic within the subject. For example 'longship' if studying the Vikings.

Using The Keyword Series as part of a whole school literacy initiative
It has long been established that whole school literacy initiatives have a very positive effect on pupils' learning. It is important therefore for schools to introduce a whole school approach to the teaching of specific reading skills in each subject. A whole school initiative to learn keywords can easily be implemented using The Keyword Series.

Differentiation
It is important that all pupils work at a level that enables them to learn, achieve success and reach their full potential. Many worksheets are presented at two levels. A=easy / B=average.

Special Educational Needs
Provision for pupils with special educational needs is a matter for the school as a whole. All teachers are teachers of pupils with special educational needs. For pupils with SEN, the learning of keywords can be incorporated as part of their IEPs.

Teachers' Notes

How to use The Keyword Series

- Introduce the concept of keywords to the class. Explain the difference between subject/topic keywords.
- Introduce students to the first group of five words and explain/discuss the definition. Begin by teaching the reading and understanding of the keyword. Correct spelling, whilst highly desirable, is secondary to the understanding of the keyword.
- When all fifteen have been introduced start using the appropriate worksheets and doing the suggested activities.

Additional suggestions for teaching keywords

- Display keywords in the classroom. Use The Keyword Series wall charts.
- Organise the class into groups. Using the current group of keywords the class is learning, ask each group to write down the fifteen words from this group. As soon as one group completes their list everyone has to stop writing. Points are awarded according to the number of correct words (less any misspelled).
- Use mnemonics to help with the spelling of keywords. Organise the class into groups. Each group is given a keyword from the group currently being learnt. Each group devises a mnemonic for that keyword.
- Find synonyms for keywords.
- Oral quiz at the end of each lesson. Make it fun. Students stay in set teams to try and beat others. This gives a sense of competition and will encourage students to learn the keywords and their definitions. Ask additional related questions. In English, for example, if the keyword is 'metaphor', ask pupils to give examples of metaphors for bonus points.
- In pairs, pupils have to write down the current fifteen keywords being learnt with definitions. Give them ten minutes. At the end of the time pairs swap sheets. One point is awarded for each keyword and definition (must be written out properly). The pair with the most points wins.
- Play card games using The Keyword Series card games.
- Involve parents. Students take keyword lists home and parents test them. Students can use The Keyword Series student dictionaries for use at home and in the classroom.

Have Fun!

Contents

General Terms

Keywords in Science

experiment	A test to find something out.
apparatus	Things needed to carry out an experiment.
method	An orderly way of doing something.
result	What happens at the end of an experiment.
conclusion	Things that can be worked out from an experiment.
fair test	Controlling some of the things used or done in a test so they do not change.
reliable	Things that can be taken to be true.
variables	Things that can change during an experiment.
reaction	Something that happens in response to something else.
process	A number of actions for making or doing something.
observations	Things that can be seen.
function	The special purpose or use of something.
evidence	Anything that gives a reason to believe something.
formula	A way of writing scientific information using letters, numbers and signs.
catalyst	Something that speeds up a reaction or change without being used up.

General Terms
Matching

Link the keyword with the correct definition.

experiment	Things that can be worked out from an experiment.
apparatus	The special purpose or use of something.
method	A way of writing scientific information using letters, numbers and signs.
result	A test to find something out.
conclusion	Things needed to carry out an experiment.
fair test	What happens at the end of an experiment.
reliable	Something that happens in response to something else.
variables	Things that can change during an experiment.
reaction	An orderly way of doing something.
process	Something that speeds up a reaction or change without being used up.
observations	Anything that gives a reason to believe something.
function	Controlling some of the things used or done in a test so they do not change.
evidence	Things that can be seen.
formula	Things that can be taken to be true.
catalyst	A number of actions for making or doing something.

General Terms

Choose the Word

experiment	A (*question, trial, test*) to find something out.
apparatus	(*Things, Test tubes, Chemicals*) needed to carry out an experiment.
method	An (*easy, orderly, odd*) way of doing something.
result	What happens at the (*end, beginning, middle*) of an experiment.
conclusion	Things that can be (*spread, worked, pulled*) out from an experiment.
fair test	Controlling some of the things used or done in a test so they do not (*remain, stay, change*).
reliable	Things that can be taken to be (*true, untrue, punctual*).
variables	Things that can (*explode, change, dissolve*) during an experiment.
reaction	Something that (*dissolves, melts, happens*) in response to something else.
process	A number of (*actions, objects, instructions*) for making or doing something.
observations	Things that can be (*heard, felt, seen*).
function	The special purpose or (*colour, use, weight*) of something.
evidence	Anything that gives a (*clue, tip, reason*) to believe something.
formula	A way of writing (*scientific, specific, symmetric*) information using letters, numbers and signs.
catalyst	Something that (*slows down, speeds up, stops*) a reaction or change without being used up.

General Terms

Wordsearch

e	x	p	e	r	i	m	e	n	t	r	t	o	w	a
z	x	c	v	b	n	m	j	h	g	f	d	b	s	p
m	c	o	n	c	l	u	s	i	o	n	s	s	d	p
e	e	r	r	e	s	u	l	t	z	x	c	e	x	a
t	z	f	a	i	r	t	e	s	t	z	x	r	s	r
h	q	a	s	d	f	g	h	h	h	h	g	v	e	a
o	x	z	r	e	l	i	a	b	l	e	z	a	x	t
d	v	a	r	i	a	b	l	e	s	e	r	t	p	u
p	o	i	u	y	t	r	e	w	q	a	s	i	d	s
r	e	a	c	t	i	o	n	d	f	g	t	o	c	z
z	p	r	o	c	e	s	s	z	x	c	v	n	v	c
c	v	f	u	n	c	t	i	o	n	v	c	s	d	s
a	s	d	f	g	h	j	k	l	n	b	v	c	x	z
e	v	i	d	e	n	c	e	f	o	r	m	u	l	a
z	x	c	v	c	a	t	a	l	y	s	t	b	b	v

experiment	apparatus	method	result	conclusion
fair test	reliable	variables	reaction	process
function	evidence	formula	catalyst	observations

Extension exercise:

What reaction would you expect if you added sodium to water?

General Terms

Wordsearch

e	x	p	e	r	i	m	e	n	t	s	a	s	d	f
a	s	d	f	g	h	c	c	v	f	u	g	t	r	d
d	q	w	s	e	d	a	c	r	f	t	t	g	y	h
o	r	a	s	d	f	t	o	g	h	a	j	e	k	l
h	l	e	k	j	h	a	n	g	f	r	d	v	f	s
t	s	a	s	z	x	l	c	c	v	a	v	i	o	c
e	p	o	i	u	u	y	l	y	t	p	r	d	r	e
m	e	r	t	y	l	s	u	u	y	p	h	e	m	f
b	v	c	x	z	s	t	s	a	s	a	s	n	u	a
v	b	r	e	a	c	t	i	o	n	b	v	c	l	i
d	f	r	t	h	p	r	o	c	e	s	s	e	a	r
f	u	n	c	t	i	o	n	r	t	y	u	i	o	t
r	e	l	i	a	b	l	e	b	v	g	h	j	k	e
v	v	a	r	i	a	b	l	e	s	s	d	f	v	s
o	b	s	e	r	v	a	t	i	o	n	s	v	g	t

experiment	apparatus	method	result	conclusion
fair test	reliable	variables	reaction	process
function	evidence	formula	catalyst	observations

Extension exercise:

What reaction would you expect if you added sodium to water?

General Terms
Jumbled Sentences

Unjumble the words to give the correct definition. The underlined words are in the right order.

experiment	A test find to something out.
apparatus	Things needed out to carry an experiment.
method	An doing of orderly way something.
result	What an the at of happens end experiment.
conclusion	Things out can an that be from worked experiment.
fair test	Controlling some the in done so they do of test used a things or not change.
reliable	Things taken can that be be to true.
variables	Things can during that change an experiment.
reaction	Something that happens response in to something else.
process	A number or actions making of for doing something.
observations	Things can that be seen.
function	The purpose special use of or something.
evidence	Anything gives that believe a reason to something.
formula	A way scientific letters, of numbers writing information using and signs.
catalyst	Something that up reaction a or without change being speeds used up.

General Terms
Jumbled Sentences

Unjumble the words to give the correct definition.

experiment	*find out to a test something*
apparatus	*needed an things out experiment to carry*
method	*doing an of orderly something way*
result	*an what the at experiment of happens end*
conclusion	*out things can an that be experiment from worked*
fair test	*the some in controlling done so they change not do of test used a things or*
reliable	*taken things can true that be be to*
variables	*can during things that experiment change an*
reaction	*happens that something else response something in to*
process	*number a or actions making something doing of for*
observations	*can things seen that be*
function	*purpose the special something use of or*
evidence	*gives anything that something believe a reason to*
formula	*scientific a letters of and signs numbers writing information way using*
catalyst	*up used something up reaction that a or without change being speeds*

General Terms

Code Breaking

A	B	C	D	E	F	G	H	I	J	K	L	M	N	O	P	Q	R	S	T	U	V	W	X	Y	Z
z	y	x	w	v	u	t	s	r	q	p	o	n	m	l	k	j	i	h	g	f	e	d	c	b	a

Decode the CAPITAL letters to find each keyword.

1. Z p p Z r Z t u s
2. X a t Z l y H t
3. V x p e I R N e n t
4. N e G S o d
5. I e s F l t
6. X o n X l u H R o n
7. U a R I G e s t
8. E a r R Z b l e H
9. V E R d e n c V
10. I e l R Z b l V
11. K I o c e H H
12. L b s e r E a t R o n H
13. f F n c t R o n
14. r e Z c G R o n
15. U o r N u O a

Extension exercise:

Do plants need light to grow?
Explain how you would set up a fair test to find out.

Word Group: Subject Name:

General Terms

Code Breaking

A	B	C	D	E	F	G	H	I	J	K	L	M	N	O	P	Q	R	S	T	U	V	W	X	Y	Z
z	y	x	w	v	u	t	s	r	q	p	o	n	m	l	k	j	i	h	g	f	e	d	c	b	a

Decode the CAPITAL letters to find each keyword.

1. Z K K Z I Z G F H
2. X Z G Z O B H G
3. V C K V I R N V M G
4. N V G S L W
5. I V H F O G
6. X L M X O F H R L M
7. U Z R I G V H G
8. E Z I R Z Y O V H
9. V E R W V M X V
10. I V O R Z Y O V
11. K I L X V H H
12. L Y H V I E Z G R L M H
13. U F M X G R L M
14. I V Z X G R L M
15. U L I N F O Z

Extension exercise:

Do plants need light to grow?
Explain how you would set up a fair test to find out.

General Terms
Cloze

experiment	A t________ to find something out.
apparatus	Things needed to carry out an e______________.
method	An o____________ way of doing something.
result	What happens at the e_______ of an experiment.
conclusion	Things that can be w___________ out from an experiment.
fair test	C________________ some of the things used or done in a test so they do not change.
reliable	Things that can be taken to be t________.
variables	Things that can c___________ during an experiment.
reaction	Something that happens in r_____________ to something else.
process	A number of a____________ for making or doing something.
observations	Things that can be s_________.
function	The special p____________ or use of something.
evidence	Anything that gives a r___________ to believe something.
formula	A way of w____________ scientific information using letters, numbers and signs.
catalyst	Something that speeds up a r_____________ or change without being used up.

General Terms
Cloze

experiment	A __________ to find something out.
apparatus	Things needed to carry out an _________________.
method	An ______________ way of doing something.
result	What happens at the _________ of an experiment.
conclusion	Things that can be _____________ out from an experiment.
fair test	___________________ some of the things used or done in a test so they do not change.
reliable	Things that can be taken to be __________.
variables	Things that can _____________ during an experiment.
reaction	Something that happens in _______________ to something else.
process	A number of ______________ for making or doing something.
observations	Things that can be __________.
function	The special ______________ or use of something.
evidence	Anything that gives a _____________ to believe something.
formula	A way of ______________ scientific information using letters, numbers and signs.
catalyst	Something that speeds up a _______________ or change without being used up.

General Terms

Anagrams

Unjumble the letters to find each keyword.

1. e x p e r i t e m n
2. t h o d m e
3. c l u c o n s i o n
4. l i a r e b l e
5. a c t i o n e r
6. t i o n v a s o b s e r
7. d e n c e e v i
8. l y s t a c a t
9. t u s a p p r a a
10. e s r u l t
11. r i f a t e t s
12. a b l e s v a r i
13. r o p s s e c
14. t i o n c f u n
15. m u f o r l a

Extension exercise:

What method would you use to separate sand from salt water?
Describe the stages and draw a diagram to illustrate your answer.

General Terms

Anagrams

Unjumble the letters to find each keyword.

1. n x p e i r t e m e
2. o e h d m t
3. n l c o u n s i o c
4. e i a r e b l l
5. r o c t i n e a
6. i n v a s o o s e r b t
7. i n c e e e v d
8. t y t a c a l s
9. a u s a p r a t p
10. t s r u l e
11. i a f r t e t s
12. i b a l e s v r a
13. c o p s s e r
14. n i n c f o u t
15. a o u f r l m

Extension exercise:

What method would you use to separate sand from salt water?
Describe the stages and draw a diagram to illustrate your answer.

Word Group: Subject Name:

General Terms

Crossword

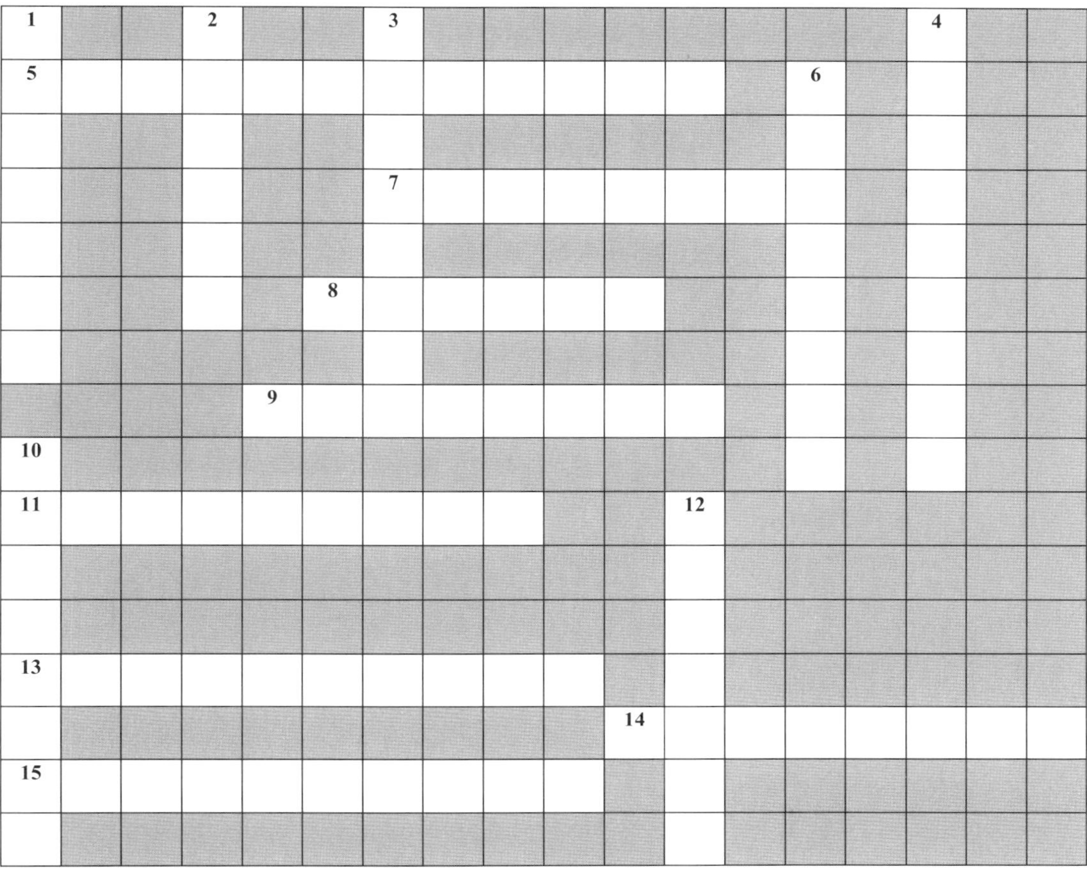

Clues Across

5 After the experiment we made our o-----------.(12)

7 The r------- of potassium with water is violent.(8)

8 The best m----- will be used for the experiment.(6)

9 C-------(s) allow reactions to happen at lower temperatures than usual.(8)

11 One of the v-------- was the length of the elastic band.(9)

13 Use a test tube for the e---------.(10)

14 We need r------- evidence.(8)

15 After analysing the results we made our c---------.(10)

Clues Down

1 The f------ for water is H^2O.(7)

2 After an experiment record the r-----.(6)

3 We controlled some factors to make it a f--- t---.(4,4)

4 The a-------- needed was a test tube and Bunsen burner.(9)

6 The f------- of a microscope is to make things look bigger.(8)

10The e------- wasn't reliable enough to make a firm conclusion.(8)

12 Plants use sunlight to make food. This p------ is called photosynthesis.(7)

Word Group: Subject Name:

General Terms

Crossword

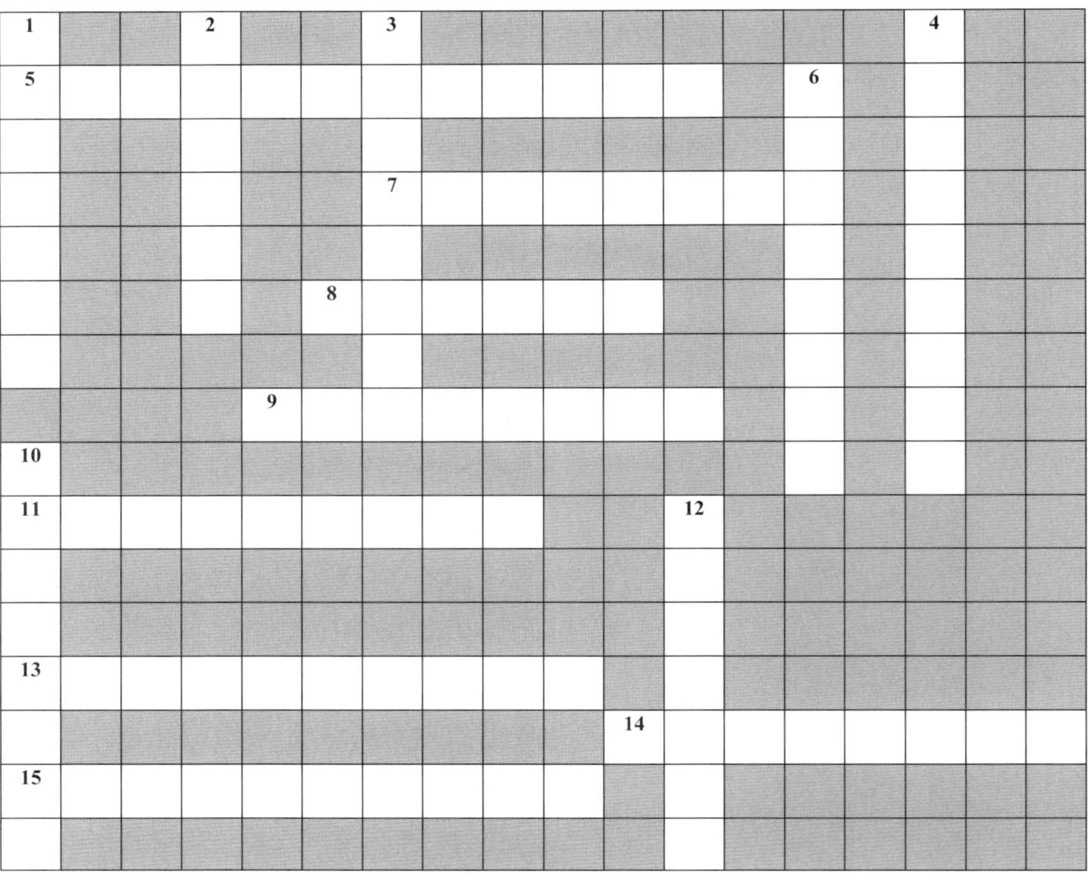

Clues Across

5 After the experiment we made our ------------.(12)
7 The -------- of potassium with water is violent.(8)
8 The best ------ will be used for the experiment.(6)
9 --------(s) allow reactions to happen at lower temperatures than usual.(8)
11 One of the --------- was the length of the elastic band.(9)
13 Use a test tube for the ----------.(10)
14 We need -------- evidence.(8)
15 After analysing the results we made our ----------.(10)

Clues Down

1 The ------- for water is H^2O.(7)
2 After an experiment record the ------.(6)
3 We controlled some factors to make it a ---- ----.(4,4)
4 The --------- needed was a test tube and Bunsen burner.(9)
6 The -------- of a microscope is to make things look bigger.(8)
10The -------- wasn't reliable enough to make a firm conclusion.(8)
12 Plants use sunlight to make food. This ------- is called photosynthesis.(7)

Word Group : Subject Name:

General Terms
Keywords in Context

Use the correct keyword to complete the sentence.

~~*When an experiment is finished it is important to consider and discuss your o*~~ *_ _ _ _ _ _ _ _ _ _ _.*

The class were asked to make a list of the a _ _ _ _ _ _ _ _ they would need to carry out the experiment.

The r _ _ _ _ _ _ _ of sodium when mixed with cold water is violent.

After the experiment the students were asked to write down the r _ _ _ _ _.

As Paul could see a shadow on the sundial his c _ _ _ _ _ _ _ _ _ was that the sun must be shining.

The f _ _ _ _ _ _ for copper oxide is CuO.

Scientists have to have proof that something is r _ _ _ _ _ _ _ or really true.

In an experiment to see how high a ball bounces on different surfaces, the different surfaces will be one of the v _ _ _ _ _ _ _ _.

It is important to know the m _ _ _ _ _ for an experiment before you start.

The p _ _ _ _ _ _ of fractional distillation means we can separate crude oil into other substances.

Scientists carry out e _ _ _ _ _ _ _ _ _ (s) to find out things.

The f _ _ _ _ _ _ _ of your heart is to pump blood around your body.

There is good e _ _ _ _ _ _ _ to tell us that smoking is bad for your health.

To make the experiment a f _ _ _ t _ _ _ I varied the amount of water I gave each plant but kept the other variables the same.

Enzymes in washing powder are c _ _ _ _ _ _ _ (s) that help break down stains in your washing.

General Terms
Keywords in Context

Use the correct keyword to complete the sentence.

When an experiment is finished it is important to consider and discuss your _ _ _ _ _ _ _ _ _ _ _ _.

The class were asked to make a list of the _ _ _ _ _ _ _ _ _ they would need to carry out the experiment.

The _ _ _ _ _ _ _ _ of sodium when mixed with cold water is violent.

After the experiment the students were asked to write down the _ _ _ _ _ _.

As Paul could see a shadow on the sundial his _ _ _ _ _ _ _ _ _ _ was that the sun must be shining.

The _ _ _ _ _ _ _ for copper oxide is CuO.

Scientists have to have proof that something is _ _ _ _ _ _ _ _ or really true.

In an experiment to see how high a ball bounces on different surfaces, the different surfaces will be one of the _ _ _ _ _ _ _ _ _.

It is important to know the _ _ _ _ _ _ for an experiment before you start.

The _ _ _ _ _ _ _ of fractional distillation means we can separate crude oil into other substances.

Scientists carry out _ _ _ _ _ _ _ _ _ _ (s) to find out things.

The _ _ _ _ _ _ _ _ of your heart is to pump blood around your body.

There is good _ _ _ _ _ _ _ _ to tell us that smoking is bad for your health.

To make the experiment a _ _ _ _ _ _ _ _ I varied the amount of water I gave each plant but kept the other variables the same.

Enzymes in washing powder are _ _ _ _ _ _ _ _ (s) that help break down stains in your washing.

General Terms

Look, Say, Cover, Write, Check

experiment	____________	____________	____________
apparatus	____________	____________	____________
method	____________	____________	____________
result	____________	____________	____________
conclusion	____________	____________	____________
fair test	____________	____________	____________
reliable	____________	____________	____________
variables	____________	____________	____________
reaction	____________	____________	____________
process	____________	____________	____________
observations	____________	____________	____________
function	____________	____________	____________
evidence	____________	____________	____________
formula	____________	____________	____________
catalyst	____________	____________	____________

General Terms

Name the Keyword

c_______________ Things that can be worked out from an experiment.

a_______________ Things needed to carry out an experiment.

f_______________ The special purpose or use of something.

r_______________ What happens at the end of an experiment.

e_______________ A test to find something out.

f_______________ A way of writing scientific information using letters, numbers and signs.

r_______________ Things that can be taken to be true.

v_______________ Things that can change during an experiment.

r_______________ Something that happens in response to something else.

p_______________ A number of actions for making or doing something.

o_______________ Things that can be seen.

m_______________ An orderly way of doing something.

e_______________ Anything that gives a reason to believe something.

f_______________ Controlling some of the things used or done in a test so they do not change.

c_______________ Something that speeds up a reaction or change without being used up.

General Terms

Name the Keyword

_______________ Things that can be worked out from an experiment.

_______________ Things needed to carry out an experiment.

_______________ The special purpose or use of something.

_______________ What happens at the end of an experiment.

_______________ A test to find something out.

_______________ A way of writing scientific information using letters, numbers and signs.

_______________ Things that can be taken to be true.

_______________ Things that can change during an experiment.

_______________ Something that happens in response to something else.

_______________ A number of actions for making or doing something.

_______________ Things that can be seen.

_______________ An orderly way of doing something.

_______________ Anything that gives a reason to believe something.

_______________ Controlling some of the things used or done in a test so they do not change.

_______________ Something that speeds up a reaction or change without being used up.

General Terms
Delivering Definitions

Give the correct definition for each keyword.

experiment

apparatus

method

result

conclusion

fair test

reliable

variables

reaction

process

observations

function

evidence

formula

catalyst

Chemistry

Keywords in Science

atom	The tiniest part of a substance.
particles	Tiny parts that scientists believe everything is made of.
element	A substance that cannot be separated into simpler substances.
molecule	A group of atoms joined together.
compound	A substance that has two or more elements in it.
chemicals	The substances used in chemistry.
properties	What a material or substance is like and how it behaves.
mixture	A mixing together of two or more substances without actually joining them, so that they can be separated again.
dissolve	To mix a solid with a liquid so it becomes a liquid too.
dilute	To make a liquid weaker or thinner by adding more liquid, often water.
filter	To separate solids, that do not dissolve, from liquids.
evaporation	When a liquid turns to a gas.
condensation	The change from a gas to a liquid or solid.
distillation	To separate a liquid from other liquids, by boiling it and condensing the steam.
residue	Something that remains or is left over.

Chemistry Matching

Link the keyword with the correct definition.

atom	The tiniest part of a substance.
particles	A group of atoms joined together.
element	Something that remains or is left over.
molecule	A substance that cannot be separated into simpler substances.
compound	Tiny parts that scientists believe everything is made of.
chemicals	A substance that has two or more elements in it.
properties	To separate a liquid from other liquids, by boiling it and condensing the steam.
mixture	The substances used in chemistry.
dissolve	What a material or substance is like and how it behaves.
dilute	To separate solids, that do not dissolve, from liquids.
filter	A mixing together of two or more substances without actually joining them, so that they can be separated again.
evaporation	To make a liquid weaker or thinner by adding more liquid, often water.
condensation	When a liquid turns to a gas.
distillation	The change from a gas to a liquid or solid.
residue	To mix a solid with a liquid so it becomes a liquid too.

Chemistry

Choose the Word

atom	The (*largest, tiniest, lightest*) part of a substance.
particles	Tiny parts that scientists believe (*everything, a chemical, a metal*) is made of.
element	A substance that cannot be (*dissolved, separated, melted*) into simpler substances.
molecule	A group of (*substances, elements, atoms*) joined together.
compound	A substance that has (*two, three, four*) or more elements in it.
chemicals	The (*fuel, substances, energy*) used in chemistry.
properties	What a material or substance is like and how it (*plays, moves, behaves*).
mixture	A (*mixing, heating, sticking*) together of two or more substances without actually joining them, so that they can be separated again.
dissolve	To (*mix, melt, heat*) a solid with a liquid so it becomes a liquid too.
dilute	To make a liquid (*stronger, weaker, colder*) or thinner by adding more liquid, often water.
filter	To separate solids, that do not dissolve, from (*liquids, gases, vapours*).
evaporation	When a (*liquid, solid, vapour*) turns to a gas.
condensation	The change from a (*mixture, gas, solution*) to a liquid or solid.
distillation	To separate a liquid from other liquids, by (*stirring, cooling, boiling*) it and condensing the steam.
residue	Something that (*departs, remains, changes*) or is left over.

Chemistry

Wordsearch

a	t	o	m	q	p	a	r	t	i	c	l	e	s	e
z	x	c	v	f	d	s	a	s	w	e	r	t	d	l
v	m	o	l	e	c	u	l	e	g	c	f	g	i	e
r	e	v	a	p	o	r	a	t	i	o	n	b	s	m
c	h	e	m	i	c	a	l	s	b	m	f	d	t	e
p	e	r	t	y	u	i	o	l	k	p	j	h	i	n
r	d	i	s	s	o	l	v	e	h	o	g	f	l	t
o	a	s	d	f	g	h	j	k	l	u	w	d	l	v
p	x	f	i	l	t	e	r	x	d	n	x	x	a	z
e	z	x	c	v	b	n	m	b	i	d	v	c	t	x
r	s	r	e	s	i	d	u	e	l	f	g	h	i	j
t	y	t	r	f	g	h	y	t	u	f	g	h	o	n
i	c	o	n	d	e	n	s	a	t	i	o	n	n	o
e	b	v	g	f	d	r	e	t	e	f	g	b	v	c
s	c	m	i	x	t	u	r	e	z	x	c	d	s	a

atom particles element molecule compound

chemicals properties mixture dissolve dilute

filter evaporation condensation distillation residue

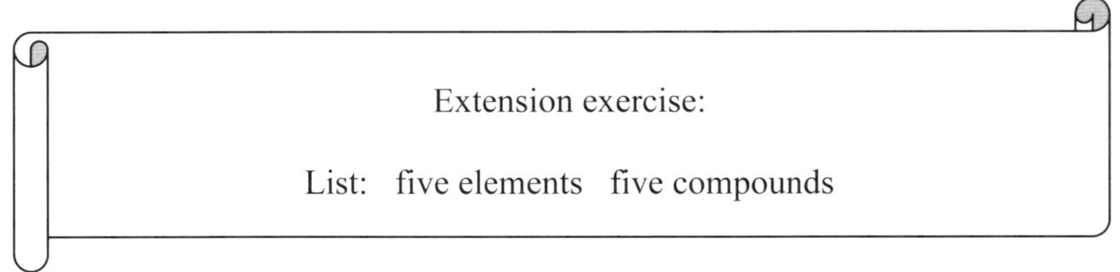
Extension exercise:
List: five elements five compounds

Name:

Chemistry

Wordsearch

a	a	s	d	p	a	r	t	i	c	l	e	s	t	d
s	t	q	w	e	r	t	y	u	i	o	p	l	n	k
j	h	o	g	m	o	l	e	c	u	l	e	f	e	d
c	s	a	m	w	r	e	s	i	d	u	e	e	m	r
o	v	c	x	s	d	f	g	h	j	y	e	t	e	d
m	c	h	e	m	i	c	a	l	s	t	r	t	l	i
p	r	o	p	e	r	t	i	e	s	z	u	x	e	s
o	f	z	x	z	x	c	v	b	n	m	t	b	v	t
u	f	d	i	s	s	o	l	v	e	c	x	q	s	a
n	i	d	i	l	u	t	e	a	s	d	i	f	g	l
d	l	v	b	g	h	j	k	l	m	n	m	h	g	l
x	t	d	i	s	t	i	l	l	a	t	i	o	n	a
x	e	x	c	v	b	g	h	j	y	t	r	e	w	t
q	r	e	v	a	p	o	r	a	t	i	o	n	q	i
c	o	n	d	e	n	s	a	t	i	o	n	q	z	x

atom	particles	element	molecule	compound
chemicals	properties	mixture	dissolve	dilute
filter	evaporation	condensation	distillation	residue

Extension exercise:

List: five elements five compounds

Chemistry
Jumbled Sentences

Unjumble the words to give the correct definition. The underlined words are in the right order.

atom	*The part a of tiniest substance.*
particles	*Tiny parts scientists everything that is believe made of.*
element	*A substance cannot that into be separated simpler substances.*
molecule	*A atoms joined of group together.*
compound	*A substance that more has elements or two in it.*
chemicals	*substances chemistry. used in The*
properties	*What a like material substance how or and is it behaves.*
mixture	*A mixing together actually so of two can substances that without more or them, be joining they separated again.*
dissolve	*To mix solid liquid a with becomes so a it a liquid too.*
dilute	*To make liquid weaker by liquid, adding a thinner more or often water.*
filter	*To separate dissolve, not solids, do that from liquids.*
evaporation	*When turns a to liquid a gas.*
condensation	*The liquid gas a or change a from to solid.*
distillation	*To separate liquid boiling and a other from liquids, condensing by it the steam.*
residue	*Something remains is that left or over.*

Chemistry
Keywords in Science

Unjumble the words to give the correct definition.

atom	part substance the a of tiniest
particles	scientists parts everything of tiny that made is believe
element	cannot that a substance substances into be simpler separated
molecule	atoms together joined a of group
compound	that more it a has elements substance or two in
chemicals	substances chemistry used in the
properties	like material behaves what substance a or it and is how
mixture	together actually again so of a two mixing can substances separated that without more or them be joining they
dissolve	to solid liquid a liquid with becomes mix so too a it a
dilute	water to liquid weaker by liquid adding make a thinner more or often
filter	dissolve liquids separate to from not solids do that
evaporation	turns a when to gas liquid a
condensation	solid liquid gas a or change a from the to
distillation	liquid boiling steam and to a other from liquids condensing the separate by it
residue	over something remains is that left or

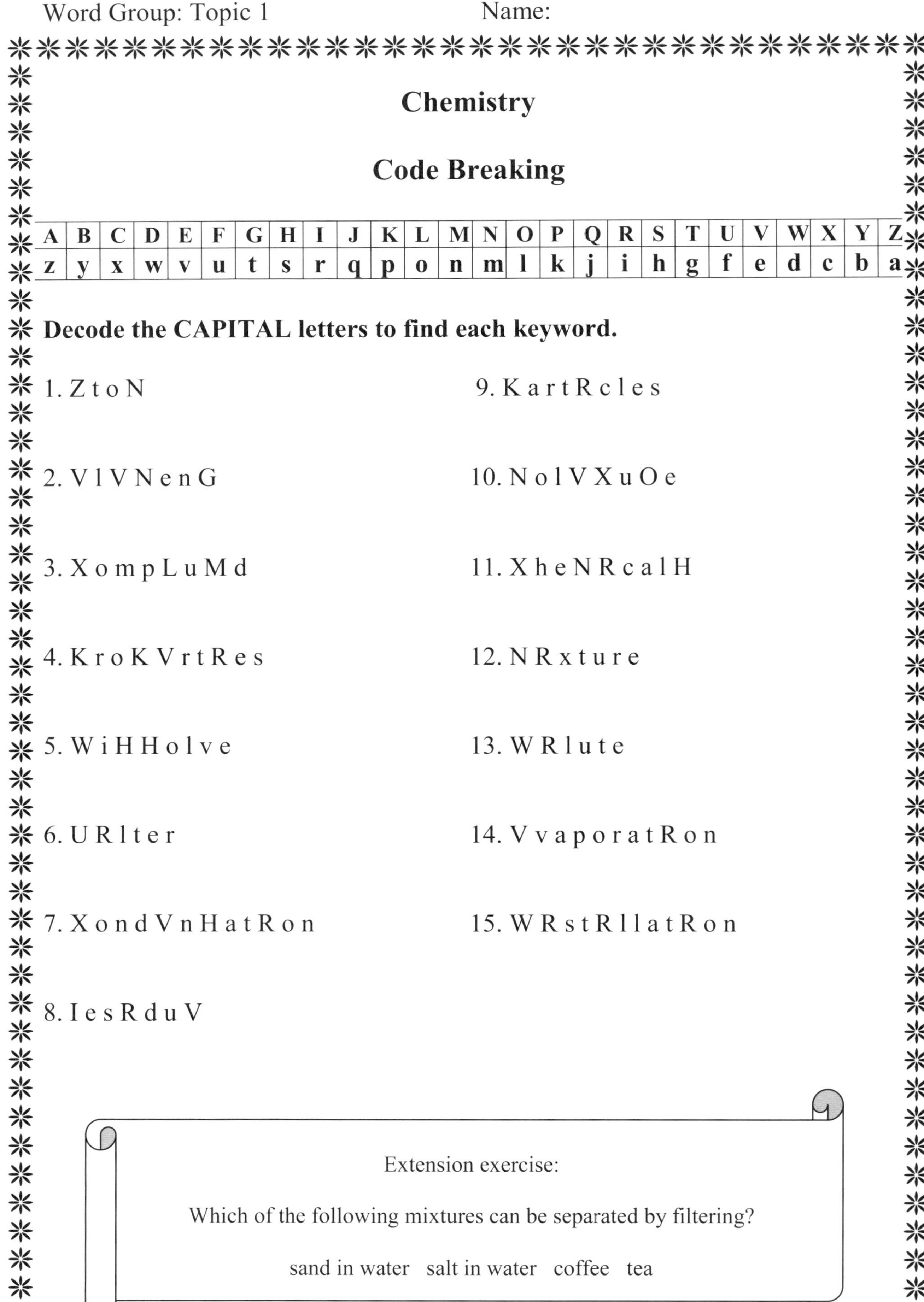

Chemistry

Code Breaking

A	B	C	D	E	F	G	H	I	J	K	L	M	N	O	P	Q	R	S	T	U	V	W	X	Y	Z
z	y	x	w	v	u	t	s	r	q	p	o	n	m	l	k	j	i	h	g	f	e	d	c	b	a

Decode the CAPITAL letters to find each keyword.

1. Z t o N
2. V l V N e n G
3. X o m p L u M d
4. K r o K V r t R e s
5. W i H H o l v e
6. U R l t e r
7. X o n d V n H a t R o n
8. I e s R d u V
9. K a r t R c l e s
10. N o l V X u O e
11. X h e N R c a l H
12. N R x t u r e
13. W R l u t e
14. V v a p o r a t R o n
15. W R s t R l l a t R o n

Extension exercise:

Which of the following mixtures can be separated by filtering?

sand in water salt in water coffee tea

Chemistry

Code Breaking

A	B	C	D	E	F	G	H	I	J	K	L	M	N	O	P	Q	R	S	T	U	V	W	X	Y	Z
z	y	x	w	v	u	t	s	r	q	p	o	n	m	l	k	j	i	h	g	f	e	d	c	b	a

Decode the CAPITAL letters to find each keyword.

1. Z G L N
2. V O V N V M G
3. X L N K L F M W
4. K I L K V I G R V H
5. W R H H L O E V
6. U R O G V I
7. X L M W V M H Z G R L M
8. I V H R W F V
9. K Z I G R X O V H
10. N L O V X F O V
11. X S V N R X Z O H
12. N R C G F I V
13. W R O F G V
14. V E Z K L I Z G R L M
15. W R H G R O O Z G R L M

Extension exercise:

Which of the following mixtures can be separated by filtering?

sand in water salt in water coffee tea

Chemistry
Cloze

atom	The t____________ part of a substance.
particles	Tiny parts that scientists believe e________________ is made of.
element	A substance that cannot be s______________ into simpler substances.
molecule	A group of a__________ joined together.
compound	A substance that has two or more e_____________ in it.
chemicals	The s_______________ used in chemistry.
properties	What a m_____________ or substance is like and how it behaves.
mixture	A mixing together of two or more substances without actually joining them, so that they can be s_______________ again.
dissolve	To m________ a solid with a liquid so it becomes a liquid too.
dilute	To make a liquid w____________ or thinner by adding more liquid, often water.
filter	To s_____________ solids, that do not dissolve, from liquids.
evaporation	When a l___________ turns to a gas.
condensation	The change from a g________ to a liquid or solid.
distillation	To s_____________ a liquid from other liquids, by boiling it and condensing the steam.
residue	Something that r_____________ or is left over.

Chemistry
Cloze

atom	The ______________ part of a substance.
particles	Tiny parts that scientists believe _________________ is made of.
element	A substance that cannot be ________________ into simpler substances.
molecule	A group of ____________ joined together.
compound	A substance that has two or more _______________ in it.
chemicals	The _________________ used in chemistry.
properties	What a _______________ or substance is like and how it behaves.
mixture	A mixing together of two or more substances without actually joining them, so that they can be ________________ again.
dissolve	To _________ a solid with a liquid so it becomes a liquid too.
dilute	To make a liquid _____________ or thinner by adding more liquid, often water.
filter	To _______________ solids, that do not dissolve, from liquids.
evaporation	When a _____________ turns to a gas.
condensation	The change from a _________ to a liquid or solid.
distillation	To _______________ a liquid from other liquids, by boiling it and condensing the steam.
residue	Something that ______________ or is left over.

Chemistry

Anagrams

Unjumble the letters to find each keyword.

1. o m a t
2. m e n t e l e
3. m p c o o u n d
4. p e r t i e s o r p
5. o l v d s s i e
6. t e r l i f
7. e n s a t i o n c o n d
8. s i d r e u e
9. i c l e s p a r t
10. c u l e m o l e
11. i c a l s e m c h
12. t u e r m i x
13. l u t e d i
14. t e v a p a i o n o r
15. l l a t i o n d i s t i

Extension exercise:

Give the properties of the following materials:

wood glass wool stainless steel cotton

Chemistry

Anagrams

Unjumble the letters to find each keyword.

1. t m a o

2. e e n t e l m

3. d p c o o u m n

4. p p r t i s o r e e

5. e l d s v s i o

6. f e r l i t

7. d n s o a t i n c n o e

8. d e i r e u s

9. t c a l e s p r i

10. e u o l e m l c

11. h c l a s e m c i

12. x u i e r m t

13. t i u e d l

14. a r e v p a i o n o t

15. a i l t i n d i s t o l

Extension exercise:

Give the properties of the following materials:

wood glass wool stainless steel cotton

Word Group: Topic 1 Name:

Chemistry

Crossword

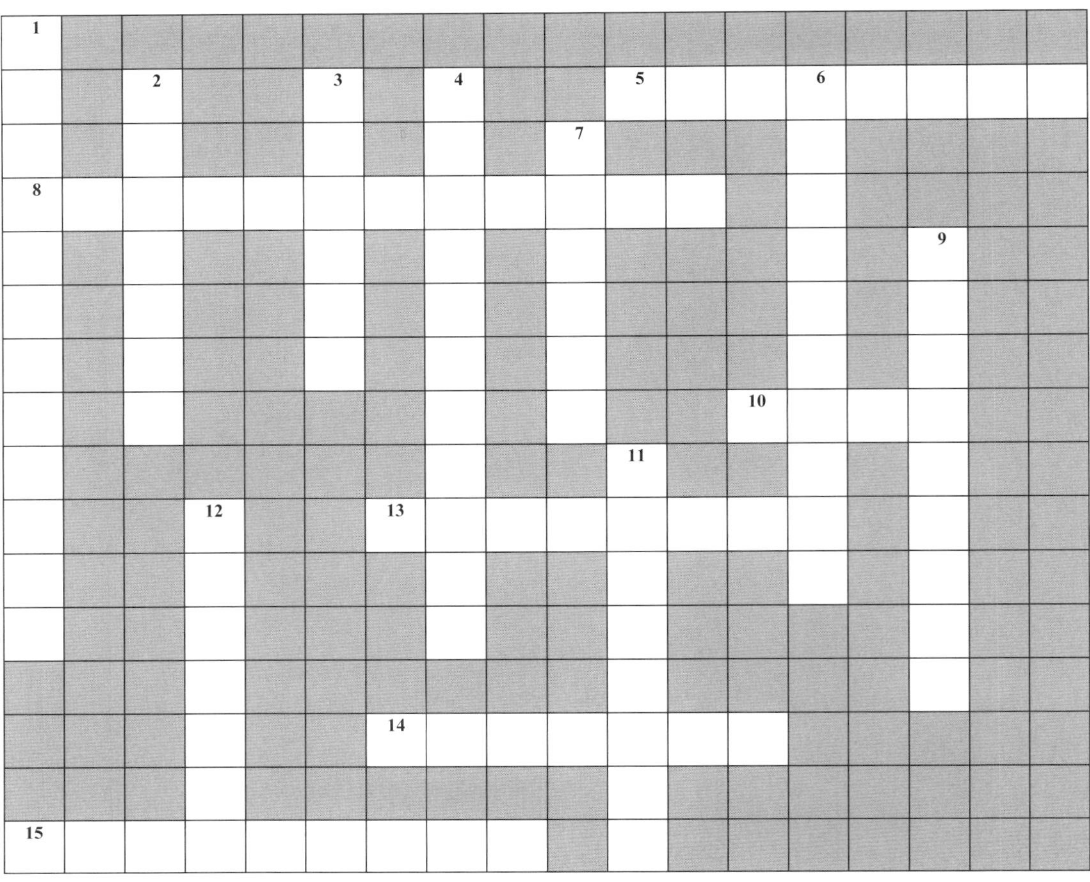

Clues Across

5 H^2O is a c-------.(8)
8 During the fractional d----------- of crude oil we get diesel for fuel.(12)
10 Elements have one type of a---.(4)
13 Oven cleaner is used to d------- baked on grease and food.(8)
14 Lots of m------(s) need to be separated before we can use them, e.g. salt from the sea.(7)
15 In solids, liquids and gases p-------- are arranged in different ways.(9)

Clues Down

1 We often see the effects of c----------- as water on our windows.(12)
2 The r------ left after filtering the water was pretty nasty.(7)
3 A f----- is often used in the home to clean water.(6)
4 The e---------- of sea water is part of the water cycle.(11)
6 Two p--------- that materials have are strength and hardness.(10)
7 I d-----(d) the orange squash with water to make it weaker.(6)
9 Leo Baekeland, a chemist, researched c-------- and discovered plastic!(9)
11 Atoms joined together make a ?(8)
12 Gold is an e------.(7)

Word Group: Topic 1 Name:

Chemistry

Crossword

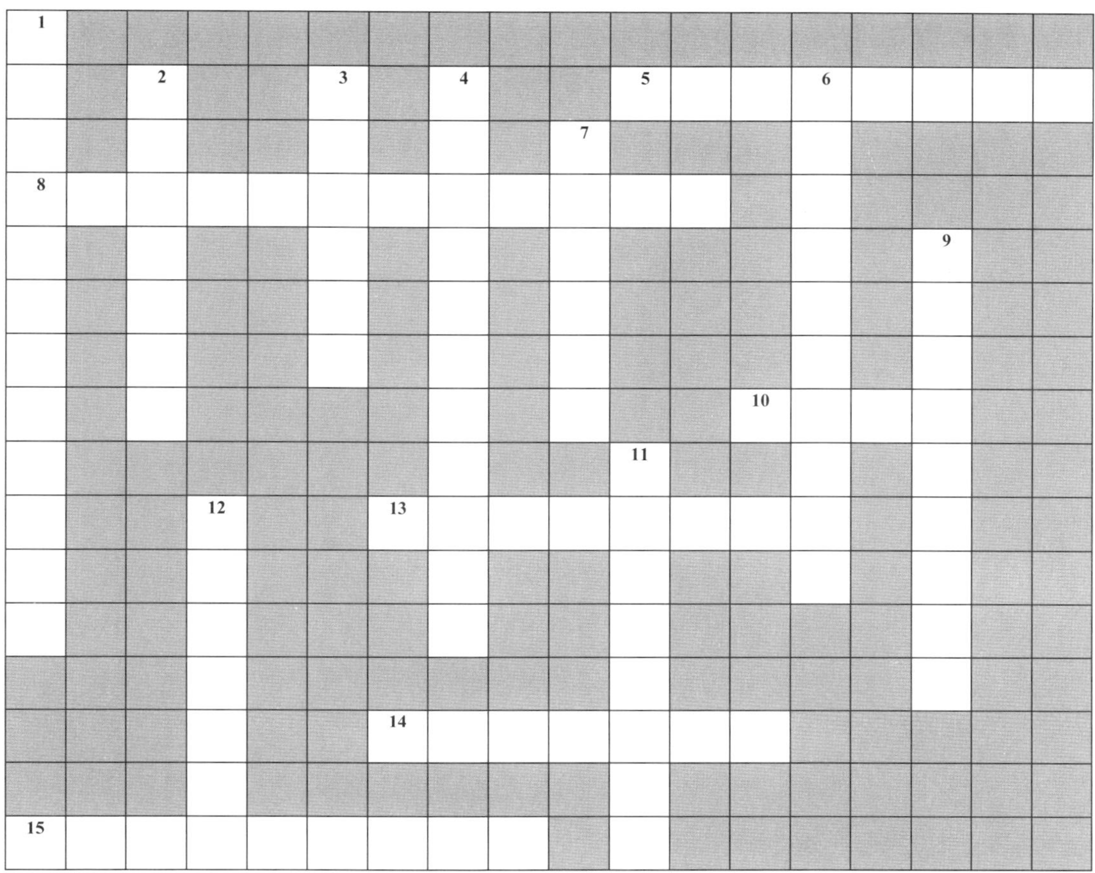

Clues Across

5 H^2O is a --------.(8)

8 During the fractional ------------ of crude oil we get diesel for fuel.(12)

10 Elements have one type of ----.(4)

13 Oven cleaner is used to -------- baked on grease and food.(8)

14 Lots of -------(s) need to be separated before we can use them, e.g. salt from the sea.(7)

15 In solids, liquids and gases --------- are arranged in different ways.(9)

Clues Down

1 We often see the effects of ------------ as water on our windows.(12)

2 The ------- left after filtering the water was pretty nasty.(7)

3 A ------ is often used in the home to clean water.(6)

4 The ----------- of sea water is part of the water cycle.(11)

6 Two ---------- that materials have are strength and hardness.(10)

7 I ------(d) the orange squash with water to make it weaker.(6)

9 Leo Baekeland, a chemist, researched --------- and discovered plastic!(9)

11 Atoms joined together make a ?(8)

12 Gold is an -------.(7)

Chemistry
Keywords in Context

Use the correct keyword to complete the sentence.

In 1661 Robert Boyle gave a name to the simplest substances on Earth and called them e _ _ _ _ _ _ (s).

Everything around us is an element, a c _ _ _ _ _ _ _ or a mixture.

Making new materials or c _ _ _ _ _ _ _ _ is a very important part of a chemist's work.

A _ _ _ (s) can join together to make molecules.

Light has three important p_ _ _ _ _ _ _ _ _: straight lines, shadow, very fast.

A colander and teabag are both f _ _ _ _ _ (s) used in the home.

The r _ _ _ _ _ _ of crude oil after being separated by fractional distillation can be used for fuel, lubrication or road tar.

P _ _ _ _ _ _ _ _ in a liquid move about less quickly than they do in a gas.

Crude oil is not one pure substance but a m _ _ _ _ _ _ of many different chemicals.

When clothes dry e _ _ _ _ _ _ _ _ _ _ takes place.

The d _ _ _ _ _ _ _ _ _ _ _ of sea water produces pure water.

Sugar d _ _ _ _ _ _ _ (s) in a hot cup of tea.

If we want to make something less concentrated we can d _ _ _ _ _ it with water.

The effects of c _ _ _ _ _ _ _ _ _ _ _ can often be seen on kitchen windows after boiling the kettle.

Two oxygen atoms can join together to make an oxygen m _ _ _ _ _ _ _.

Chemistry
Keywords in Context

Use the correct keyword to complete the sentence.

In 1661 Robert Boyle gave a name to the simplest substances on Earth and called them _ _ _ _ _ _ _ (s).

Everything around us is an element, a _ _ _ _ _ _ _ _ or a mixture.

Making new materials or _ _ _ _ _ _ _ _ _ is a very important part of a chemist's work.

_ _ _ _ (s) can join together to make molecules.

Light has three important _ _ _ _ _ _ _ _ _ _: straight lines, shadow, very fast.

A colander and teabag are both _ _ _ _ _ _ (s) used in the home.

The _ _ _ _ _ _ _ of crude oil after being separated by fractional distillation can be used for fuel, lubrication or road tar.

_ _ _ _ _ _ _ _ _ in a liquid move about less quickly than they do in a gas.

Crude oil is not one pure substance but a _ _ _ _ _ _ _ of many different chemicals.

When clothes dry _ _ _ _ _ _ _ _ _ _ _ takes place.

The _ _ _ _ _ _ _ _ _ _ _ _ of sea water produces pure water.

Sugar _ _ _ _ _ _ _ _ (s) in a hot cup of tea.

If we want to make something less concentrated we can _ _ _ _ _ _ it with water.

The effects of _ _ _ _ _ _ _ _ _ _ _ _ can often be seen on kitchen windows after boiling the kettle.

Two oxygen atoms can join together to make an oxygen _ _ _ _ _ _ _ _.

Chemistry

Look, Say, Cover, Write, Check

atom ______ ______ ______

particles ______ ______ ______

element ______ ______ ______

molecule ______ ______ ______

compound ______ ______ ______

chemicals ______ ______ ______

properties ______ ______ ______

mixture ______ ______ ______

dissolve ______ ______ ______

dilute ______ ______ ______

filter ______ ______ ______

evaporation ______ ______ ______

condensation ______ ______ ______

distillation ______ ______ ______

residue ______ ______ ______

Chemistry

Name the Keyword

a________________	The tiniest part of a substance.
p________________	Tiny parts that scientists believe everything is made of.
e________________	A substance that cannot be separated into simpler substances.
m________________	A mixing together of two or more substances without actually joining them, so that they can be separated again.
c________________	A substance that has two or more elements in it.
c________________	The substances used in chemistry.
p________________	What a material or substance is like and how it behaves.
m________________	A group of atoms joined together.
f________________	To separate solids, that do not dissolve, from liquids.
d________________	To make a liquid weaker or thinner by adding more liquid, often water.
d________________	To mix a solid with a liquid so it becomes a liquid too.
r________________	Something that remains or is left over.
c________________	The change from a gas to a liquid or solid.
d________________	To separate a liquid from other liquids, by boiling it and condensing the steam.
e________________	When a liquid turns to a gas.

Chemistry

Name the Keyword

________________ The tiniest part of a substance.

________________ Tiny parts that scientists believe everything is made of.

________________ A substance that cannot be separated into simpler substances.

________________ A mixing together of two or more substances without actually joining them, so that they can be separated again.

________________ A substance that has two or more elements in it.

________________ The substances used in chemistry.

________________ What a material or substance is like and how it behaves.

________________ A group of atoms joined together.

________________ To separate solids, that do not dissolve, from liquids.

________________ To make a liquid weaker or thinner by adding more liquid, often water.

________________ To mix a solid with a liquid so it becomes a liquid too.

________________ Something that remains or is left over.

________________ The change from a gas to a liquid or solid.

________________ To separate a liquid from other liquids, by boiling it and condensing the steam.

________________ When a liquid turns to a gas.

Name:

Chemistry
Delivering Definitions

Give the correct definition for each keyword.

atom ______________________________

particles ______________________________

element ______________________________

molecule ______________________________

compound ______________________________

chemicals ______________________________

properties ______________________________

mixture ______________________________

dissolve ______________________________

dilute ______________________________

filter ______________________________

evaporation ______________________________

condensation ______________________________

distillation ______________________________

residue ______________________________

Physics

Keywords in Science

force	A push or pull.
friction	A force that slows things down when they rub together.
resistance	Slows something down or stops it.
tension	How much something is being stretched.
gravity	The force that pulls things towards the centre of the Earth.
repel	To push away.
attract	To pull towards itself.
vibration	When something moves backwards and forwards quickly, making a sound.
rotate	Moves around a central point.
pivot	The point on which something turns.
component	A part of something.
radiation	When energy travels through the air.
renewable energy	It cannot be used up, it is always there, e.g. wind.
non-renewable energy	Once it is used, it is gone forever, e.g. coal.
vacuum	A space without any air in it.

Physics
Matching

Link the keyword with the correct definition.

force	A force that slows things down when they rub together.
friction	How much something is being stretched.
resistance	A space without any air in it.
tension	When energy travels through the air.
gravity	When something moves backwards and forwards quickly, making a sound.
repel	A push or pull.
attract	Moves around a central point.
vibration	Slows something down or stops it.
rotate	The point on which something turns.
pivot	The force that pulls things towards the centre of the Earth.
component	To pull towards itself.
radiation	It cannot be used up, it is always there, e.g. wind.
renewable energy	A part of something.
non-renewable energy	To push away.
vacuum	Once it is used, it is gone forever, e.g. coal.

Physics

Choose the Word

force	A push or (*hit, slap, pull*).
friction	A force that (*slows, speeds, helps*) things down when they rub together.
resistance	Slows something down or (*hits, traps, stops*) it.
tension	How much something is being (*weighed, stretched, forced*).
gravity	The force that (*pushes, pulls, blows*) things towards the centre of the Earth.
repel	To (*push, pull, drive*) away.
attract	To (*pull, push, steer*) towards itself.
vibration	When something moves backwards and forwards (*quickly, slowly, quietly*), making a sound.
rotate	(*Runs, Moves, Slides*) around a central point.
pivot	The point on which something (*turns, breaks, vibrates*).
component	A (*weight, part, colour*) of something.
radiation	When (*rain, energy, sound*) travels through the air.
renewable energy	It (*cannot, can, shouldn't*) be used up, it is always there, e.g. wind.
non-renewable energy	Once it is used, it is gone (*forever, temporarily, occasionally*), e.g. coal.
vacuum	A space without any (*water, air, dust*) in it.

Physics

Wordsearch

f	o	r	c	e	q	f	r	i	c	t	i	o	n	r
d	f	g	h	j	k	l	u	y	t	r	p	e	r	e
t	e	n	s	i	o	n	g	r	a	v	i	t	y	s
r	t	y	h	g	f	d	c	v	b	n	v	z	x	i
r	z	x	c	v	b	b	n	m	j	h	o	f	d	s
e	d	a	t	t	r	a	c	t	f	d	t	s	e	t
p	v	i	b	r	a	t	i	o	n	r	t	y	u	i
e	d	n	o	n	r	e	n	e	w	a	b	l	e	e
l	v	c	b	f	d	e	r	t	h	g	j	p	o	n
v	c	r	o	t	a	t	e	a	s	w	q	w	s	e
c	o	m	p	o	n	e	n	t	a	s	e	d	r	r
f	g	r	a	d	i	a	t	i	o	n	z	x	z	g
r	e	n	e	w	a	b	l	e	e	n	e	r	g	y
z	x	z	x	r	e	s	i	s	t	a	n	c	e	z
v	a	c	u	u	m	z	x	c	v	b	n	m	n	b

force friction resistance tension gravity

repel attract vibration rotate pivot

component radiation vacuum renewable energy

non-renewable energy

Extension exercise:

Give three examples of: renewable energy non-renewable energy

Physics

Wordsearch

n	o	n	r	e	n	e	w	a	b	l	e	a	t	a
q	r	w	e	d	s	p	a	s	d	f	e	g	c	h
w	d	e	n	b	m	j	i	k	j	h	n	g	a	f
d	f	c	p	v	f	g	t	v	e	d	e	f	r	h
c	v	b	n	e	z	x	z	x	o	z	r	z	t	a
a	s	d	f	g	l	g	f	d	s	t	g	a	t	a
r	o	t	a	t	e	a	s	d	e	w	y	a	a	c
r	e	n	e	w	a	b	l	e	e	n	e	r	g	y
f	o	r	c	e	c	f	r	i	c	t	i	o	n	g
r	e	s	i	s	t	a	n	c	e	c	f	v	g	r
z	x	c	v	t	e	n	s	i	o	n	d	a	f	a
g	f	c	o	m	p	o	n	e	n	t	f	c	f	v
r	r	r	a	d	i	a	t	i	o	n	e	u	g	i
a	b	n	m	j	h	g	f	r	t	y	u	u	z	t
r	v	i	b	r	a	t	i	o	n	c	v	m	c	y

force friction resistance tension gravity

repel attract vibration rotate pivot

component radiation vacuum renewable energy

non-renewable energy

Extension exercise:

Give three examples of: renewable energy non-renewable energy

Physics
Jumbled Sentences

Unjumble the words to give the correct definition. The underlined words are in the right order.

force	push pull. A or
friction	A force slows down when that things they rub together.
resistance	Slows down or stops something it.
tension	How much being something is stretched.
gravity	The force centre the pulls that things of towards the Earth.
repel	away. To push
attract	pull itself. towards To
vibration	When something quickly, moves forwards and backwards making a sound.
rotate	central Moves point. a around
pivot	The which point something on turns.
component	of part something. A
radiation	When travels energy through the air.
renewable energy	It cannot up, used be there, is it always e.g. wind.
non-renewable energy	Once e.g. forever, used, gone is it is it coal.
vacuum	A air without space in any it.

Physics
Jumbled Sentences

Unjumble the words to give the correct definition.

force	*push pull a or*
friction	*slows a down together when rub that things force they*
resistance	*down it or slows stops something*
tension	*much how being something stretched is*
gravity	*centre the pulls Earth the that the force things of towards*
repel	*away to push*
attract	*pull itself towards to*
vibration	*sound something quickly moves forwards when and a backwards making*
rotate	*central moves point a around*
pivot	*which the turns point something on*
component	*of part something a*
radiation	*travels energy air through the when*
renewable energy	*cannot up it used be there is it always e.g. wind*
non-renewable energy	*e.g. forever coal once used gone is it is it*
vacuum	*air without it a space in any*

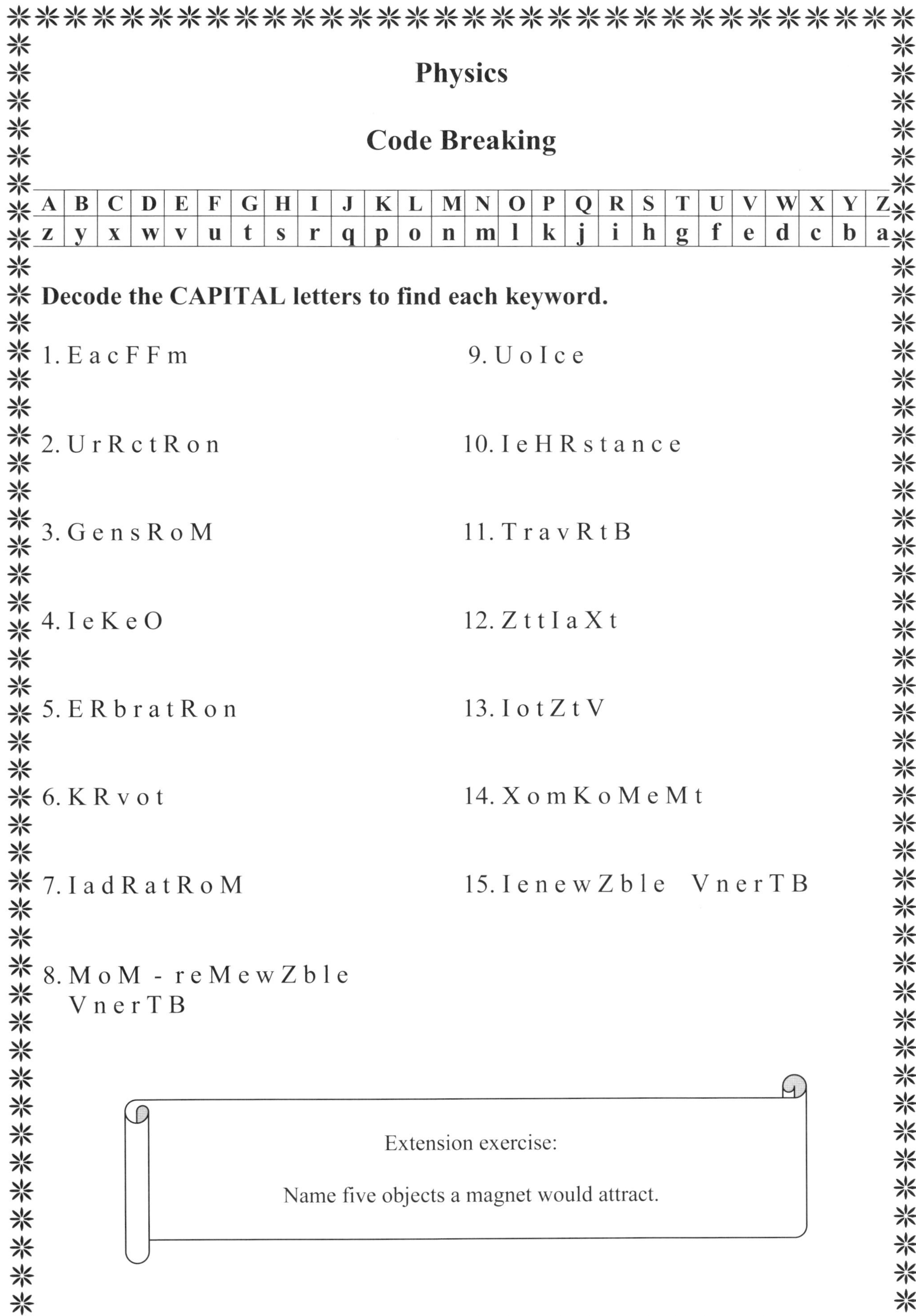

Physics

Code Breaking

A	B	C	D	E	F	G	H	I	J	K	L	M	N	O	P	Q	R	S	T	U	V	W	X	Y	Z
z	y	x	w	v	u	t	s	r	q	p	o	n	m	l	k	j	i	h	g	f	e	d	c	b	a

Decode the CAPITAL letters to find each keyword.

1. E a c F F m
2. U r R c t R o n
3. G e n s R o M
4. I e K e O
5. E R b r a t R o n
6. K R v o t
7. I a d R a t R o M
8. M o M - r e M e w Z b l e V n e r T B
9. U o I c e
10. I e H R s t a n c e
11. T r a v R t B
12. Z t t I a X t
13. I o t Z t V
14. X o m K o M e M t
15. I e n e w Z b l e V n e r T B

Extension exercise:

Name five objects a magnet would attract.

Physics

Code Breaking

A	B	C	D	E	F	G	H	I	J	K	L	M	N	O	P	Q	R	S	T	U	V	W	X	Y	Z
z	y	x	w	v	u	t	s	r	q	p	o	n	m	l	k	j	i	h	g	f	e	d	c	b	a

Decode the CAPITAL letters to find each keyword.

1. E Z X F F N
2. U I R X G R L M
3. G V M H R L M
4. I V K V O
5. E R Y I Z G R L M
6. K R E L G
7. I Z W R Z G R L M
8. M L M - I V M V D Z Y O V V M V I T B
9. U L I X V
10. I V H R H G Z M X V
11. T I Z E R G B
12. Z G G I Z X G
13. I L G Z G V
14. X L N K L M V M G
15. I V M V D Z Y O V V M V I T B

Extension exercise:

Name five objects a magnet would attract.

Physics
Cloze

force	A p________ or pull.
friction	A f_________ that slows things down when they rub together.
resistance	S_________ something down or stops it.
tension	How much something is being s_____________.
gravity	The f_________ that pulls things towards the centre of the Earth.
repel	To p________ away.
attract	To p________ towards itself.
vibration	When something moves backwards and forwards quickly, making a s_________.
rotate	Moves around a c___________ point.
pivot	The p_________ on which something turns.
component	A p________ of something.
radiation	When e__________ travels through the air.
renewable energy	It c__________ be used up, it is always there, e.g. wind.
non-renewable energy	Once it is used, it is gone f___________, e.g. coal.
vacuum	A space without any a_______ in it.

Physics
Cloze

force	A __________ or pull.
friction	A ___________ that slows things down when they rub together.
resistance	___________ something down or stops it.
tension	How much something is being _______________.
gravity	The ___________ that pulls things towards the centre of the Earth.
repel	To __________ away.
attract	To __________ towards itself.
vibration	When something moves backwards and forwards quickly, making a ___________.
rotate	Moves around a ______________ point.
pivot	The ___________ on which something turns.
component	A __________ of something.
radiation	When ____________ travels through the air.
renewable energy	It ____________ be used up, it is always there, e.g. wind.
non-renewable energy	Once it is used, it is gone ______________, e.g. coal.
vacuum	A space without any _________ in it.

Physics

Anagrams

Unjumble the letters to find each keyword.

1. r c e f o
2. s t a n c e r e s i
3. s i o n t e n
4. p e l r e
5. r a t i o n b i v
6. v o t p i
7. d i a r a t i o n
8. o n n – e r n e w b l e a e n g y e r
9. i c t i o n f r
10. u u m v a c
11. g r a t y i v
12. r a c t a t t
13. t a t e o r
14. p o n e n t c o m
15. n e r e a b l e w e n g y e r

Extension exercise:

Draw a diagram of a vacuum flask.
Write an explanation about how it keeps things warm.

Physics

Anagrams

Unjumble the letters to find each keyword.

1. o c e f r
2. n i t a c e r e s s
3. n i n t o e s
4. e l r p e
5. v a o t i n b i r
6. i o t p v
7. n i a r a t i o d
8. o n n - e r w e n b a e l e g e r y n
9. r o c t i n f i
10. a c u m v u
11. a v r t y i g
12. c t a t a t r
13. r t a e o t
14. m e o n t c n o p
15. e e r a b e l n w r n y e g e

Extension exercise:

Draw a diagram of a vacuum flask.
Write an explanation about how it keeps things warm.

Physics

Crossword

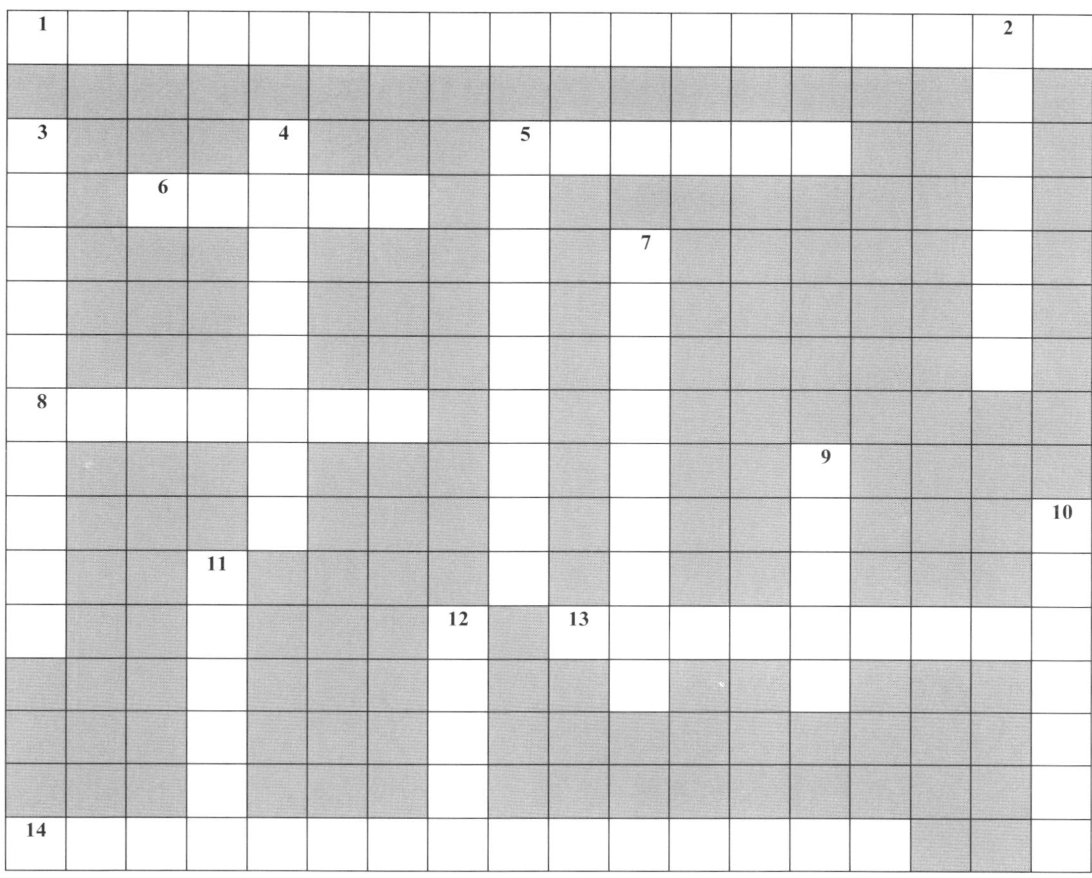

Clues Across

1 Oil is a n-- - --------- e-----.(12,6)
5 I keep my tea hot in a v----- flask.(6)
6 If two f----(s) are equal and opposite they are balanced.(5)
8 We pulled the rope and created t------.(7)
13 In a series circuit the same current goes through all the c--------(s).(9)
14 An example of r-------- e----- is solar.(9,6)

Clues Down

2 Isaac Newton thought a lot about the force of g------.(7)
3 A feather falls more slowly than an apple because of air r---------.(10)
4 Grease and oil reduce f-------.(8)
5 The v-------- of the guitar strings made the sound.(9)
7 Our bodies give out r--------, we radiate energy.(9)
9 A see-saw will have one of these.(5)
10 Magnets can a------ and repel.(7)
11 To move around? (6)
12 The opposite of attract.(5)

Physics

Crossword

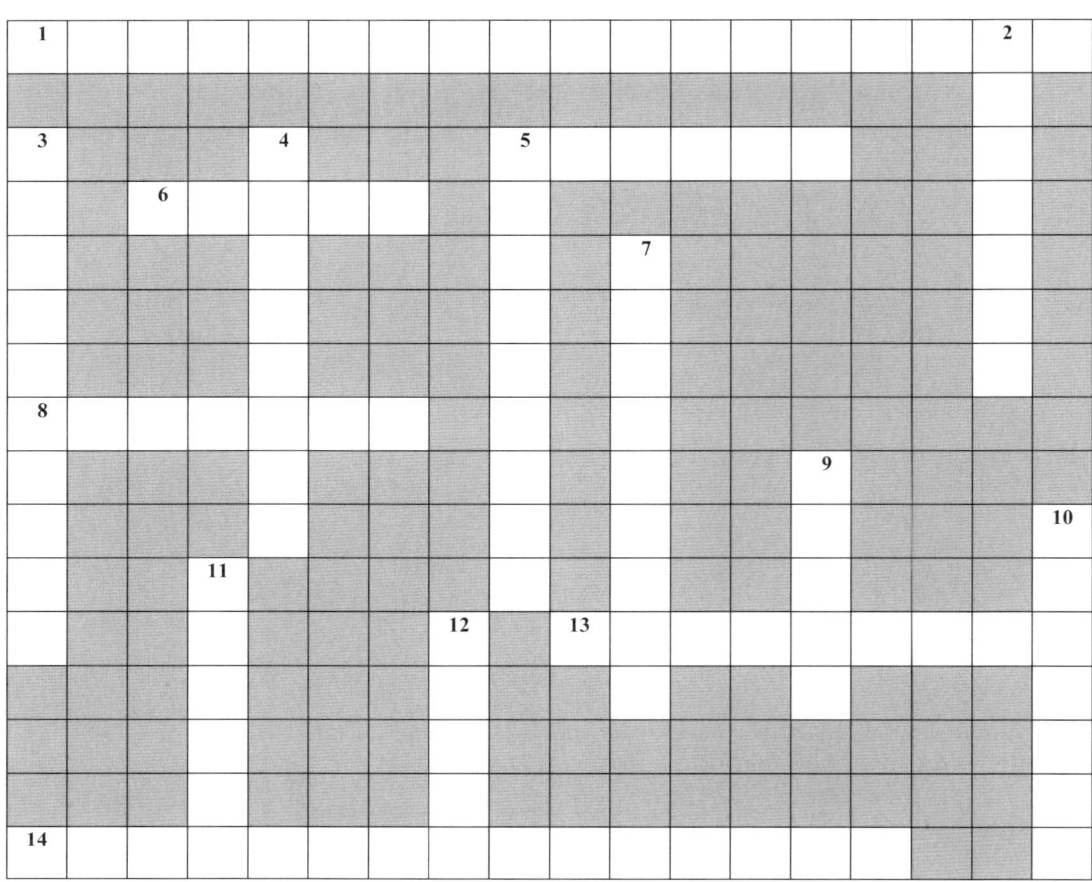

Clues Across

1 Oil is a --- - --------- ------.(12,6)
5 I keep my tea hot in a ------ flask.(6)
6 If two -----(s) are equal and opposite they are balanced.(5)
8 We pulled the rope and created -------.(7)
13 In a series circuit the same current goes through all the ---------(s).(9)
14 An example of --------- ------ is solar.(9,6)

Clues Down

2 Isaac Newton thought a lot about the force of -------.(7)
3 A feather falls more slowly than an apple because of air ----------.(10)
4 Grease and oil reduce --------.(8)
5 The --------- of the guitar strings made the sound.(9)
7 Our bodies give out ---------, we radiate energy.(9)
9 A see-saw will have one of these.(5)
10 Magnets can ------- and repel.(7)
11 To move around? (6)
12 The opposite of attract.(5)

Physics
Keywords in Context

Use the correct keyword to complete the sentence.

If an object is standing still, then a f_ _ _ _ is needed to start it moving.

When things rub together the force of f _ _ _ _ _ _ _ slows them down.

The v _ _ _ _ _ _ _ _ _ of air molecules make the sound when you speak.

The hands of a clock r _ _ _ _ _ around a central point.

R _ _ _ _ _ _ _ _ is one of three ways in which energy can be transferred.

A conductor has a low r _ _ _ _ _ _ _ _ _ because it lets electrons pass through it easily.

Fulcrum is another word for p _ _ _ _, the point on which something turns.

The elastic band was stretched to the limit causing great t _ _ _ _ _ _.

We are all held on Earth by the force of g _ _ _ _ _ _.

Sound cannot travel through a v _ _ _ _ _ because there isn't air to vibrate.

Wind power is an example of r _ _ _ _ _ _ _ _ e _ _ _ _ _.

Coal is an example of n _ _ - _ _ _ _ _ _ _ _ _ _ e _ _ _ _ _.

Like poles repel, unlike poles a _ _ _ _ _ _.

A magnet can r _ _ _ _ another magnet.

In a circuit diagram the c _ _ _ _ _ _ _ _ (s) can be in series or parallel.

Physics
Keywords in Context

Use the correct keyword to complete the sentence.

If an object is standing still, then a _ _ _ _ _ is needed to start it moving.

When things rub together the force of _ _ _ _ _ _ _ _ slows them down.

The _ _ _ _ _ _ _ _ _ _ of air molecules make the sound when you speak.

The hands of a clock _ _ _ _ _ _ around a central point.

_ _ _ _ _ _ _ _ _ _ is one of three ways in which energy can be transferred.

A conductor has a low _ _ _ _ _ _ _ _ _ _ _ because it lets electrons pass through it easily.

Fulcrum is another word for _ _ _ _ _, the point on which something turns.

The elastic band was stretched to the limit causing great _ _ _ _ _ _ _.

We are all held on Earth by the force of _ _ _ _ _ _ _.

Sound cannot travel through a _ _ _ _ _ _ because there isn't air to vibrate.

Wind power is an example of _ _ _ _ _ _ _ _ _ _ _ _ _ _ _ _.

Coal is an example of _ _ _ - _ _ _ _ _ _ _ _ _ _ _ _ _ _ _ _.

Like poles repel, unlike poles _ _ _ _ _ _ _.

A magnet can _ _ _ _ _ another magnet.

In a circuit diagram the _ _ _ _ _ _ _ _ _ _ (s) can be in series or parallel.

Physics

Look, Say, Cover, Write, Check

force	________	________	________
friction	________	________	________
resistance	________	________	________
tension	________	________	________
gravity	________	________	________
repel	________	________	________
attract	________	________	________
vibration	________	________	________
rotate	________	________	________
pivot	________	________	________
component	________	________	________
radiation	________	________	________
renewable energy	________	________	________
non-renewable energy	________	________	________
	________	________	________
vacuum	________	________	________

Physics

Name the Keyword

g_______________	The force that pulls things towards the centre of the Earth.
v_______________	When something moves backwards and forwards quickly, making a sound.
r_______________	Slows something down or stops it.
t_______________	How much something is being stretched.
f_______________	A push or pull.
r_______________	To push away.
a_______________	To pull towards itself.
f_______________	A force that slows things down when they rub together.
r_______________	Moves around a central point.
p_______________	The point on which something turns.
n_______________	Once it is used, it is gone forever, e.g. coal.
r_______________	When energy travels through the air.
r_______________	It cannot be used up, it is always there, e.g. wind.
c_______________	A part of something.
v_______________	A space without any air in it.

Physics

Name the Keyword

_______________ The force that pulls things towards the centre of the Earth.

_______________ When something moves backwards and forwards quickly, making a sound.

_______________ Slows something down or stops it.

_______________ How much something is being stretched.

_______________ A push or pull.

_______________ To push away.

_______________ To pull towards itself.

_______________ A force that slows things down when they rub together.

_______________ Moves around a central point.

_______________ The point on which something turns.

_______________ Once it is used, it is gone forever, e.g. coal.

_______________ When energy travels through the air.

_______________ It cannot be used up, it is always there, e.g. wind.

_______________ A part of something.

_______________ A space without any air in it.

Physics
Delivering Definitions

Give the correct definition for each keyword.

force ______________________________

friction ______________________________

resistance ______________________________

tension ______________________________

gravity ______________________________

repel ______________________________

attract ______________________________

vibration ______________________________

rotate ______________________________

pivot ______________________________

component ______________________________

radiation ______________________________

renewable energy ______________________________

non-renewable energy ______________________________

vacuum ______________________________

Biology

Keywords in Science

invertebrates	Animals without a backbone.
vertebrates	Animals with a backbone.
omnivores	Animals that eat both plants and animals.
herbivores	Animals that eat only plants.
carnivores	Animals that eat other animals.
mammals	Warm-blooded animals usually with fur or hair, that feed their young with milk from the mother.
fish	Cold-blooded animals that live in water; have a backbone, scaly skin, gills for breathing and fins and tails for swimming.
amphibians	Animals that live on land and in water; have smooth, moist skins and lay their eggs in water.
reptiles	Animals that have dry, scaly skin, live mainly on land and lay eggs with soft shells.
birds	Animals that have feathers and wings, usually fly and lay eggs with hard shells.
flowering plants	Have flowers and seeds made inside fruits.
ferns	Have strong stems, roots and leaves and do not have seeds.
mosses	Have weak roots; thin, delicate leaves and do not have seeds.
conifers	Do not have flowers and their seeds are made in cones.
photosynthesis	The way in which a plant uses light energy from the sun to make food.

Biology
Matching

Link the keyword with the correct definition.

invertebrates	Animals without a backbone.
vertebrates	Animals that live on land and in water; have smooth, moist skins and lay their eggs in water.
omnivores	Animals that eat both plants and animals.
herbivores	Have strong stems, roots and leaves and do not have seeds.
carnivores	Cold-blooded animals that live in water; have a backbone, scaly skin, gills for breathing and fins and tails for swimming.
mammals	Have weak roots; thin, delicate leaves and do not have seeds.
fish	Animals that have dry, scaly skin, live mainly on land and lay eggs with soft shells.
amphibians	The way in which a plant uses light energy from the sun to make food.
reptiles	Animals that eat only plants.
birds	Warm-blooded animals usually with fur or hair, that feed their young with milk from the mother.
flowering plants	Animals with a backbone.
ferns	Do not have flowers and their seeds are made in cones.
mosses	Animals that eat other animals.
conifers	Have flowers and seeds made inside fruits.
photosynthesis	Animals that have feathers and wings, usually fly and lay eggs with hard shells.

Biology

Choose the Word

invertebrates	Animals (*without, with, chasing*) a backbone.
vertebrates	Animals (*without, with, chasing*) a backbone.
omnivores	Animals that eat both plants and (*fish, people, animals*).
herbivores	Animals that eat only (*herbs, plants, flowers*).
carnivores	Animals that eat other (*things, animals, people*).
mammals	(*Warm-blooded, Red-blooded, Cold-blooded*) animals usually with fur or hair, that feed their young with milk from the mother.
fish	(*Cold-blooded, Warm-blooded, Red-blooded*) animals that live in water; have a backbone, scaly skin, gills for breathing and fins and tails for swimming.
amphibians	Animals that live on land and in (*caves, water, trees*); have smooth, moist skins and lay their eggs in water.
reptiles	Animals that have (*dry, wet, cold*), scaly skin, live mainly on land and lay eggs with soft shells.
birds	Animals that have feathers and wings, usually fly and lay eggs with (*hard, soft, chocolate*) shells.
flowering plants	Have flowers and seeds made inside (*fruits, leaves, stems*).
ferns	Have (*weak, strong, thin*) stems, roots and leaves and do not have seeds.
mosses	Have weak roots; (*thin, thick, hard*), delicate leaves and do not have seeds.
conifers	Do not have flowers and their (*seeds, fruits, petals*) are made in cones.
photosynthesis	The way in which a plant uses light energy from the (*moon, sky, sun*) to make food.

Biology

Wordsearch

i	n	v	e	r	t	e	b	r	a	t	e	s	p	v
z	x	c	v	b	n	m	k	j	h	g	g	f	h	e
o	m	n	i	v	o	r	e	s	f	g	h	y	o	r
a	s	d	h	e	r	b	i	v	o	r	e	s	t	t
c	d	f	r	t	y	u	i	o	p	f	f	g	o	e
a	m	a	m	m	a	l	s	z	x	i	z	x	s	b
r	q	w	e	r	t	y	u	i	o	s	p	o	y	r
n	p	o	i	u	y	t	r	e	d	h	d	d	n	a
i	a	m	p	h	i	b	i	a	n	s	s	s	t	t
v	d	r	e	p	t	i	l	e	s	s	b	s	h	e
o	c	v	b	n	h	j	k	m	i	u	i	f	e	s
r	f	e	r	n	s	f	d	f	g	h	r	n	s	b
e	z	m	o	s	s	e	s	z	x	c	d	x	i	v
s	v	c	o	n	i	f	e	r	s	v	s	v	s	v
f	l	o	w	e	r	i	n	g	p	l	a	n	t	s

omnivores	herbivores	carnivores	vertebrates	invertebrates
mammals	fish	amphibians	reptiles	photosynthesis
birds	ferns	mosses	conifers	flowering plants

Extension exercise:

Name five amphibians. Write about one in detail.

Biology

Wordsearch

i	n	v	e	r	t	e	b	r	a	t	e	s	c	v
h	e	r	b	i	v	o	r	e	s	c	v	b	o	e
s	q	w	e	r	t	y	u	i	o	p	s	l	n	r
i	p	o	i	u	y	t	r	e	w	q	l	q	i	t
f	o	m	n	i	v	o	r	e	s	x	a	z	f	e
b	c	a	r	n	i	v	o	r	e	s	m	z	e	b
z	i	z	x	c	x	z	x	c	x	z	m	d	r	r
d	f	r	g	h	j	k	l	o	u	p	a	y	s	a
y	u	i	d	o	i	u	j	h	g	d	m	x	c	t
c	v	b	n	s	m	n	j	h	b	g	v	f	r	e
a	m	p	h	i	b	i	a	n	s	d	f	g	h	s
r	e	p	t	i	l	e	s	e	r	t	y	u	i	o
f	l	o	w	e	r	i	n	g	p	l	a	n	t	s
f	e	r	n	s	v	v	m	o	s	s	e	s	v	x
p	h	o	t	o	s	y	n	t	h	e	s	i	s	z

omnivores	herbivores	carnivores	vertebrates	invertebrates
mammals	fish	amphibians	reptiles	photosynthesis
birds	ferns	mosses	conifers	flowering plants

Extension exercise:

Name five amphibians. Write about one in detail.

Biology
Jumbled Words

Unjumble the words to give the correct definition. The underlined words are in the right order.

invertebrates	a without backbone. Animals
vertebrates	with a Animals backbone.
omnivores	Animals both that and plants eat animals.
herbivores	Animals eat only that plants.
carnivores	Animals that other eat animals.
mammals	Warm-blooded animals milk young their feed hair, usually fur from with or that with the mother.
fish	Cold-blooded animals skin, tails water; a in that backbone, for live have scaly and breathing gills fins and for swimming.
amphibians	Animals that eggs on in smooth, land and water; moist live and their have skins lay in water.
reptiles	Animals that land dry, skin, have on scaly with and mainly lay live eggs soft shells.
birds	Animals that wings, eggs feathers fly usually have and and with lay hard shells.
flowering plants	Have seeds flowers inside and made fruits.
ferns	Have strong leaves not stems, roots do and and have seeds.
mosses	Have weak thin, roots; leaves not do delicate and have seeds.
conifers	Do not flowers seeds made and have are their in cones.
photosynthesis	The way plant the a to in sun which uses energy light from make food.

Biology
Jumbled Words

Unjumble the words to give the correct definition.

invertebrates	*a without backbone animals*
vertebrates	*with a animals backbone*
omnivores	*both that and plants animals animals eat*
herbivores	*eat plants animals only that*
carnivores	*that animals other eat animals*
mammals	*the milk young their feed hair warm-blooded usually fur mother animals from with or that with*
fish	*skin tails animals water swimming cold-blooded a in that backbone for live have scaly and breathing gills fins and for*
amphibians	*eggs that on in animals smooth land and water moist live and their have skins lay in water*
reptiles	*land dry that skin animals have on soft scaly shells with and mainly lay live eggs*
birds	*wings eggs shells animals feathers fly hard that usually have and and with lay*
flowering plants	*seeds fruits flowers inside and have made*
ferns	*leaves seeds not stems strong roots have do and and have*
mosses	*thin seeds have have roots weak leaves not do delicate and*
conifers	*in not do flowers seeds made cones and have are their*
photosynthesis	*food the way make plant the a to in sun which uses energy light from*

Biology

Code Breaking

A	B	C	D	E	F	G	H	I	J	K	L	M	N	O	P	Q	R	S	T	U	V	W	X	Y	Z
z	y	x	w	v	u	t	s	r	q	p	o	n	m	l	k	j	i	h	g	f	e	d	c	b	a

Decode the CAPITAL letters to find each keyword.

1. X o n R f e r s
2. R n v e r t V b r Z t e s
3. S e r Y R v o r e s
4. N Z m m Z l s
5. Z m p h R b R a n s
6. Y R r d s
7. U e r n H
8. K h o t L s B n t h e s R s
9. E e r t V b r a t V H
10. L m n R v o r e s
11. X a r n R v o r e H
12. U R s h
13. I e p G R l e s
14. U l o w e r R n g K l Z n t s
15. N L s s e s

Extension exercise:

Name three of the following:

omnivore herbivore carnivore

Biology

Code Breaking

A	B	C	D	E	F	G	H	I	J	K	L	M	N	O	P	Q	R	S	T	U	V	W	X	Y	Z
z	y	x	w	v	u	t	s	r	q	p	o	n	m	l	k	j	i	h	g	f	e	d	c	b	a

Decode the CAPITAL letters to find each keyword.

1. X L M R U V I H
2. R M E V I G V Y I Z G V H
3. S V I Y R E L I V H
4. N Z N N Z O H
5. Z N K S R Y R Z M H
6. Y R I W H
7. U V I M H
8. K S L G L H B M G S V H R H
9. E V I G V Y I Z G V H
10. L N M R E L I V H
11. X Z I M R E L I V H
12. U R H S
13. I V K G R O V H
14. U O L D V I R M T K O Z M G H
15. N L H H V H

Extension exercise:

Name three of the following:

omnivore herbivore carnivore

Biology
Cloze

invertebrates	Animals w____________ a backbone.
vertebrates	Animals w_________ a backbone.
omnivores	Animals that eat both p___________ and animals.
herbivores	Animals that eat only p___________.
carnivores	Animals that eat other a____________.
mammals	W_________________ animals usually with fur or hair, that feed their young with milk from the mother.
fish	C_________________ animals that live in water; have a backbone, scaly skin, gills for breathing and fins and tails for swimming.
amphibians	Animals that live on l_________ and in water; have smooth, moist skins and lay their eggs in water.
reptiles	Animals that have dry, s__________ skin, live mainly on land and lay eggs with soft shells.
birds	Animals that have f______________ and wings, usually fly and lay eggs with hard shells.
flowering plants	Have f____________ and seeds made inside fruits.
ferns	Have strong s__________, roots and leaves and do not have seeds.
mosses	Have weak r__________; thin, delicate leaves and do not have seeds.
conifers	Do not have f____________ and their seeds are made in cones.
photosynthesis	The way in which a plant uses light energy from the s________ to make food.

Biology
Cloze

invertebrates	Animals ______________ a backbone.
vertebrates	Animals __________ a backbone.
omnivores	Animals that eat both _____________ and animals.
herbivores	Animals that eat only _____________.
carnivores	Animals that eat other ______________.
mammals	____________________ animals usually with fur or hair, that feed their young with milk from the mother.
fish	____________________ animals that live in water; have a backbone, scaly skin, gills for breathing and fins and tails for swimming.
amphibians	Animals that live on __________ and in water; have smooth, moist skins and lay their eggs in water.
reptiles	Animals that have dry, ____________ skin, live mainly on land and lay eggs with soft shells.
birds	Animals that have _______________ and wings, usually fly and lay eggs with hard shells.
flowering plants	Have ______________ and seeds made inside fruits.
ferns	Have strong ____________, roots and leaves and do not have seeds.
mosses	Have weak ____________; thin, delicate leaves and do not have seeds.
conifers	Do not have ______________ and their seeds are made in cones.
photosynthesis	The way in which a plant uses light energy from the _________ to make food.

Biology

Anagrams

Unjumble the letters to find each keyword.

1. b r a t e s i n v e r t e
2. v o r e s c a r n i
3. i v o r e s h e r b
4. m m a l s m a
5. p h i b i a n s m a
6. i r d s b
7. r n s f e
8. f e r s c o n i
9. b r a t e s v e r t e
10. v o r e s o m i n
11. s y n t h e s i s p h o t o
12. s h i f
13. t i l e s r e p
14. r i n g f l o w e a n t s p l
15. s s e s m o

Extension exercise:

Name five: vertebrates invertebrates
Write about one in detail.

Biology

Anagrams

Unjumble the letters to find each keyword.

1. e r a e t e n s i v r t b
2. i o r s c r a n v e
3. r b v o e s h r i e
4. a m a s m m l
5. a h i b i n s m p a
6. i d r s b
7. n r s f e
8. i e o r s c n f
9. e r t a e s v e t b r
10. n o m r e s o i v
11. e n o y t h s i s p h o t s
12. s i f h
13. p i e s r e t l
14. e i n g f o l w r l t n s p a
15. s e s m s o

Extension exercise:

Name five: vertebrates invertebrates
Write about one in detail.

Biology

Crossword

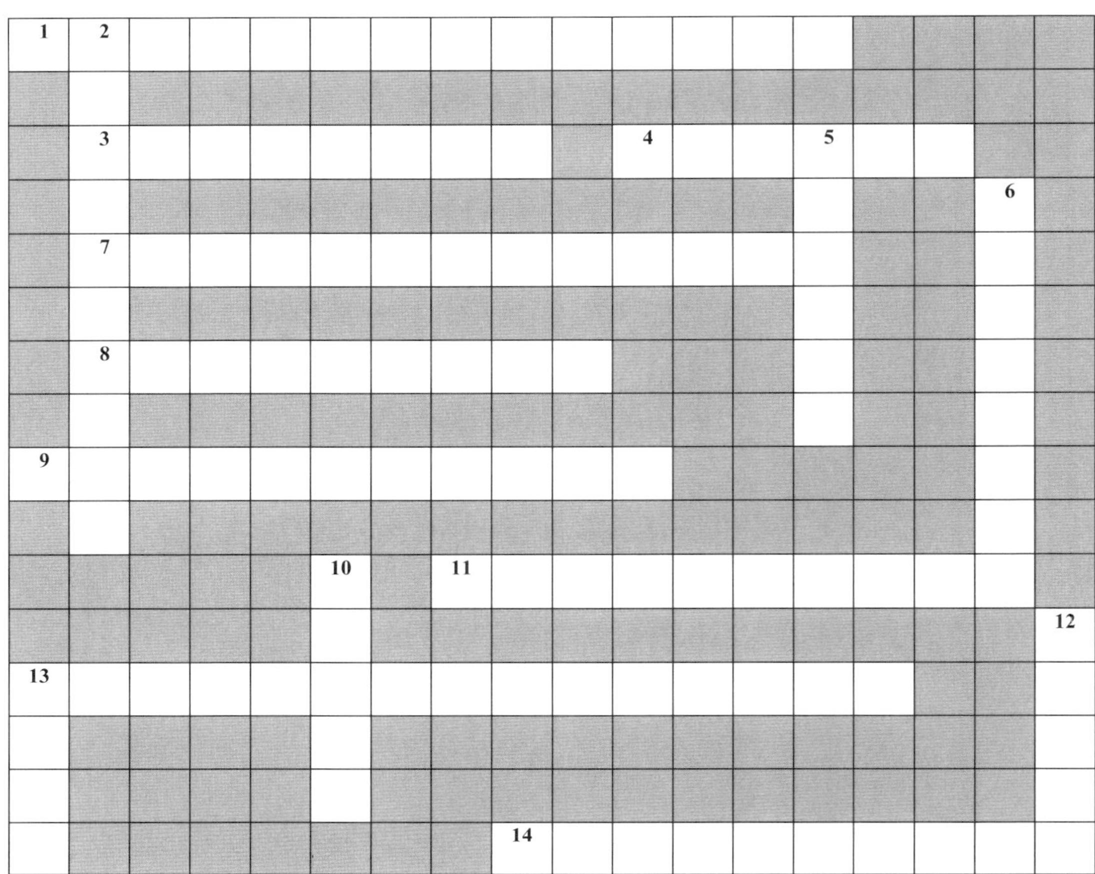

Clues Across

1 During p------------- sugar and oxygen are made.(14)
3 Lizards are r-------.(8)
4 A llama is a m-----.(6)
7 Worms are i------------.(13)
8 These animals aren't fussy what they eat.(9)
9 All v---------- belong to one of five main groups of animals.(11)
11 Foxes are c---------.(10)
13 Most f-------- p----- live on the land and lose water through their leaves.(9,6)
14 Toads are a---------.(10)

Clues Down

2 Horses are h---------.(10)
5 The leaves of m----- lose water easily.(6)
6 The cones c------- produce are very attractive.(8)
10 Crows are b----.(5)
12 F---- are very popular for use in bouquets.(5)
13 A bream is a f---.(4)

Biology

Crossword

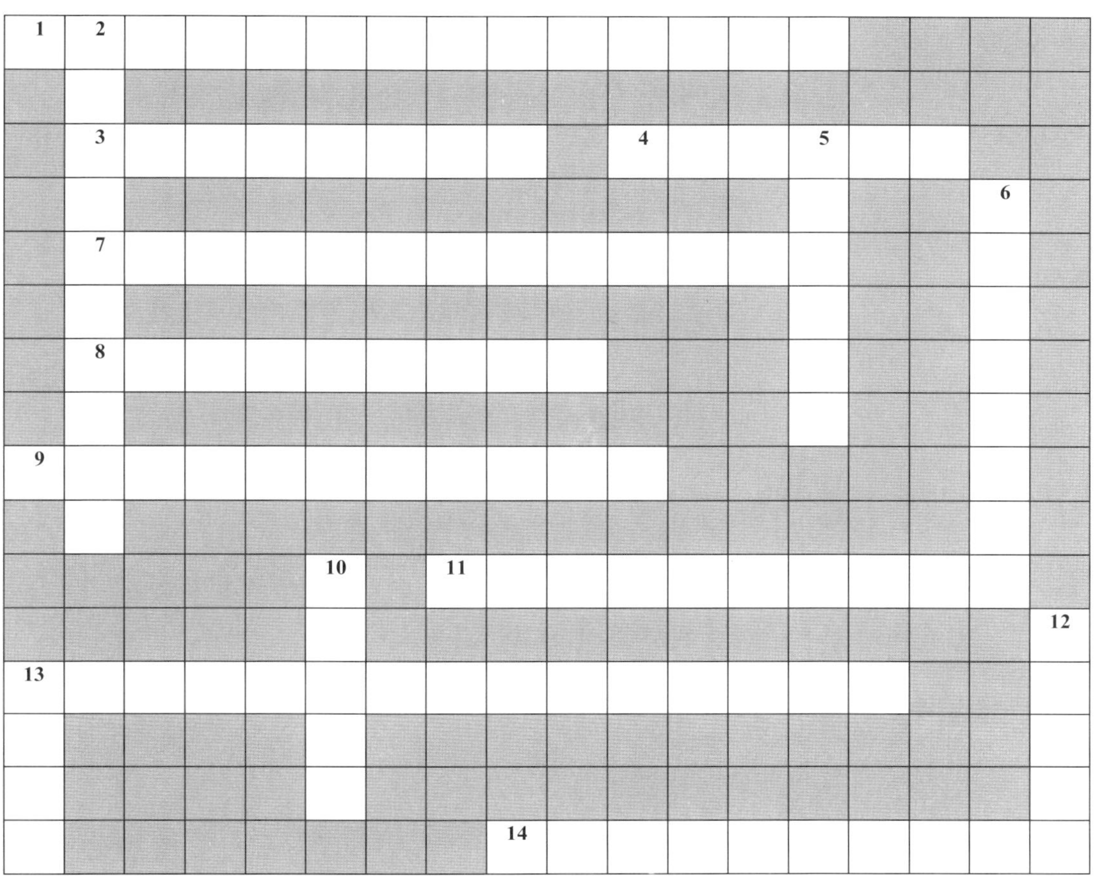

Clues Across

1 During -------------- sugar and oxygen are made.(14)
3 Lizards are --------.(8)
4 A llama is a ------.(6)
7 Worms are -------------.(13)
8 These animals aren't fussy what they eat.(9)
9 All ----------- belong to one of five main groups of animals.(11)
11 Foxes are ----------.(10)
13 Most --------- ------ live on the land and lose water through their leaves.(9,6)
14 Toads are ----------.(10)

Clues Down

2 Horses are ----------.(10)
5 The leaves of ------ lose water easily.(6)
6 The cones -------- produce are very attractive.(8)
10 Crows are -----.(5)
12 ----- are very popular for use in bouquets.(5)
13 A bream is a ----.(4)

Biology
Keywords in Context

Use the correct keyword to complete the sentence.

I _ _ _ _ _ _ _ _ _ _ _ _ _ are small and usually found in the sea.

Fish, birds, reptiles, mammals and amphibians are all v _ _ _ _ _ _ _ _ _ _.

Most c _ _ _ _ _ _ _ have evergreen leaves.

M _ _ _ _ _ often grow together in clumps and live in damp places.

O _ _ _ _ _ _ _ _ include human beings as we eat both plants and animals.

Cows and tortoises are examples of h _ _ _ _ _ _ _ _ _.

Most c _ _ _ _ _ _ _ _ _ _ are predators and survive by hunting and eating other animals.

There are many different species of m _ _ _ _ _ _ including elephants, whales and bats.

F _ _ _ will be found almost anywhere where there is water.

The a _ _ _ _ _ _ _ _ _ _ were the first vertebrates to develop legs instead of fins and so were able to move on to dry land.

Snakes and crocodiles are all types of r _ _ _ _ _ _ _.

B _ _ _ _ are the only animals to have feathers.

F _ _ _ _ _ _ _ _ p _ _ _ _ _ are to be found all over the world and offer us some of the most beautiful sights of nature.

F _ _ _ _ do not have flowers but can still look very attractive.

P _ _ _ _ _ _ _ _ _ _ _ _ _ is vital to life on Earth because it provides food, directly or indirectly, for the living world.

Biology
Keywords in Context

Use the correct keyword to complete the sentence.

_ _ _ _ _ _ _ _ _ _ _ _ _ _ are small and usually found in the sea.

Fish, birds, reptiles, mammals and amphibians are all _ _ _ _ _ _ _ _ _ _ _ _.

Most _ _ _ _ _ _ _ _ _ have evergreen leaves.

_ _ _ _ _ _ often grow together in clumps and live in damp places.

_ _ _ _ _ _ _ _ _ _ include human beings as we eat both plants and animals.

Cows and tortoises are examples of _ _ _ _ _ _ _ _ _ _ _.

Most _ _ _ _ _ _ _ _ _ _ _ are predators and survive by hunting and eating other animals.

There are many different species of _ _ _ _ _ _ _ including elephants, whales and bats.

_ _ _ _ will be found almost anywhere where there is water.

The _ _ _ _ _ _ _ _ _ _ _ were the first vertebrates to develop legs instead of fins and so were able to move on to dry land.

Snakes and crocodiles are all types of _ _ _ _ _ _ _ _ _.

_ _ _ _ _ are the only animals to have feathers.

_ _ _ _ _ _ _ _ _ _ _ _ _ _ _ _ are to be found all over the world and offer us some of the most beautiful sights of nature.

_ _ _ _ _ do not have flowers but can still look very attractive.

_ _ _ _ _ _ _ _ _ _ _ _ _ _ _ is vital to life on Earth because it provides food, directly or indirectly, for the living world.

Name:

Biology

Look, Say, Cover, Write, Check

invertebrates			
vertebrates			
omnivores			
herbivores			
carnivores			
mammals			
fish			
amphibians			
reptiles			
birds			
flowering plants			
ferns			
mosses			
conifers			
photosynthesis			

Biology

Name the Keyword

c_______________	Animals that eat other animals.
v_______________	Animals with a backbone.
f_______________	Have flowers and seeds made inside fruits.
h_______________	Animals that eat only plants.
i_______________	Animals without a backbone.
m_______________	Warm-blooded animals usually with fur or hair, that feed their young with milk from the mother.
f_______________	Cold-blooded animals that live in water; have a backbone, scaly skin, gills for breathing and fins and tails for swimming.
m_______________	Have weak roots; thin, delicate leaves and do not have seeds.
r_______________	Animals that have dry, scaly skin, live mainly on land and lay eggs with soft shells.
b_______________	Animals that have feathers and wings, usually fly and lay eggs with hard shells.
o_______________	Animals that eat both plants and animals.
f_______________	Have strong stems, roots and leaves and do not have seeds.
a_______________	Animals that live on land and in water; have smooth, moist skins and lay their eggs in water.
c_______________	Do not have flowers and their seeds are made in cones.
p_______________	The way in which a plant uses light energy from the sun to make food.

Biology

Name the Keyword

________________ Animals that eat other animals.

________________ Animals with a backbone.

________________ Have flowers and seeds made inside fruits.

________________ Animals that eat only plants.

________________ Animals without a backbone.

________________ Warm-blooded animals usually with fur or hair, that feed their young with milk from the mother.

________________ Cold-blooded animals that live in water; have a backbone, scaly skin, gills for breathing and fins and tails for swimming.

________________ Have weak roots; thin, delicate leaves and do not have seeds.

________________ Animals that have dry, scaly skin, live mainly on land and lay eggs with soft shells.

________________ Animals that have feathers and wings, usually fly and lay eggs with hard shells.

________________ Animals that eat both plants and animals.

________________ Have strong stems, roots and leaves and do not have seeds.

________________ Animals that live on land and in water; have smooth, moist skins and lay their eggs in water.

________________ Do not have flowers and their seeds are made in cones.

________________ The way in which a plant uses light energy from the sun to make food.

Biology
Delivering Definitions

Give the correct definition for each keyword.

invertebrates ______________________________

____

vertebrates ______________________________

____

omnivores ______________________________

____

herbivores ______________________________

____

carnivores ______________________________

____

mammals ______________________________

____

fish ______________________________

____

amphibians ______________________________

____

reptiles ______________________________

____

birds ______________________________

____

flowering plants ______________________________

____

ferns ______________________________

____

mosses ______________________________

____

conifers ______________________________

____

photosynthesis ______________________________

____

Sure S[illegible]s

literacy

Tutor Support Pack

Entry 1 & 2 • Access 1 & 2

Linda Richards

www.heinemann.co.uk

✓ Free online support
✓ Useful weblinks
✓ 24 hour online ordering

01865 888118

Heinemann

Heinemann is an imprint of Pearson Education Limited, a company incorporated in England and Wales, having its registered office at Edinburgh Gate, Harlow, Essex, CM20 2JE. Registered company number: 872828

www.heinemann.co.uk

Heinemann is a registered trademark of Pearson Education Limited

First published 2008

12 11 10 09 08
10 9 8 7 6 5 4 3 2 1

British Library Cataloguing in Publication Data is available from the British Library on request.

ISBN 978 0 435 46513 1

Typeset by TechType
Illustrated by TechType
Cover design by Tower Designs
Printed in the UK by Ashford Colour Press

The author and publisher would like to thank the following individuals and organizations for their kind permission to reproduce material: Bob Tapp, Lead Tutor in Business and General Education at South Devon College, Paignton for the Bingo and Domino Generators; safetyshop.com for the health and safety signs (Activity Sheets 2.1.1, 2.2.2, 2.2.3, 3.2.9); UNISON for the 'Slips and Trips' poster (Activity Sheet 5.2.4); ENCAMS for the 'Tidy Man' logo (Activity Sheet 11.1.1)

Every effort has been made to contact copyright holders of material reproduced in this book. Any omissions will be rectified in subsequent printings if notice is given to the publishers.

Contents

Introduction

How to use this pack

The *Sure Skills Literacy Tutor Support Pack for Entry 1 and 2/ Access 1 and 2* takes a themed approach to the literacy skills that learners at these levels need. Each theme draws together the relevant objectives from the Adult Literacy Core Curriculum, with references to the Adult Literacy and Numeracy Framework for Scotland, providing a holistic approach to developing key literacy skills and abilities. The themes are set in everyday contexts which will be most useful to adult learners, and can be easily adapted to work in different settings and contexts.

It is not intended that you work through the pack from start to finish, completing every activity. The themes can be used flexibly, in any order, and there is no set time given for the themes. How long you spend on each theme or activity will depend on the skills and needs of your particular group of learners.

A range of activities is given for each theme – you may wish to pick and mix from these activities, providing your learners with the particular level of consolidation and reinforcement that they need. Most of the activities are suitable for learners working at either Entry 1/Access 1 or Entry 2/Access 2; where appropriate, specific activities or variations are given for working with a particular level. References are given both within the notes and on the activity sheets themselves.

The pack is fully photocopiable, and you will find copies of the activity sheets and presentations on the CD for you to customise.

Using and adapting the activities

The first activity in each theme is intended to introduce the learning outcomes, and set learners' expectations for what is to come. These activities are suitable for adults working at Entry 1/ Access 1 and Entry 2/Access 2.

Each theme then contains several activities with a different focus; these can usually be used flexibly, and do not have to be followed in sequential order.

A comprehensive bank of activity sheets is provided both in print and in Word format on the CD, all of which can be adapted to suit your learners' specific requirements.

Many activities have suggestions for working in specific contexts, such as vocational settings, home and leisure, work and employment.

Using the Microsoft PowerPoint® presentations

P Many of the themes include Powerpoint® presentations, which can be accessed via the CD in the pack.

The presentations are there to give you alternative ways of introducing or reinforcing key concepts and learning points, and are ideal for supporting group or whole class discussions. They can be used with a whiteboard or projector, or you could work directly from a computer if you are working with a small group.

The theme notes include suggestions for setting the scene before showing the presentation, along with points to bring out for each slide.

We hope that you will find these presentations a useful starting point – they are ideal for stimulating discussions and canvassing and recording the opinions or experience of your learners. You can edit the slides, adding notes and suggestions that come up during your sessions, and save your versions for future use.

Using the CD

On the CD, you will find all the teaching notes, presentations and activity sheets, along with some templates for developing your own activities that we hope you will find useful. The contents are arranged by theme and also by resource type, e.g. presentations, activities, notes for easy navigation.

Bingo generator

This Excel spreadsheet is included with the kind permission of Bob Tapp (Lead Tutor in Business and General Education at South Devon College) You can use this to create your own bingo cards for use with any of the themes, quickly and easily. Simply follow the instructions on the spreadsheet, and save your own variations. The Bingo generator is particularly useful for Theme 3 and 4.

Domino generator

Also provided with the kind permission of Bob Tapp, the Domino generator can be used with any theme, particularly those which require 'matching' exercises, such as matching upper and lower case versions of the alphabet. Again, simply complete the Excel spreadsheet and save your own variations.

For details on how to load the CD, please see the notes in the CD wallet.

Sure Skills literacy

Theme 3

Some themes are closely related, and you may wish to combine activities, or where prior knowledge is required, ensure that you have covered these topics.

words

Links

Theme 2 Signs and symbols; Theme 7 Using the alphabet.

Key words

letter, sound, word.

Try to introduce these key words and phrases to learners during teaching. You may wish to suggest that these are recorded in personal dictionaries or notebooks.

Key:

 Activity Sheet

 PowerPoint® presentation on CD

 Resource available on CD, e.g. colour version of activity sheet, Excel spreadsheet

Where you will need resources other than those supplied with this pack, these are highlighted at the start of an activity.

Other resources

Examples of company/product logos, examples of other words from the learners' environment, highlighter pens.

It is important for learners to see the correlation between written and spoken words if they are to improve their reading skills. Length, shape, initial letters, association with other words and personal experience of language are all clues that can be used to work out and remember a new word.

In this theme the main focus is on visual recognition of social sight vocabulary. Learners are given the opportunity to become familiar with common words and are asked to compile or add to a personal dictionary of words that has particular relevance to their own lives and habits. It is important in these activities to include words that have meaning to the learner in his or her context and suggestions are given throughout to help with ways of doing this.

Learning outcomes	Adult Literacy Curriculum references	ALAN Curriculum Framework for Scotland
To be able to build a meaningful vocabulary of personal key words	Rw/E1.1 Rw/E1.2 Rw/E2.2 Rw/E2.3 Ww/E1.1 Ww/E1.3 Ww/E2.1 Ww/E2.2	A1/A2 • Recognising social sight words
To be able to use their own language experience to help recognise sight vocabulary		
To be able to recognise the correlation between graphemes and phonemes		
To be able to decode regular words		

Activity notes

Activity 1 Introducing the theme

Reassure learners that they already have a bank of words they recognise by discussing the words we see around us, such as logos on shops and products and signs in the street, workplace or hospital.

- How do we recognise them?
- What information are they giving us?

Start a collection of product/shop names or logos that the learners will recognise, which they can add to during the course of the theme. Create a poster or wall display if possible. Do the same with words and phrases that are of interest to your learners, e.g. road signs if they are learner drivers, hospital signs if they need to visit hospital often, words to do with a particular job, words that are used on computers and the Internet.

This symbol denotes where an activity sheet is included. Some activity sheets are in colour – these are provided on the CD in the relevant theme; a black and white version is included in the printed pack for reference.

A 3.1.1 The interview story 3.1.2 Words from the interview(Entry 1 and 2/Access 1 and 2)

Introduce the concept of the value of words as useful tools to negotiate a new environment by telling a story about a journey or new experience likely to be faced by the learners. Use the example given on Activity Sheet 3.1.1 or customise your own sheet. Other examples might be a shopping trip or going to the sports centre.

- Give each learner a sign from Activity Sheet 3.1.2 and make sure he or she is familiar with the word. Discuss each word briefly.
- Where else might it be seen?
- What makes it easy to recognise?
- Talk about the shape, first letter, similarities and differences from other words. Ask learners to share any techniques they may have developed for remembering words. Prompt for: repeating a word over and over, making up a story to associate the word with; picturing the word in the mind's eye. Confirm that these ways are all valid – whatever works for one individual is right for them. Also point out that many techniques are available and it is up to each learner to try new ones to see if they work for him or her.
- Explain that you are going to tell the learners what happened to you when you went for an interview for a new job. At several points during the morning you needed to know where to go and what to do next. If learners think they are holding a sign that may have given you the information you needed, they should hold it up at the appropriate moment. Read the 'story' on Activity Sheet 3.1.1, using the first paragraph, to ensure learners know what to do.

After telling the story, go through it briefly again and discuss each sign.

Differentiation

Where appropriate, ideas for further work are included. These may be suggestions for working with learners at a particular level, or extending the activity to different contexts.

Most learners will not need to see the story written down. However, some may wish to use the words on Activity Sheet 3.1.2 to match the words in the story. Others may wish to use a highlighter pen to highlight words from the story.

Theme 1

What is it all about?

Introduction

In this theme, learners work with a variety of texts in the activity sheets, as well as a selection based on their personal experience. They are given the opportunity to recognise the skills they already have in deciphering these texts, as well as those they need to develop in order to access texts more effectively.

You can use this theme as an assessment of existing skills and make use of the information to add to the ILPs of the learners. Themes from throughout the pack can then be used to support them.

Learning outcomes	**Adult Literacy Curriculum references**	**ALAN Curriculum Framework for Scotland**
To be able to recognise the importance of text To be able to recognise different formats To be able to recognise different text features	Rt/E1.2 Rt/E2.1 Rt/E2.2	A1/A2 • Reading for understanding • Reading for particular purposes • Recognising signs, symbols and social sight words

Links

All other themes.

Key words

bold, describe, entertain, explain, font, graphic, inform, instruct, italic, leaflet, logo, notice, persuade, poster, table, text.

Activity notes

Activity 1 Introducing the theme

This activity looks at what text is and what forms it takes. It introduces some of the vocabulary used throughout the theme.

P Presentation 1 What is text? (Entry 1 and 2/Access 1 and 2)

Slide 1

Discuss why and when people read and collate suggestions on the slide. Prompt for reasons such as 'to find information', 'for enjoyment on holiday'.

Slide 2

Explain that each person in the illustration is looking at some text. Ask for suggestions about the type of each text and the purpose of it. Use vocabulary associated with the text. The woman is reading a holiday brochure that is describing holiday destinations; the man is reading a car manual that is giving him instructions about how to repair his car; the boy is reading a comic for entertainment; the girl is looking for some information on the Internet. Ask learners to say what other types of texts each person could be reading.

Slide 3

Symbols can be recognised by everyone. Ask learners to contribute other examples of symbols.

Sometimes words are needed. Discuss how logos include words. Ask learners to think of some examples from their clothing, bags, etc.

Slide 4

This slide gives a list of reasons why text is important. Read through it with the learners and add to the list.

Other resources

A selection of everyday texts, e.g. newspapers, timetables, magazines.

Activity 2 What do you need to read?

Share your experiences of the consequences of misreading text, e.g. missing a dental appointment (and being charged for it) because you misread the appointment card; being late for a job interview because you had not read where to go; missing a bus because you looked up the bus times for a weekday on a Saturday. If learners are willing, ask them to add any experiences of their own. Stress that everybody makes mistakes when reading.

Discuss how words convey meaning and we have to decide what is important and what we can safely ignore, e.g. the consequences of ignoring a sign for a one-way street while driving versus the consequences of not reading an advert for a new deodorant while waiting for a bus.

Display a selection of different types of texts around the room. Ask learners to pick a text they would choose to read and one they would ignore. Ask learners to explain their choices. Expect and acknowledge a variety of responses.

Discuss texts that have a particular purpose.

- What text would you use to find the time of the next bus home?
- What text would you use to see what is on television tonight?
- What text would you use to buy a second-hand car?
- What text would you use to find a job?

As learners make their choices, briefly look at each text and ask them to pick out the main features of that text:

- How do you know this is a newspaper? (A newspaper uses particular paper, different-sized fonts, photographs and adverts.)

- How do you know this is a timetable? (A timetable has information arranged in columns and rows.)
- Acknowledge all contributions by emphasising how much they already know about texts.

Ask learners to start collecting their own resource bank of useful texts, e.g. timetables, surgery opening times and phone numbers, rubbish collection dates, work rotas, college timetables, car manuals.

Differentiation

Observe learners who need support and add to their ILPs as necessary.

Activity 3 Different texts

This section looks at different types of texts and encourages learners to explore what makes them different.

Decide on a selection of texts appropriate to your learners. These can be from this tutor pack, actual texts that the learners might use, or a mixture of both. Depending on the needs and interests of the learners, the texts could be limited to just workplace items, those to do with leisure activities, those based around home life, or a mixture of them all.

Other resources

A selection of everyday texts.

 **1.3.1 What would you use to find...? (Entry 1/Access 1)**

Cut up the sheet, select any appropriate cards and add some if necessary. Read out each card and ask learners to find a text that matches it.

Using the same technique, ask learners to select some texts and challenge fellow learners.

Activity 4 What does it look like?

This activity uses notices and noticeboards to look at the message we get from the way a piece of text is presented.

Other resources

Access to computers, access to noticeboards.

Arrange for learners to see a noticeboard in the learning environment and discuss the notices.

- What is the first thing they notice?
- Why do they think that is?
- What is easy to read and why?
- What is difficult to read and why?

Steer the discussion towards font styles, type and colour, use of upper case letters, bold, italic, underlining, background colour and graphics.

1.4.1 Workplace noticeboard (Entry 1 and 2/Access 1 and 2)

1.4.2 Sports and leisure centre noticeboard (Entry 1 and 2/Access 1 and 2)

1.4.3 Family noticeboard (Entry 1 and 2/Access 1 and 2)

Display one of these activity sheets from the presentation or the pack and discuss the noticeboard shown.

- What stands out and why?
- What graphics are used?
- What messages do the logos convey?

Discuss each notice in more detail, paying particular attention to the format. Read each notice for learners to follow and check their understanding.

- Is the notice a list? Is the graphic important?

1.4.4 Change a notice: gardener (Entry 1 and 2/ Access 1 and 2)

1.4.5 Change a notice: tai chi (Entry 1 and 2/ Access 1 and 2)

1.4.6 Change a notice: new windows (Entry 1 and 2/Access 1 and 2)

- Use these activity sheets for learners who are familiar with Microsoft Word. They can customise the notices by altering the font, adding clip art, etc.
- Display the finished results on a noticeboard and discuss which ones stand out and why.
- Discuss the intended audience for each notice. What difference does audience make to how the text is presented?

Differentiation

Less confident learners may require more time to become familiar with different texts.

Read the words on the notices for learners to follow.

Pair learners with more competent partners to read the notices.

Learners who are less confident with Microsoft Word can work with a partner to alter the format of the notices.

Learners who need more practice to become familiar with different word-processing tasks can customise other activities from this support pack.

Extension

Ask learners to create and print out a notice for use in your learning environment or for a club, society or work placement.

Learners who are in work could read the health and safety law poster at their workplace to find out who their health and safety representative is.

Activity 5 Who is it for and what is it for?

This activity looks at the purpose and audience of different texts and is suitable for learners working at E2/A2.

Other resources

A selection of everyday texts.

- Ensure learners understand the key words used (entertain, instruct, inform, describe and persuade). Show an example of each type of text, e.g. a novel, flat-pack furniture instructions, a recycling leaflet, a holiday brochure and an advert.
- From a selection of texts, ask learners to collect one text for each category.
- Alternatively, select a category and ask learners to select one text that belongs to that category until all the texts have been sorted.
- Discuss the selections. Do some texts fit into more than one category? (A magazine might contain all five categories.)

A 1.5.1 Who is it for? (Entry 2/Access 2)

- Allocate each learner a character from the activity sheet and ask them to select a text that might be chosen by their character from a range of texts you have provided. Ask learners to explain their choice.

1.3.1 What would you use to find…?

Match the things to find with the places.

a crossword puzzle	an application for a job
an application for a bank account	what to put in the recycling box
how to cook a chicken	when the surgery is open
how to get a television licence	how to use a fire extinguisher
how to look after a plant	what time the shop opens
how to send a fax	how to change a tyre
how to wash a new jumper	when the school trip is
if you can turn left	how to get to Land's End
information about health and safety	information about a holiday
the local school	the phone number of a business
the phone number of a friend	details about today's weather in Scotland
the time of a bus	when the next home game is being played
the workplace policy on smoking	when the swimming pool is open
what courses are available at college	how to put flat-pack furniture together
what is on television	how to work a photocopier
what time the film starts	

1.4.1 Workplace noticeboard

NOTICES
Want to learn something new?
Talk to your union rep
AUSW
HEALTH AND SAFETY LAW
What you should know
For sale
LADIES' BIKE £25 ONO
CONTACT PAVEEN 01234 567890
LOST
BLACK LEATHER PURSE
Last seen in the car park
Contact Sharon
! CHRISTMAS PARTY !
on Saturday 20th December
8 till late
FREE bar till 10 o'clock
Come and join in the fun!
See Matt or Val in Sales for tickets
Is your floor surface an accident waiting to happen?
Talk to your safety rep
TODAY!
Car share - why share?
Car sharing is when two or more people share a lift. By sharing a lift, you will spend less money on fuel and car repairs (so more cash to spend on the things that really matter). It might even mean that you do not need a second car. It is sociable and helps make our roads less congested.
Interested?
Ring Chris on extension 33

Note for tutor: Discuss the notices. What stands out?

1.4.2 Sports and leisure centre noticeboard

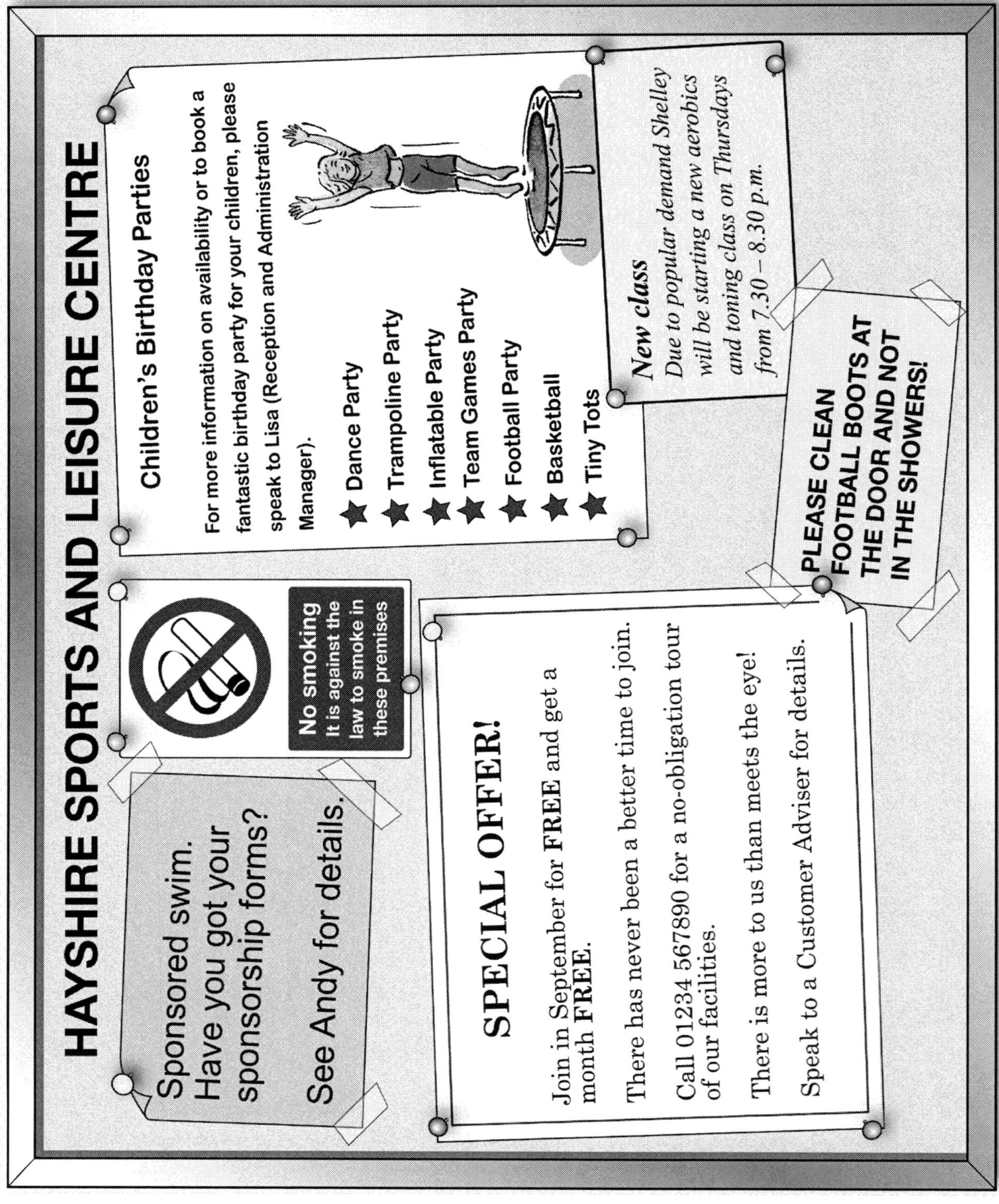
HAYSHIRE SPORTS AND LEISURE CENTRE
Children's Birthday Parties
For more information on availability or to book a fantastic birthday party for your children, please speak to Lisa (Reception and Administration Manager).
Dance Party
Trampoline Party
Inflatable Party
Team Games Party
Football Party
Basketball
Tiny Tots
New class
Due to popular demand Shelley will be starting a new aerobics and toning class on Thursdays from 7.30 – 8.30 p.m.
PLEASE CLEAN FOOTBALL BOOTS AT THE DOOR AND NOT IN THE SHOWERS!
No smoking
It is against the law to smoke in these premises
Sponsored swim.
Have you got your sponsorship forms?
See Andy for details.
SPECIAL OFFER!
Join in September for FREE and get a month FREE.
There has never been a better time to join.
Call 01234 567890 for a no-obligation tour of our facilities.
There is more to us than meets the eye!
Speak to a Customer Adviser for details.

Note for tutor: Discuss the notices. What stands out?

1.4.3 Family noticeboard

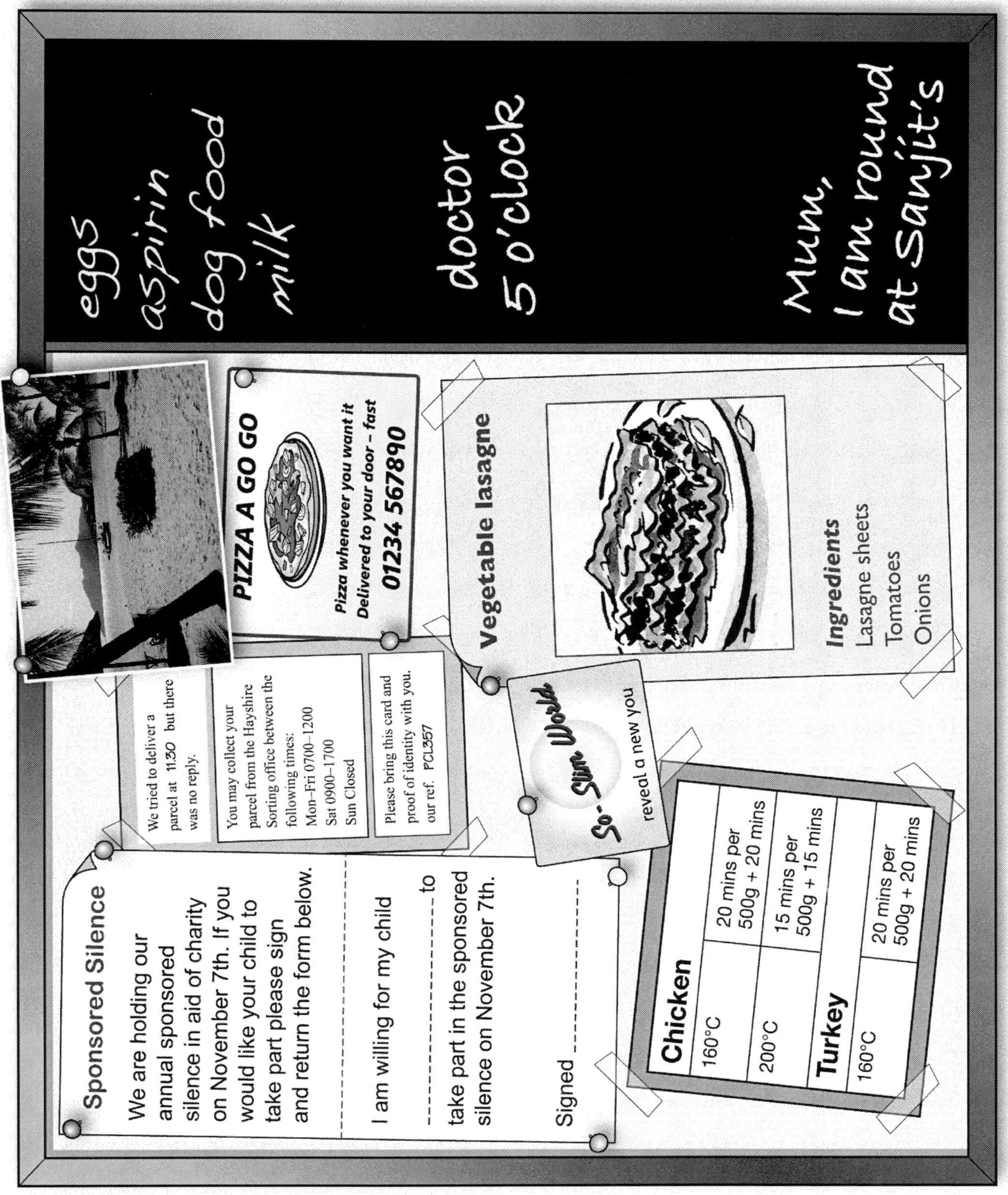

eggs
aspirin
dog food
milk
doctor
5 o'clock
Mum,
I am round
at Sanjit's
PIZZA A GO GO
Pizza whenever you want it
Delivered to your door – fast
01234 567890
Vegetable lasagne
Ingredients
Lasagne sheets
Tomatoes
Onions
We tried to deliver a parcel at 11.30 but there was no reply.
You may collect your parcel from the Hayshire Sorting office between the following times:
Mon–Fri 0700–1200
Sat 0900–1700
Sun Closed
Please bring this card and proof of identity with you.
our ref. PCL357
So-Slim World
reveal a new you
Chicken
160°C
20 mins per 500g + 20 mins
200°C
15 mins per 500g + 15 mins
Turkey
160°C
20 mins per 500g + 20 mins
Sponsored Silence
We are holding our annual sponsored silence in aid of charity on November 7th. If you would like your child to take part please sign and return the form below.
I am willing for my child
---------------- to
take part in the sponsored silence on November 7th.
Signed ----------------

Note for tutor: Discuss the notices. What stands out?

1.4.4 Change a notice: gardener

Change the notice.

You can change the font.

You can make it bigger or smaller.

You can make it **bold**, *italic* or underlined.

You can change the colour of the font.

You can make the font UPPER CASE or lower case.

You can change the colour of the background.

You can add a graphic.

GARDENER WANTED

Part-time gardener wanted for large garden near Kingstown

20 hours per week

Must be reliable and honest

References essential

Ring Mrs Evans

01234 567890

1.4.5 Change a notice: tai chi

Change the notice.

You can change the font.

You can make it bigger or smaller.

You can make it **bold**, *italic* or underlined.

You can change the colour of the font.

You can make the font UPPER CASE or lower case.

You can change the colour of the background.

You can add a graphic.

Tai chi
Gentle exercises for all ages

Classes every Thursday

6.30 – 7.30p.m. juniors

7.30 – 8.30p.m. adult beginners

8.30 – 9.30p.m. adult improvers

For more details contact Ronan 01234 567890

1.4.6 Change a notice: new windows

Change the notice.

You can change the font.

You can make it bigger or smaller.

You can make it **bold**, *italic* or underlined.

You can change the colour of the font.

You can make the font UPPER CASE or lower case.

You can change the colour of the background.

You can add a graphic.

New windows

Is your house looking tired?

Do you need new windows?

July special offer!

Buy four new windows and get a door absolutely free!

Windows 4 All

01234 567890

1.5.1 Who is it for?

Note for tutor: ask learners to select a text from your list for each character.

Theme 2

Signs and symbols

Links
Theme 3 Words, words, words.

Key words
blue, circle, green, health and safety, rectangle, red, sign, square, symbol, triangle, yellow.

Other resources
Examples of signs from the learning environment, a digital camera, a copy of the Highway Code.

Introduction

Signs and symbols are everywhere around us. They communicate information quickly without the use of words, so it is important that everyone is familiar with them.

At work, health and safety information is often conveyed using signs and symbols. A clear understanding of them can help employees contribute to a safe workplace. At home, symbols are used for instructions such as how to care for clothing or put together flat-pack furniture. Often the key to these symbols is arranged in a table.

In this theme, learners will be able to explore how signs are constructed. They are given the opportunity to recognise, respond to and interpret a wide range of everyday signs in each of the different contexts. You can adapt the activities to suit the interests and abilities of each learner.

Learning outcomes	**Adult Literacy Curriculum references**	**ALAN Curriculum Framework for Scotland**
To be able to recognise and respond to signs and symbols in different situations	Rw/E1.1 Rt/E1.2 Rt/E2.4	A1/A2 • Recognising signs, symbols and social sight words
To be able to name and interpret signs and symbols in different situations		

Activity notes

Activity 1 Introducing the theme

These activities introduce the concept of signs and symbols and are suitable for all learners at Entry 1 and 2/Access 1.

Conduct a short quiz using examples from the Highway Code, health and safety information and signs from the learning environment. Hold up each sign and ask learners what message they get from it. Briefly discuss the colours and shapes of signs, and discuss the symbols used.

Create a maze or trail around the room using furniture as barriers and signs indicating that in order to navigate the maze learners should turn right, stop, go left, etc. The key message here is that signs give information without using words.

Walk around the learning environment with your learners. Take photos of any signs seen and discuss what they might mean and what you would need to do in order to 'obey' the sign. Be aware that learners at Entry 1/Access 1 may not be familiar with wording on signs; instead concentrate their attention on the colours, shapes and symbols while pointing out that the words often make the meaning clearer, especially when the same symbol is used in different contexts.

2.1.1 I spy (Entry 1/Access 1)

Conduct an 'I spy' trail. Together, walk around the learning environment matching the signs seen to those on the activity sheet.

Activity 2 Shapes, colours and symbols at work

This activity uses some of the signs and symbols found on health and safety signs in the workplace as well as in public buildings. The activities can be used with all Entry 1 and 2 learners. Before starting on this activity, make sure learners understand the concept of health and safety.

Other resources

Examples of signs from different categories.

2.2.1 Health and safety: shapes and colours (Entry 1/Access 1)

Ensure learners are familiar with the colours and shapes involved in health and safety signs. If not, use the cards on the activity sheet to introduce them as part of a naming or snap game. Use Activity Sheet 2.2.1 to practise matching shapes and colours. Note that 'safety' can be represented by a square or a rectangular sign. Use the 'Domino Generator' on the CD to create more examples.

Presentation 2 Health and safety signs (Entry 1 and 2/ Access 1 and 2)

Each slide follows a similar pattern. A health and safety sign appears followed by three others. Ask questions such as 'What shape is this sign?', 'What colour is it?' This will help to reinforce the message that the colours and shapes – as well as the symbols – have specific meanings on health and safety signs and to draw learners' attention to the detail of the signs.

Take one slide at a time and demonstrate how the shape and then the colour of a sign can give a message even before a symbol is added. More information about health and safety signs can be obtained at www.hse.gov.uk.

Involve learners by asking them to describe shape and colour, to guess meanings or to link to other resources in the activity sheets. Write up any key words as they occur.

Slide 1

Set the scene by saying that this presentation is about health and safety signs that are set down by law. They have certain shapes and colours to send clear messages so that everyone can understand them and follow the information given to keep themselves healthy and safe.

Slide 2

Mandatory signs show things that must be obeyed. They are round, have a blue background and a white symbol. The slide shows signs for washing hands, wearing gloves, putting out cigarettes and wearing protective clothing.

If possible, show learners more signs that have the same shape and colour scheme but a different symbol on them, e.g. hair covering must be worn; eye protection must be worn; report all accidents immediately.

Slide 3

Warning (hazard) signs are triangular, have a yellow background and a black symbol. Show learners more signs that have the same shape and colour scheme but a different symbol on them, e.g. hazardous area; industrial trucks; arc welding; mind your head.

Slide 4

Prohibitory signs stop people from doing things that are likely to increase or cause danger. They are round, have a white background, a red edge and diagonal line, and a black symbol. Show learners more signs that have the same shape and colour scheme but a different symbol on them, e.g. no smoking; do not touch; cameras prohibited.

Slide 5

General safety information appears as a white symbol on a green square or rectangle. They are commonly fire safety signs. Show learners more signs that have the same shape and colour scheme but a different symbol on them, e.g. drinking water; smoking area; fire exit.

Slide 6

Fire equipment signs are red squares or rectangles with white symbols. If possible, show learners more signs that have the same shape and colour scheme but a different symbol on them, e.g. fire point; fire hydrant; fire blanket.

  2.2.2 Make a sign (Entry 1/Access 1)

Using the activity sheet, ask learners to reconstruct the types of signs they have seen in the presentation.

Using an enlarged and laminated version of the activity sheet, demonstrate how a new sign could be made. Ask learners to invent signs using shapes, colours and symbols in different combinations. Blank shapes are provided for learners to invent their own symbols.

Discuss with learners signs they would like to see, such as a sign preventing people from using MP3 players, a sign to ask supermarket users to return their trolleys, a sign asking people not to drop chewing gum. Customise the activity sheet so that learners can invent their own signs as appropriate.

  2.2.3 Signs in the workplace (Entry 1/Access 1)

- Using the activity sheet and/or your own examples of signs, ask learners to sort the signs into different categories, e.g. all the triangular ones, all the blue ones. Ask learners to talk about the reasons for their choices.
- To familiarise learners with signs and symbols, make sets of domino or snap cards using the 'Domino generator' on the CD. Add to the selection using signs from the learning environment or workplace with which the learners must become familiar.
- In pairs or small groups, ask learners to look at a sign and describe its colour, shape and symbol to their partner, who has to guess which sign it is. Add to the signs on the sheet with your own examples if possible.

Differentiation

Some learners may require more practice in order to recognise and name health and safety signs. Give these learners plenty of opportunity to sort and match signs. Assist them in describing signs. Ensure they are given plenty of opportunity to talk about signs in real settings and to describe any actions that should be taken when they see each sign.

Using Activity Sheet 2.2.2, ask more confident learners to read and write the appropriate words to accompany each sign. They could add useful words to a personal dictionary.

Extension

Invent a trail of directional signs (no entry; no left turn; no pedestrians; right turn only) around the building for learners to follow.

Investigate road signs and the way they are constructed using examples from the Highway Code and real life.

Activity 3 Symbols at home

Signs and symbols are important in the home as a quick way of accessing information such as how to put together flat-pack furniture, wash a favourite jumper or cook and store food. In some circumstances, symbols are changed in subtle ways to mean different things. For example, on a weather map a black cloud shape can mean low-level cloud, a black cloud with one rain drop can mean drizzle and a black cloud shape with two rain drops can mean heavy rain. This activity asks learners to look carefully at how symbols can change to mean different things.

A 2.3.1 What is your weather like? (Entry 1 and 2/Access 1 and 2)

- Discuss with learners the weather forecasts they have seen or heard. Ensure they have an understanding of the map and where they live in relation to it.

Other resources

Examples of recent weather maps from local or national newspapers, care labels from items of clothing, menus using symbols.

- If possible, display the map on a whiteboard. Discuss the symbols used on the map.
- How are they formed?
- What do they mean?
- What is the weather like where they live?

Talk about the symbols to role-play a weather forecast as seen on TV.

  **2.3.2 Make a weather map (Entry 1/Access 1)**

- Ask learners to create a weather map, using the symbols.

Demonstrate how a weather forecaster would describe the map. Ask learners to take it in turns to describe their own maps.

 **2.3.3 Clothing care labels (Entry 1/Access 1)**

2.3.4 How should you care for these clothes? (Entry 1 and 2/Access 1 and 2)

- Ask learners to work out how to care for the clothes.

This activity sheet can be used in conjunction with Activity Sheet 2.3.3 Clothing care labels.

Show how clothing care symbols change according to their meaning. Ask learners to sort the symbols into 'wash', 'tumble dry', 'iron', etc. Ensure learners talk about and name the symbols as they use them in the games.

Extension

If a whiteboard is available, go to www.bbc.co.uk/weather. Enter your postcode to see the five-day forecast for the area. Roll the mouse over each symbol for an explanation of its meaning. A full list of symbols can be found at www.bbc.co.uk/weather/bbcweather/features/symbols.shtml.

In pairs or small groups, ask learners to role-play a scene in a restaurant or café using menus with symbols as a guide to the food on offer, e.g. suitable for vegetarians, hot or mild curry, children's portions. Show what is required and practise forming the questions, e.g. 'Is there anything on the menu that is suitable for vegetarians?', 'Is this curry hot or mild?' Ensure each learner knows the role he or she should play (waiter, customer, etc.).

Other resources

L-shaped cards, rulers.

Activity 4 Symbols in leisure activities

Introduce learners to tables that help people to understand symbols. Tables are dealt with in more detail in Theme 5 Everyday information. Learners at E1 will need support to read the explanations.

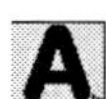 **2.4.1 Pool safety (Entry 1 and 2/Access 1 and 2)**

Explain how information can be arranged in a table. Read the explanations aloud to the group.

Ask learners to point to each symbol in turn and then to move their fingers across to the explanation of the symbol. Read the words together.

Some learners may prefer to use a piece of card or a ruler to cover information not yet seen or to cover information already seen.

Some learners may like to use an L-shaped piece of card to keep their place in the table.

2.4.2 What does the notice in the local pool say? (Entry 1 and 2/Access 1 and 2)

This activity sheet can be used in conjunction with Activity Sheet 2.4.1. Working in pairs, learners can ask their partners to say what each sign means. Ask more confident learners to write the meanings using Activity Sheet 2.4.1 to help them.

2.4.3 Choose a caravan park (Entry 2/Access 2)

Read through the descriptions of the families (on 2.4.4). Ask learners to decide which of the two caravan parks (on 2.4.3) would be most appropriate for each family.

2.4.4 What is at the caravan park? (Entry 2/Access 2)

- Talk through the caravan park descriptions Activity Sheet 2.4.3 with the learners.
- Has anyone been to a caravan park?
- What could you do there?

Differentiation

Ask less able learners to play matching, snap and domino games using the symbols to consolidate their learning. More able learners can match each symbol to the explanation for it.

Extension

Ask learners confident with using ICT to create a table and make an easy reference chart that explains the symbols used on the buttons of the toolbar, e.g. = Save.

Ask learners to use real brochures or care labels to extract information from symbols and to explain it to a partner.

2.1.1 I spy

Can you find these signs?

2.2.1 Health and safety: shapes and colours

Match the colours and the words to the shapes.

		you must do
		watch out for
		you must not
		safety!

2.2.2 Make a sign

Make up your own signs.

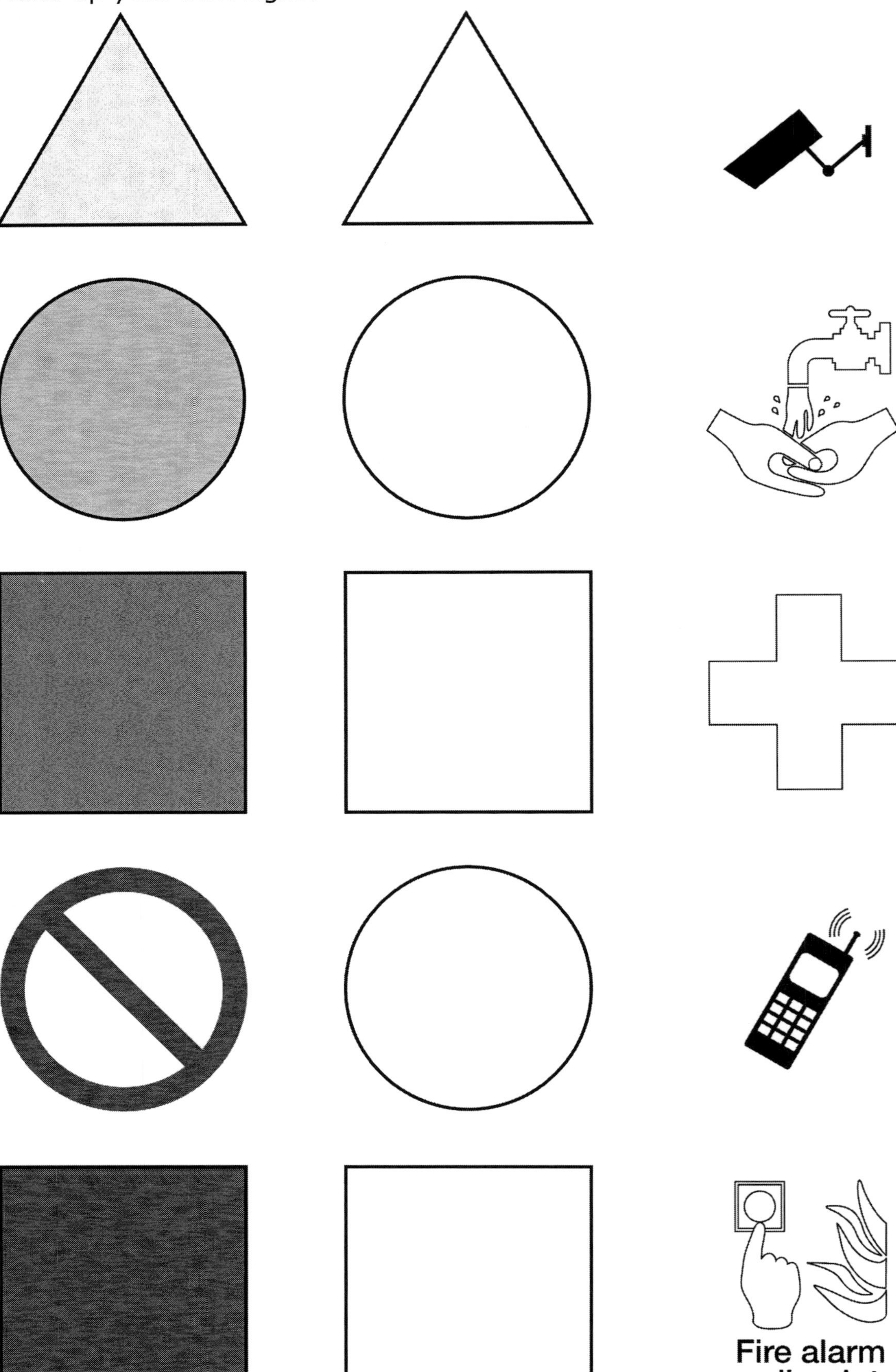

2.2.3 Signs in the workplace

Sort the signs into different groups.

2.3.1 What is your weather like?

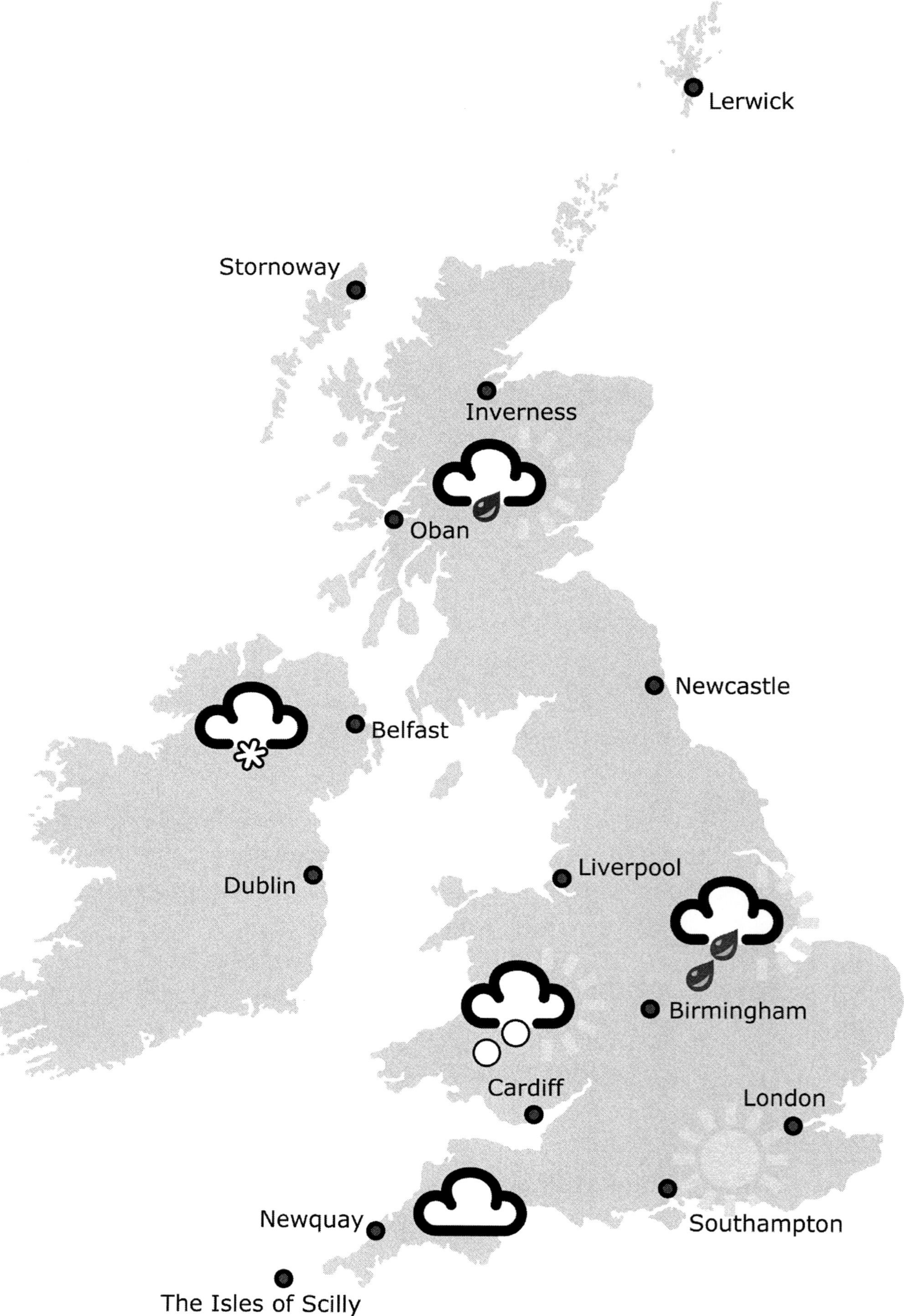

2.3.2 Make a weather symbol

Draw your own weather map.

2.3.3 Clothing care labels

Cut out these symbols. Sort them into 'Wash', 'Bleach', 'Tumble dry', 'Iron' and 'Dry clean'.

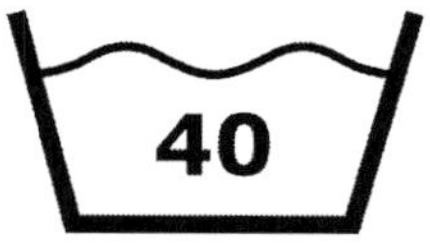 Wash at 40°C	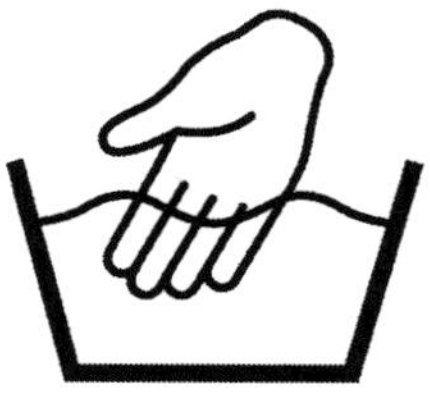 Wash by hand	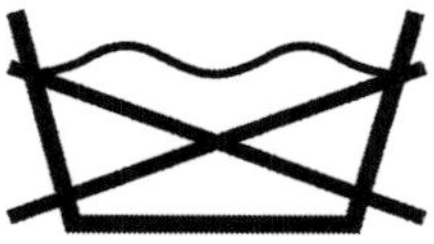 Do not wash
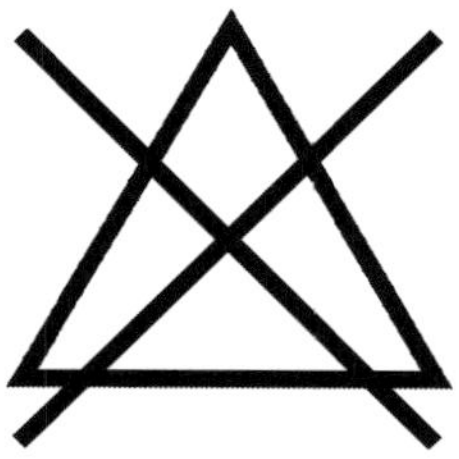 Do not bleach	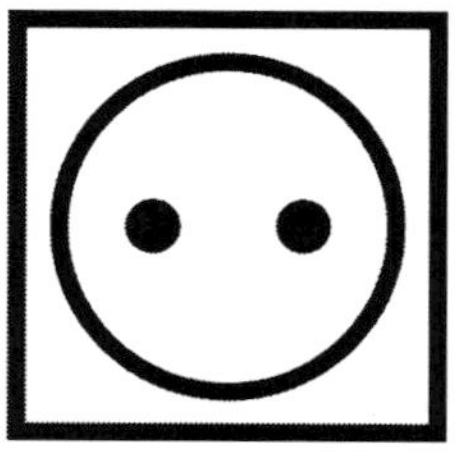 Tumble dry after washing on high heat	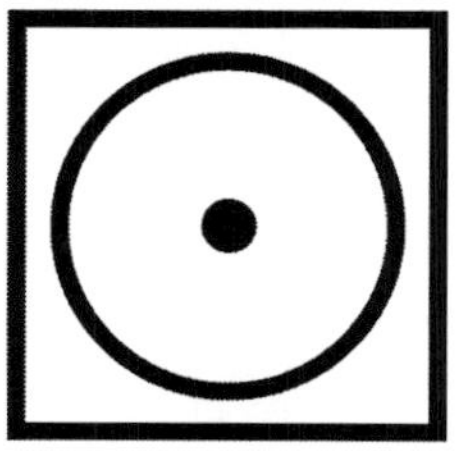 Tumble dry after washing on low heat
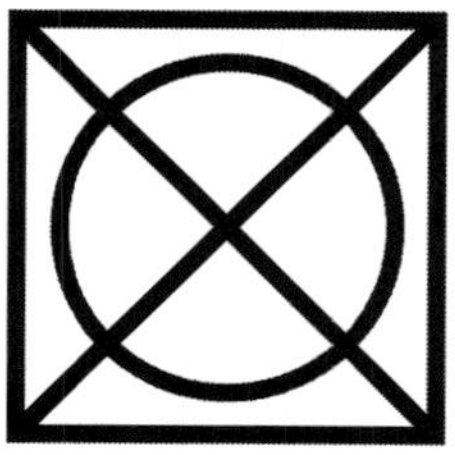 Do not tumble dry	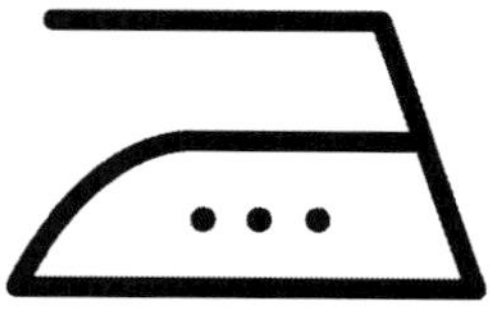 Hot iron	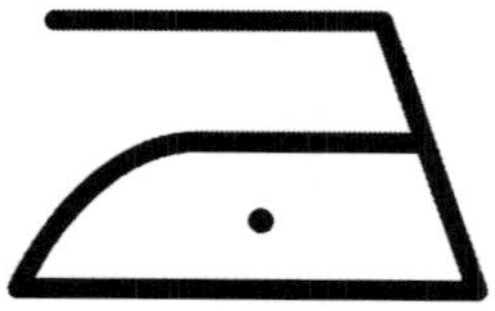 Cool iron
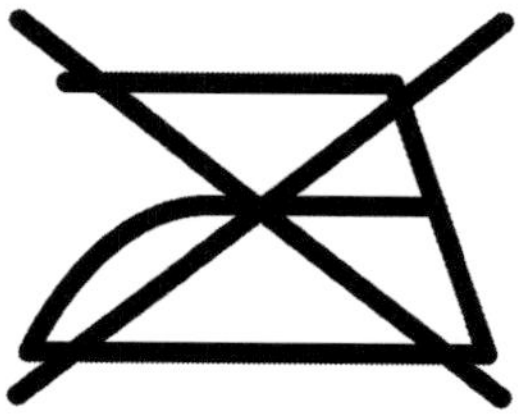 Do not iron	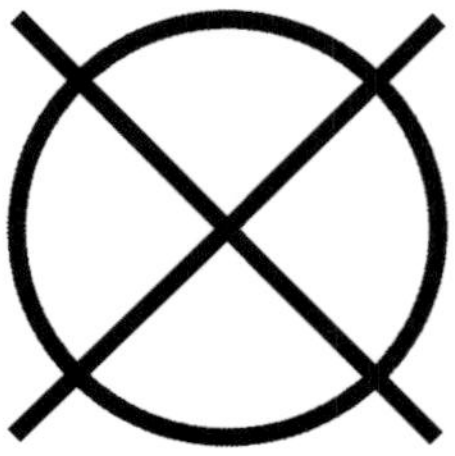 Do not dry clean	

2.3.4 How should you care for these clothes?

What do these signs mean?

1.  ______________________________

2.  ______________________________

3. 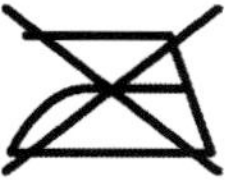 ______________________________

4.  ______________________________

5. 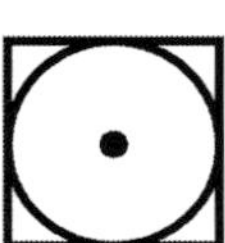 ______________________________

6. 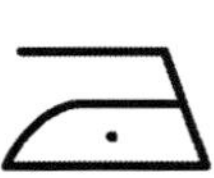 ______________________________

7. 

____

8.  ______________________________

9.  ______________________________

2.4.1 Pool safety

These signs can all be found at your local swimming pool.

	✗	No running
	✗	No bombing
	✗	No pushing
	✗	No eating
	✗	No glass bottles

	✓	Read the warning signs
	✓	Listen to the lifeguards
	✓	Check for lifeguards
	✓	Check for safety equipment
	✓	Check the depth of the pool

2.4.2 What does the notice in the local pool say?

Can you work out what these signs mean?

1.  ______________________________

2.  ______________________________

3.  ______________________________

4.  ______________________________

2.4.3 Choose a caravan park

Match these families to the caravan parks.

John and Jess want to take their children on a caravan holiday. Which site would be best for them?

Alan and Margaret play golf. Which site would be best for them?

This family want to learn to ride horses. Which site would be best for them?

Kim and Pete have a young child. Which site would be best for them?

Ivy and Stan like to eat out. Which site would be best for them?

2.4.4 What is at the caravan park?

Here are two different caravan parks. Which would you choose?

Happy Days Caravan Park

☆ ***Right on the beach***

☆ ***A short walk to the shops***

☆ ***Social club***

Children's playground

Baby listening service

Take away

Laundry room

Indoor pool

Blue Pines Caravan Park

☆ ***Open all year round***

☆ ***In a peaceful setting***

☆ ***Plenty to do for the energetic holiday-maker***

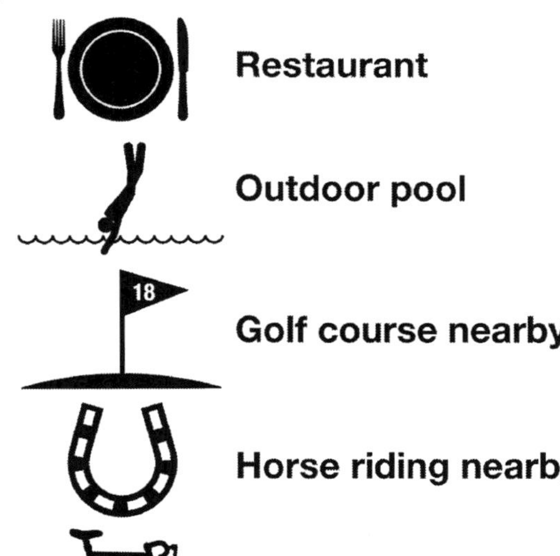

Theme 3

Words, words, words

Links

Theme 2 Signs and symbols; Theme 7 Using the alphabet.

Key words

letter, sound, word.

Other resources

Examples of company/product logos, examples of other words from the learners' environment, highlighter pens.

Introduction

It is important for learners to see the correlation between written and spoken words if they are to improve their reading skills. Length, shape, initial letters, association with other words and personal experience of language are all clues that can be used to work out and remember a new word.

In this theme the main focus is on visual recognition of social sight vocabulary. Learners are given the opportunity to become familiar with common words and are asked to compile or add to a personal dictionary of words that has particular relevance to their own lives and habits. It is important in these activities to include words that have meaning to the learner in his or her context and suggestions are given throughout to help with ways of doing this.

Learning outcomes	**Adult Literacy Curriculum references**	**ALAN Curriculum Framework for Scotland**
To be able to build a meaningful vocabulary of personal key words	Rw/E1.1 Rw/E1.2 Rw/E2.2 Rw/E2.3 Ww/E1.1 Ww/E1.3 Ww/E2.1 Ww/E2.2	A1/A2 • Recognising social sight words
To be able to use their own language experience to help recognise sight vocabulary		
To be able to recognise the correlation between graphemes and phonemes		
To be able to decode regular words		

Activity notes

Activity 1 Introducing the theme

Reassure learners that they already have a bank of words they recognise by discussing the words we see around us, such as logos on shops and products and signs in the street, workplace or hospital.

- How do we recognise them?
- What information are they giving us?

Start a collection of product/shop names or logos that the learners will recognise, which they can add to during the course of the theme. Create a poster or wall display if possible. Do the same with words and phrases that are of interest to your learners, e.g. road signs if they are learner drivers, hospital signs if they need to visit hospital often, words to do with a particular job, words that are used on computers and the Internet.

A 3.1.1 The interview story 3.1.2 Words from the interview(Entry 1 and 2/Access 1 and 2)

Introduce the concept of the value of words as useful tools to negotiate a new environment by telling a story about a journey or new experience likely to be faced by the learners. Use the example given on Activity Sheet 3.1.1 or customise your own sheet. Other examples might be a shopping trip or going to the sports centre.

- Give each learner a sign from Activity Sheet 3.1.2 and make sure he or she is familiar with the word. Discuss each word briefly.
- Where else might it be seen?
- What makes it easy to recognise?
- Talk about the shape, first letter, similarities and differences from other words. Ask learners to share any techniques they may have developed for remembering words. Prompt for: repeating a word over and over, making up a story to associate the word with; picturing the word in the mind's eye. Confirm that these ways are all valid – whatever works for one individual is right for them. Also point out that many techniques are available and it is up to each learner to try new ones to see if they work for him or her.
- Explain that you are going to tell the learners what happened to you when you went for an interview for a new job. At several points during the morning you needed to know where to go and what to do next. If learners think they are holding a sign that may have given you the information you needed, they should hold it up at the appropriate moment. Read the 'story' on Activity Sheet 3.1.1, using the first paragraph, to ensure learners know what to do.

After telling the story, go through it briefly again and discuss each sign.

Differentiation

Most learners will not need to see the story written down. However, some may wish to use the words on Activity Sheet 3.1.2 to match the words in the story. Others may wish to use a highlighter pen to highlight words from the story.

Extension

Make two sets of cards from Activity Sheet 3.1.2 for learners to match, use as snap cards or as a pelmanism game.

Ask learners to tell the story of a journey or experience they have had using signs or other words that are relevant, e.g. the journey to college, work or home.

Other resources

A small notebook in which learners can write their personal dictionaries or a small card if fewer words are to be remembered.

Activity 2 Words we need

There are certain words we all need to recognise in our daily lives. These vary from person to person. Ask learners to start a personal dictionary of words that are of value to them and to develop some strategies for learning these words. Make sure they include words of relevance to their work as well as their personal lives. For example, a typical personal dictionary for someone who works in a care home might include the names of family members as well as words from signs such as *wash*, *hands*, *lift*, *restless* and *peaceful*.

Ask learners to suggest ways they have discovered for learning words. What clues do they use to help remember words? Say that there are many methods and that each person will develop a method that suits them best. Here are some examples.

- Write words in a notebook: words can be listed in alphabetical order or under topic headings.
- Crib cards may help with learning words related to a specific task or subject (e.g. for ICT: *file*, *close*, *yes*, *no*, *cancel*, *exit*) or with words related to particular vocational areas (e.g. in a horticultural setting: *compost*, *pesticide*, *growing medium*). Do not give learners too many words at once.
- When remembering a word or a list of words, ask learners to think about how they did it and to tell someone else the method.
- Repetition is the key to remembering words. Suggest learners develop a method such as reading a word, covering it, saying it aloud, looking at it again and then reading it again.
- Some learners may prefer to use clues from the shape or length of the word.
- Others may look at initial letters, letter combinations or words within words.
- A spelling method such as 'look, say, cover, remember, write, check' can be used.
- Some learners may like to weave a story around the words they need to remember.
- Others may be able to visualise a word. Font style and colour may be important aids here.
- Games such as snap, dominoes and pelmanism can help some learners.

Throughout the theme, give learners the opportunity to experience different methods of learning but do not overburden them.

Ask learners for five or six words that are important for them to recognise or provide learners with a list of common words they meet in their daily environment. Ask them to write these into their notebook or card. Ensure they are copied correctly. At a later date, check whether the words have been useful.

P Presentation 3a Railway station signs (Entry 1 and 2/ Access 1 and 2)

In this presentation, the idea is that learners should work out what the signs will say before they are completed, while you give them clues. Use the prompts for each slide below to tell the story of your journey to the station.

Slide 1

Set the scene by saying that each slide shows a sign you can find at a railway station.

Slide 2

I was going on holiday and I had a big suitcase, so I got a taxi to the station. Where did it drop me off? (Answer: Taxi rank.) (Click to reveal sign.)

Slide 3

When I got to the station I needed to find out where to catch my train. Where could I find that out? (Answer: Information.) (Click to reveal sign.)

Slide 4

I had plenty of time before my train left. Where could I get a coffee? (Answer: Station café.) (Click to reveal sign.)

Slide 5

Before I got on the train I needed to wash my hands. Where could I do that? (Answer: Toilets.) (Click to reveal sign.)

Slide 6

At last it was time to catch the train. Where did I catch the train from? (Answer: Platform.) (Click to reveal sign.)

At the end of the presentation, ask learners to continue the story. Add other signs that might be seen at a railway station such as:

- newsagent (Where could I buy a magazine?)
- ticket machine (Where could I buy a ticket?)
- timetable (Where could I find out what time the train was leaving?)

Ask learners to extend the story to the arrival at a destination. Add the signs to the presentation and save a copy for future reference.

Extension

Ask learners to make the signs that would be needed to get off the train, find a taxi, etc. and stick them to a large photo or drawing of a railway station.

Invite learners to make and stick signs to other places of relevance to them, such as a place of work or a leisure centre.

3.2.1 In reception/3.2.2 Signs around the office (Entry 1 and 2/Access 1 and 2)

- Ask learners to discuss the words, make up a story around them and then copy them into a personal dictionary.
- Invite learners to match the words with those on Activity Sheet 3.2.2.
- Use this activity sheet as a matching, snap or pelmanism game with learners at Entry 1/Access 1.

3.2.3 Office wordsearch (Entry 1/Access 1)

Ask learners to look at a word they want to search for from the list and try to remember the first letter or group of letters in it. Then they track left to right across the wordsearch to locate the word. When they are sure they have found it, they should say the word, say the letters in it, draw a line through it and move on to the next one.

3.2.4 On the street (Entry 1 and 2/Access 1 and 2)

Ask learners to discuss the words, make up a story around them and then copy them into a personal dictionary. Be aware that most street signs are written in upper case letters and are therefore more difficult to read. Supplement the signs already used by adding more from the Highway Code.

3.2.5 On the street bingo/3.2.6 On the street wordsearch (Entry 1/Access 1)

- Words seen on the street are often written in capital letters, which makes them more difficult to read as they have no outer shape, so learners may need more support and consolidation.
- Play 'bingo' or wordsearch using words commonly found on the street.
- Use the 'Bingo generator' on the CD to make a bingo game using words relevant to the learners.

3.2.7 The supermarket (Entry 1 and 2/Access 1 and 2)

Ask learners to discuss the words, make up a story around them and then copy them into a personal dictionary. Some learners will benefit from seeing the signs in real life so, if possible, organise a trip to a local supermarket and devise a trail where learners have to tick off words as they see them or collect items from particular locations.

3.2.8 Supermarket dominoes (Entry 1/Access 1)

Use this activity sheet to match items with words. Ask learners to create a shopping list using the words. The CD contains a

Bingo/Domino generator to help you to customise your own games.

Extension

Activity Sheets 3.2.3, 3.2.4 and 3.2.6 are all suitable for use in extending learners' speaking and listening skills.

Encourage learners to add useful words to their personal dictionaries and to learn them.

3.2.9 Health and safety signs (Entry 1 and 2/ Access 1 and 2)

Use this activity sheet to get learners who prefer to remember words from shapes and other non-phonic clues to match the signs with the words. Encourage learners to look at the symbols and decide what the sign might be about. They can also get clues from the shape and colour of the sign.

If necessary, explain words such as *caution* and *prohibited* and ask learners to substitute a more familiar word or phrase such as *be careful* or *banned*.

Ensure learners add any significant words to their personal dictionaries.

3.2.10 Health and safety signs wordsearch (Entry 1/ Access 1)

Use this activity sheet to familiarise learners with words commonly found on signs. Some learners may prefer to work in pairs.

Differentiation

For Activity Sheet 3.2.10, you could limit the number of words for less confident learners.

Extension

Extend Activity Sheet 3.2.10 to include some signs learners see in their daily lives at work.

Activity 3 Letters and words

Learners at this level will require lots of practice when reading words. It is suggested that some of the following ideas are developed with each person's learning style in mind.

Initial consonants

- For initial consonants, play sound word games such as I spy and Beat the clock. Work as a team to think of things in one category beginning with each sound in the alphabet such as plants, breeds of dog or television programmes.
- Play team games in which the next person in the team has to think of a word that begins with the last sound of the previous word, e.g. *dog/get*, *toy/yam*, *mum/man*.

 **3.3.1 Shopping list (Entry 1/Access 1)**

Use this activity sheet for work on initial consonants. Ensure learners look at the image and verbalise each item before deciding what letter it begins with. Repeat the exercise for final consonants.

Consonant clusters

- In pairs, get learners to highlight consonant clusters in a prepared text such as from a newspaper or magazine. They can then read the text, paying particular attention to the highlighted sounds.
- Dictate short sentences that include words that have consonant clusters, e.g. 'Shall we have fish and chips for tea?' Give instant feedback.
- Provide learners with a letter each. Check they know the sound of the letter they have. Ask learners to find a partner that has been given a letter that goes with theirs to make a new sound (e.g. *ch*, *sh*, *th* as well as blends *bl*, *st*, *tr*).

 **3.3.2 Consonant blend grid (Entry 1/Access 1)**

- Use this activity sheet to practise writing words beginning with '*bl*'. Ask learners to invent their own grids to give to a partner to complete.

Vowels

 **3.3.3 Shopping for vowels (Entry 1/Access 1)**

- Use this activity sheet for learners to sort items according to the highlighted vowel sound. Discuss the other vowel sounds in the words. What sounds can learners hear? Why might this be? (e.g. words of foreign origin, two vowels together creating a different sound)
- Ask learners to list as many consonant-vowel-consonant names as they can think of, e.g. *Kim*, *Dan*, *Sam*, *Tom*.

Long vowel phonemes and vowel phonemes

- Ask learners to match a list of words with the same spelling pattern.
- Provide learners with vowel cards and ask them to find a partner to make a long vowel sound, e.g. *ee*, *ai*, *ie*, *oa*, *oo*.

 **3.3.4 Postcard/3.3.5 Note from Chris (Entry 2/Access 2)**

- Ask learners to highlight all the words that have a long vowel sound in them before checking with a partner and reading the words aloud. Together learners can find other words with the same long vowel sounds from the postcard and in other texts, list them and then read them aloud.

Syllables

- Ask learners to tap or nod to help them count the number of syllables in a word. Stress that this can be done discreetly and that recognising syllables is an important way of breaking words into manageable chunks.

- Ask learners to listen to and then invent raps or rhyming poems that must scan. These can be recorded or performed.

 3.3.6 Syllables (Entry 2/Access 2)

- Use this activity sheet to practise putting syllables together to form new words. Learners can work in pairs or on their own.
- Deal the cards so that each player has three that they put face up in front of them. They read what they have got. The rest of the cards are put in a stack in the centre. Each player in turn takes a card from the stack and tries to match it with the syllables in front of them. If this is not possible, the player must place the card on a discard stack. The next player can take either the previous player's card or an unseen one from the spare pack. The winner is the first person to make three complete words.
- To make the game simpler, only deal the beginnings of words and include only the endings in the spare pack.
- Make a pack of cards using words from the learners' personal dictionaries.

P Presentation 3b Letters and words (Entry 1 and 2/ Access 1 and 2)

This presentation gives an overview of the phonic skills required at E1 and E2. It can be shown at your discretion, at the beginning or the end of this theme.

It is not expected that learners will take on board all the features demonstrated during this presentation but rather that they should confirm or be reminded of prior knowledge.

As you show each slide, be aware that some learners may need further practice in some areas and be ready to do this.

Ensure learners hear the sounds and are given the opportunity to make them themselves. Speak the sounds and words as they appear on the slides.

Slide 1

Stress that phonics is only one way of working out a word or spelling it. Explain that some learners may not find the sounds of letters helpful and should concentrate on other approaches such as remembering the shape of the word.

Slide 2

All words are made of letters. Check that learners know the difference between letters and sounds. Can learners repeat the letters of the alphabet? Can they start saying the letters of the alphabet from the letter H (or from any other point)? Can learners name an item beginning or ending with each sound?

Slide 3

Letters have sounds. Sound out the letters in a natural manner. Have some other examples that can be sounded out easily, ready prepared for learners to use as practice. Ask for learners' suggestions too.

Slide 4

Vowels are important letters. Provide and ask learners for other examples of words where a change of vowel means a change of meaning, e.g. *stop/step*, *hip/hop*, *big/bag*.

Slide 5

Two letters together can make a different sound.

Slide 6

Ask learners to nod or tap to the beats or syllables in each word.

3.1.1 The interview story

It was the morning of my interview for a job working for **Brown Brothers Ltd**, so I made sure I was up early and gave myself plenty of time to get ready. I looked in the cupboard for some **cornflakes** and in the fridge for some **milk** for breakfast. Then I washed my face, cleaned my teeth and got dressed into my smart clothes.

Soon it was time to catch the bus. I walked to the **bus stop** and waited. I was getting nervous now. I needed to catch the number 59 bus that was going to the **town centre**. After what seemed like ages, it arrived so I climbed aboard and paid my fare. I made sure I could see the bell that said **Press** on it so that I could stop the bus at the right stop. I was really nervous now!

'Have a nice day,' said the driver as I got off the bus.

'I hope I do,' I thought to myself.

I was right outside Brown Brothers, but how could I get in? I walked along the road until I saw a notice on a door saying **Way in**. I stood and looked at that door for a while.

'This is it,' I thought to myself.

I went in through the wooden doors. Straight away I was faced with another set of glass doors with the sign **Way in**. Luckily a sign on them said **Push** so I did not make a fool of myself by trying to pull them open.

I found myself in the **reception** area. I looked at my watch. I was a bit early. I had time to go the toilets, but where were they? Gazing around, I finally spotted a sign saying **Toilets**. This time I had to **Pull** the door to get in. I smartened myself up in the mirror, took a deep breath and went back out into the reception area.

A woman was sitting behind a desk. She had a notice in front of her saying **Enquiries** so I walked over to her. She smiled and said, 'Good morning. Are you here for an interview?' There was no turning back now!

Note to tutor: use this 'story' to introduce familiar words (shown in bold) as tools. For use with Activity Sheet 3.1.2.

3.1.2 Words from the interview

Brown Brothers Ltd	**cornflakes**
milk	**bus stop**
town centre	**Press**
Way in	**Push**
reception	**Enquiries**
Toilets	**Pull**

Note to tutor: ask learners to find these words on Activity Sheet 3.1.1.

3.2.1 In Reception

Note to tutor: use this with Activity Sheet 3.2.2 to make up a story.

3.2.2 Signs around the office

OPEN	**CLOSED**
IN	**OUT**
VACANT	**ENGAGED**
HOT	**COLD**
OFF	**ON**
PUSH	**PULL**
EXIT	**ENTRANCE**

Note to tutor: ask learners to match these words with those in Activity Sheet 3.2.2.

3.2.3 Office wordsearch

Find 12 signs or words you could see in an office.

Cross off each word as you find them.

Engaged	Entrance	Hot	Out
Vacant	Off	On	Closed
Exit	Pull	Push	Open

Start here. Read this way → along each row.

↓

E	n	g	a	g	e	d	z
y	x	V	a	c	a	n	t
t	E	x	i	t	s	r	q
E	n	t	r	a	n	c	e
p	O	f	f	n	m	l	k
P	u	l	l	j	H	o	t
g	O	n	f	P	u	s	h
l	n	e	O	u	t	d	c
C	l	o	s	e	d	b	a
q	O	p	e	n	w	e	r

3.2.4 On the street

Note to tutor: use the picture to discuss signs often seen in the street.

3.2.5 On the street bingo

Caller words

SLOW	STOP	GIVE WAY
GO	BUS STOP	BUS LANE
KEEP CLEAR	SCHOOL	LONG VEHICLE
REDUCE SPEED NOW	HOSPITAL	RIGHT TURN

Player cards

SLOW	STOP
LONG VEHICLE	BUS STOP

GO	BUS STOP
REDUCE SPEED NOW	SLOW

BUS LANE	GIVE WAY
HOSPITAL	STOP

KEEP CLEAR	SCHOOL
RIGHT TURN	GIVE WAY

Note to tutor: use the 'Bingo generator' on the CD to make a bingo game.

3.2.6 On the street wordsearch

Find 11 signs or words you could see on the street.

Cross off each word as you find them.

SLOW	SCHOOL	LEFT
STOP	HOSPITAL	REDUCE SPEED NOW
BUS LANE	LONG VEHICLE	KEEP CLEAR
GIVE WAY	NO RIGHT TURN	

L	N	O	R	I	G	H	T	T	U	R	N
O	A	T	D	F	K	U	P	Q	X	E	M
N	S	E	K	E	E	O	P	W	C	D	P
G	I	V	E	W	A	Y	R	G	I	U	H
V	C	N	B	E	K	P	L	J	E	C	J
E	K	P	O	L	J	F	K	W	Q	E	S
H	O	S	P	I	T	A	L	L	P	S	W
I	K	T	P	L	C	M	E	K	W	P	A
C	L	O	A	W	W	L	F	P	K	E	Z
L	W	P	K	P	S	Z	T	K	C	E	T
E	S	C	H	O	O	L	C	M	N	D	K
J	P	O	J	L	B	U	S	L	A	N	E
I	P	C	M	K	X	O	P	S	L	O	W
K	E	E	P	C	L	E	A	R	L	W	D

3.2.7 The supermarket

Note to tutor: use the picture to discuss signs often seen in the supermarket.

3.2.8 Supermarket dominoes

	**popadoms**
	**cod**
	**loaf**
	**milk**
	**apples**
	**cabbage**
	**chicken**
	**prawns**
	**buns**
	**yoghurt**
	**carrots**
	**rice**
	**pasta**
	**eggs**
	**sausages**
	**lentils**

Note to tutor: the CD contains a 'Domino generator' to help you customise your own games.

3.2.9 Health and safety signs

Match the signs with the words.

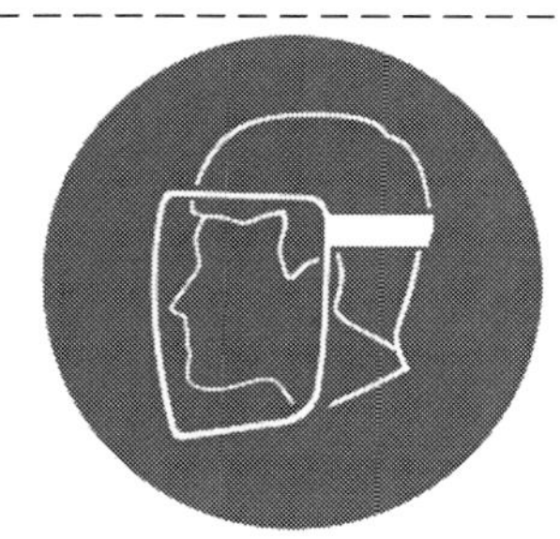

Safety Overalls must be worn

Hand protection must be worn

Face protection must be worn

No dogs except guide dogs

Eating prohibited

Cameras prohibited

CAUTION Trip hazard

CAUTION Mind your head

CAUTION Industrial trucks

3.2.10 Health and safety signs wordsearch

Find 12 signs and words you might see to do with health and safety.

Cross off each word as you find it.

Caution	Protection	HAZARD	CAUTION
PROHIBITED	must	Prohibited	BE
DANGER	be	PROTECTION	
MUST	Danger	Hazard	

Start here. Read this way ⟶ along each row.

↓

C	a	u	t	i	o	n	g	b	e
P	R	O	H	I	B	I	T	E	D
D	A	N	G	E	R	M	U	S	T
P	r	o	t	e	c	t	i	o	n
m	u	s	t	D	a	n	g	e	r
F	K	H	A	Z	A	R	D	I	m
P	r	o	h	i	b	i	t	e	d
P	R	O	T	E	C	T	I	O	N
b	j	y	t	H	a	z	a	r	d
C	A	U	T	I	O	N	x	B	E

3.3.1 Shopping list

Which letters do the words on the list start with?

Fruit

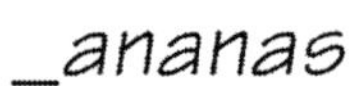
_ananas

_ranges

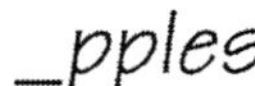
_pples

Vegetables

_arrots

_eeks

_otatoes

Meat

_ince

_oint of beef

_ausages

Fish

_od

_almon

_ish _ingers

Dairy produce

_ilk

_oghurt

_ottage cheese

Canned goods

_aked beans

_omatoes

_eaches

Frozen food

_eas

_eans

_ash browns

Cleaning products

_ashing powder

_abric softener

_oilet cleaner

Dry goods

_ice

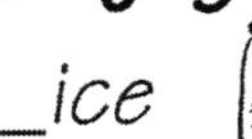

_asta

_ornflakes

Foods from the chiller

_uice

_am

_acon

3.3.2 Consonant blend grid

Fill in the missing words. All the words start with 'bl'.

				1 b				
			2	l				
		3		a				
	4			n				
5				k				
		6		e				
7				t				

1 You might do this if you have something in your eye.

2 The colour of the sky in the day.

3 The colour of the sky at night.

4 When a pencil is not sharp, it is this – what?

5 When a piece of paper has no writing on it, it is …

6 You use this to make sure things are really clean.

7 What do you call the noise that sheep make?

3.3.3 Shopping for vowels

Sort these words according to the highlighted vowel sound.

h**a**m	**e**ggs	m**i**lk
c**a**rrots	**a**pples	**o**ranges
p**o**rridge	b**i**scuits	j**a**m
t**o**matoes	p**o**tatoes	cr**a**ckers
p**a**sta	b**u**tter	c**o**ffee
pl**u**ms	b**a**nanas	p**o**lish
olives	p**i**ckle	y**o**ghurt
m**e**lon	l**e**mon	c**u**rrants
s**a**tsumas	l**e**ttuce	cr**e**ss

3.3.4 Postcard

Highlight all the words with a long vowel sound.

Hello everyone

We arrived yesterday. The train journey was OK after all.

The hotel is first-rate. We can see along the coast from our window.

The weather is fine. The sun shines all day but it can be breezy. The children can fly their kites.

The children have played in the warm sea. The beach is sandy – good for building castles.

We are all going on a boat trip tomorrow.

We will see you all when we get back.

Love Kim

3.3.5 Note from Chris

Meera and Chris have a job-share in a café at work.

Highlight all the long vowel sounds you can read in the note that Chris left for Meera.

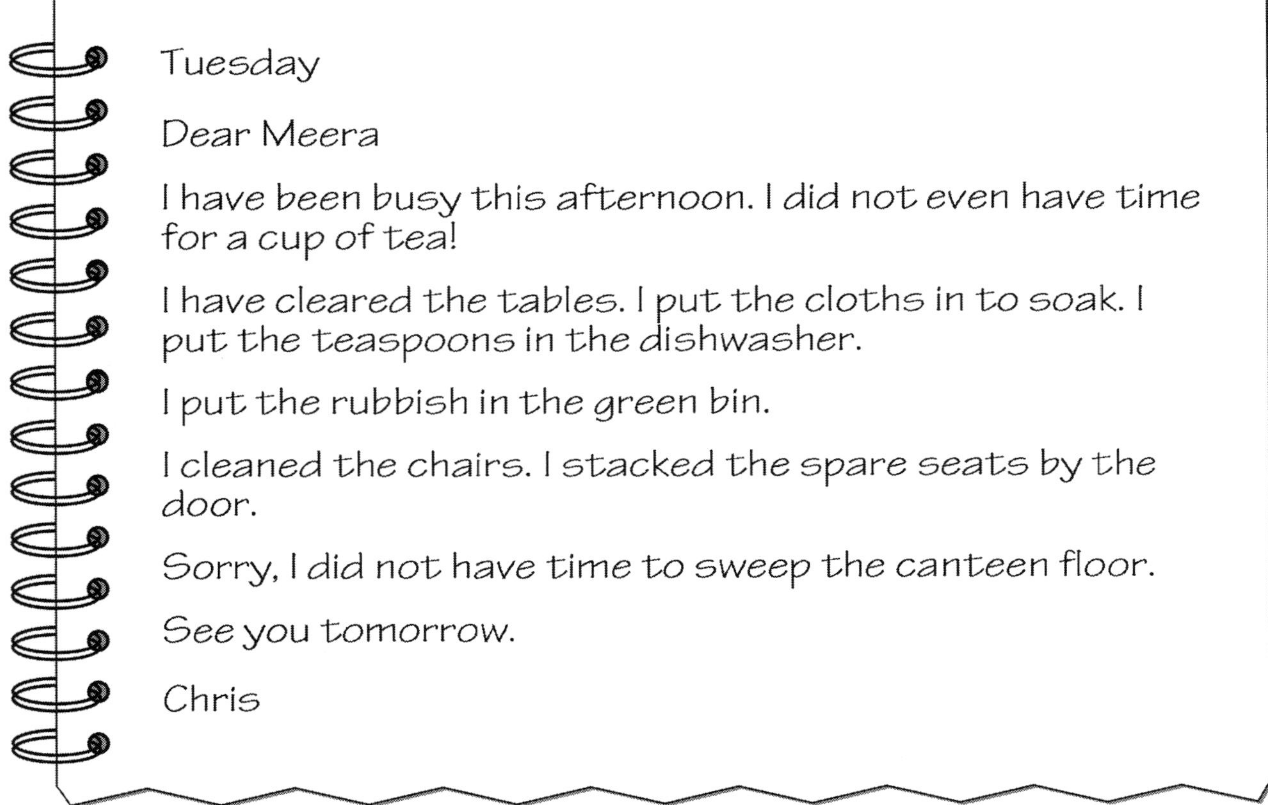

Tuesday

Dear Meera

I have been busy this afternoon. I did not even have time for a cup of tea!

I have cleared the tables. I put the cloths in to soak. I put the teaspoons in the dishwasher.

I put the rubbish in the green bin.

I cleaned the chairs. I stacked the spare seats by the door.

Sorry, I did not have time to sweep the canteen floor.

See you tomorrow.

Chris

3.3.6 Syllables

Put the syllables together to form new words.

ade	en
band	on
board	man
bout	ter
clut	min
com	plain
dom	light
ex	pect
head	thun
ket	ed
key	bat
king	high
lamp	der
lem	prom
light	kit
mag	dis
net	play
pand	tra
pete	plex
poc	mar
port	ply
ran	round
sack	a
sup	pose
ten	zig
wag	ing
wel	come
zag	an

Theme 4

Making a note

Introduction

In this theme, learners get the opportunity to consider when they need to write and to make decisions about that writing accordingly. They have the opportunity to plan their writing and to proofread it afterwards. Some spelling strategies are also addressed.

The key to this theme is to ask, 'When do people write?' In most scenarios, learners at this level will usually only be required to write single words or short notes. Learners need to be aware of the context in which they are writing and the intended audience for the writing.

A note to others needs to make sense, be correctly spelt and legible. A note that is going to be read only by the writer does not necessarily need these attributes as long as it can be read easily.

Learning outcomes	**Adult Literacy Curriculum references**	**ALAN Curriculum Framework for Scotland**
To be able to use written words and phrases to record information in different contexts and for a different intended audience	Wt/E2.1 Wt/E3.1 Ws/E1.1 Ws/E2.1 Ww/E1.1 Ww/E2.1	A1/A2 • Using language to express oneself • Using sentence length and complexity appropriately • Using spelling strategies • Using appropriate punctuation
To be able to construct simple sentences and join them together using conjunctions		
To be able to develop strategies to learn to spell personal key words and high-frequency words correctly		

Links

Theme 3 Words, words, words.

Key words

capital letter, full stop, invitation, letter, list, message, note, reply, sentence, sound, word.

Activity notes

Activity 1 Introducing the theme

Discuss briefly what and when learners need to write. Acknowledge any difficulties they express and confirm that although they may

Other resources

Pieces of paper, notebooks, pencils, pens, Post-It notes.

wish to write complex and extended texts it is important to build the basics and plug the gaps. Some learners might say that they cannot spell, so explain that this theme contains some suggestions for improving the spelling of useful words.

Begin an oral communal note, list or message by giving an example of one with which the learners are familiar, such as a note to a teacher:

Dear Miss Li, Please excuse Jamie from swimming lessons today. He has a bad cold. He should be well enough to swim again by next week. Yours sincerely, Lewis Brown.

Agree a suitable theme for the next note. Get each learner in turn to add a sentence until the note reaches a natural ending. Repeat the exercise until the ideas run out.

Discuss the contents and conventions of each note and ask questions about them.

- Was the message to the teacher the same as the list of things to do before going on holiday? Why not?
- How did it start? How did it end?
- Did it have whole sentences in it?
- Is a written message the same as a spoken one? Draw out answers concerning the intended recipient and the difference this makes to the way in which the note is written. Establish that written and spoken language are different and have different conventions.

Using a whiteboard or flip chart, write up some of their oral messages. Discuss spelling and legibility.

Differentiation

For less confident learners, present a sentence from the oral notes cut into individual words and phrases for them to rearrange into a sensible order.

For more confident learners, present the entire text from the oral notes cut into individual sentences for learners to rearrange into a sensible order.

Extension

In pairs, ask learners to compose a short note on a given theme that is relevant to their circumstances.

Activity 2 Lists

 **Presentation 4a Lists (Entry 1 and 2/Access 1 and 2)**

Most learners will be familiar with lists of things to do or shopping lists.

Slide 1

Use this presentation to demonstrate the different ways in which lists can be organised and to assist learners in selecting a method suitable for the task in hand. Stress that there is no right or wrong way, just a matter of personal preference.

Slide 2

How easy to read is this text? Be aware that learners may not be familiar with the concept of commas to divide items on a list. This slide shows the difficulty of spotting individual items when written consecutively.

Slide 3

This slide shows the same items but with each one on each line. Is it easier to read? What types of lists can this method be used for?

Slide 4

This slide uses bullet points to emphasise each point. When might this method be used? What different forms can bullet points take?

Slide 5

Here, numbers have been used for each item in the list. Explain that these can sometimes be useful if things must be done in a particular order.

Slide 6

The items in the list are crossed off after they have been done – a satisfying way to see what is left to do.

Extension

Encourage learners to add items to one of the lists from the presentation.

On the whiteboard or flip chart, write one list for something relevant to the learners. Decide how it will be organised.

A shopping list is probably the most common type of list. Ask learners to use ideas from catalogues and newspapers to create a list of presents they want to buy for friends and family for Christmas, Eid, Divali or whatever is appropriate to the learners.

 4.2.1 Make a list (Entry 1/Access 1)

Use this activity sheet to assist learners to make a list of things to do before going on holiday.

Extension

Adjust the scenario according to the needs of the learners, for example a list of things to do before a job interview. Other lists might include the order in which to perform actions when closing down a computer, things to do when leaving work if you are the last person out, how to use a photocopier, how to use the drinks machine, how to send a fax or email.

Other resources

Post-It notes.

Activity 3 Organising a list

Create a list using Post-It notes, for example around 'opening up' the shop if you are the first to arrive at work. Take their suggestions and write them on notes. Organise the 'list' in order.

Differentiation

Allow learners time to copy any useful words into a personal dictionary.

Ask confident learners to make a personal list in their notebooks.

Extension

Ask learners to write lists for other occasions, e.g. a shopping list for party food, a list of things to take into hospital, a list of things to do before cooking a special meal. Make suggestions as realistic as possible.

Other resources

'Classified ad' pages.

Activity 4 Writing 'for sale' notices

Writing 'For sale' notices can be a good way to encourage learners to think about what information is needed, as well as order. Read some notices together from your local newspaper. Pick out key features, such as, contact details, price, description.

A 4.4.1 Bicycle for sale (Entry 1/Access 1)/4.4.2 Internet advert (Entry 2/Access 2)

- Ask learners to create classified adverts for things they might sell.

Activity 5 Birthday spelling

This activity suggests some strategies that learners can employ to help fix words in their memories.

- It is not suggested that all of these strategies are tried at once, rather that they are introduced over a period of time and learners given the option of accepting or rejecting the method as suitable for them or of combining various elements and adding some of their own. It is not a definitive list of spelling techniques.

If the birthday scenario is not appropriate for your group of learners, select a number of words that the learners want to learn how to spell and use these words to adapt the activities described below. For example, someone working in a home for the elderly who needs to write daily reports on people in his or her care might choose to learn words such as *anxious*, *behaviour*, *constipation*, *dentures*, *deteriorate*, *infection*, *medication*, *mobility* and *prescription*. A learner who has to follow recipes might choose to learn *boil*, *blend*, *cream*, *dice*, *poach*, *reduce*, *seal*, *season*, *simmer* and *toss*.

4.5.1 Birthday wordsearch (Entry 1/Access 1)

Ask learners to look at a word that they want to search for from the list and try to remember the first letter or group of letters in it. Then they track left to right across the wordsearch and top to bottom to locate the letter or whole word. When they are sure they have found it, they should say the word, say the letters in it, draw a line through it and move on to the next one.

Differentiation

Learners who find it difficult to track could use a piece of card, a ruler or a finger to trace along the letters and to cover either the letters above or below the line they are looking at. To track the vertical words, hold the card vertically, to the left or right.

Extension

Learners who enjoy wordsearches can find plenty to practise on in the shops. However, be aware that most wordsearch books use capital letters, which are more difficult to differentiate. Words are also written backwards both horizontally and vertically, as well as diagonally, making them less easy for learners to decipher.

4.5.2 Birthday words (Entry 1/Access 1)

Copy several sets of the cards. Cut them up to make a snap game or pelmanism.

CD 4.5.3 Birthday bingo (Entry 1/Access 1)

The words on Activity Sheet 4.5.2 can be used in conjunction with this activity sheet. They can be pulled out of a hat and used to cover the matching word on the caller's card. Learners with 'player' cards can pick one of the words from a central pile to cover the matching word on their card.

CD Use the 'Bingo generator' on the CD to make your own sets of words.

4.5.4 Birthday 'look, say, cover, write check' (Entry 1 and 2/Access 1 and 2)

This activity sheet is an effective way to learn how to spell individual words. It should be practised regularly to be effective. Learners should:

- select a word and make sure it is spelt correctly
- write it down
- look at it carefully and imagine its shape
- say it aloud if possible
- try to remember its beginning, middle and end
- cover the word
- write the word in one go before the visual picture disappears.

- check the final word is spelt correctly
- repeat the process some time later until the word is fixed in the memory.

A 4.5.5 Birthday words missing letters (Entry 1/ Access 1)

Use this activity sheet to help some learners focus on what they need to write on a birthday card.

Differentiation

Give less confident learners one phrase at a time to master.

Ask more confident learners to cover the completed phrase and check each time they fill in the gaps lower down the sheet.

Ask learners to write a 'complete' birthday message.

Extension

Learners with good ICT skills could make a card and write an appropriate message before printing and signing it.

Differentiation

For learners who require more practice, any of these activities could be adapted using words that might be used on a card or invitation for any celebration appropriate to the learner, e.g. Christmas, Eid, Divali, a birthday, a wedding, a wedding anniversary, a children's party, a summer barbeque.

Other techniques that learners may find useful when learning to spell a word are as follows.

- Write a new word on to a piece of paper, preferably in handwriting. Trace over the word with a finger, saying each part of the word at the same time. Then, without looking at the original, try to write the word again.
- For irregular words such as *Wednesday* and *February*, deliberately mispronounce them, saying each part as it is written and emphasising the irregular part, e.g. Wed**nes**day, Feb**ru**ary.
- Use mnemonics to remember words that are often mistaken, e.g. *because* ***b****ig* ***e****lephants* ***c****an* ***a****lways* ***u****nderstand* ***s****mall* ***e****lephants because they speak the same language*. It is a good idea for learners to invent their own mnemonics as they are more likely to remember them.
- Words that can cause confusion because they sound similar but are spelt differently (*to*, *too*, *two*; *there*, *their*, *they're*) should be learnt separately with an emphasis on the meaning.
- Word games such as I spy, Hangman and Scrabble are useful ways of getting learners thinking about words and using letters and sounds.

Activity 6 Sending a message

In this activity learners are encouraged to write a message in complete sentences, focusing on the difference between spoken and written words. The activities centre around writing a holiday postcard but should be adapted to the needs of your learners. For example, learners may have to complete a daybook or report at the end of a shift, leave notes for co-workers, or complete memos or telephone messages. In each case, learners need to be aware of the difference between what they would say and how it is written.

- Discuss learner's experiences of holidays: where do learners go, where would they like to go, activities that learners do on holiday and what they would like to do, what they liked best and what was the worst aspect. During the conversation write key words on the whiteboard or flip chart for learners to use later.
- Stop every so often and give examples of how some answers would be written. For example, if the answer to the question 'Where did you go on holiday last year?' is 'Spain', it might be written as 'I went on holiday to Spain last year.' Write sentences on the whiteboard or flip chart. Show the upper case letters and full stops.
- Later in the conversation ask 'If you had to write that down, how would you write it?' Add answers to the whiteboard or flip chart. Stress the concept of the written word being more formal than the spoken word, and that what is written must be clear and make complete sense because the writer is not going to be there to explain what is meant.
- Model how to write a postcard, building on the learners' suggestions:
  - Write a salutation.
  - Choose what to write about first.
  - Discuss how to turn ideas into full sentences, using appropriate punctuation.
  - Read through the text, including the final salutation. Point out the full stops and upper case letters that follow them. Address any queries.

Differentiation

- Using Activity Sheet 4.6.1, ask a range of questions to which learners write one-word answers in the spaces provided before folding the section of paper over and passing it on to the next person. Start with 'What is your name?' and move on to 'Where did you go on holiday last year?', 'What was the best thing about it?', 'What was the worst thing about it?', 'Where are you going to go this/next year?' Collect and redistribute the sheets randomly. Learners should try to imagine they have just received the answers in the post and try to work out the meaning of what they have read.

Other resources

Examples of holiday postcards, images of skills that might be learned on holiday, examples of daybooks and notes left for work colleagues, memos and telephone messages, Post-It notes.

 4.6.2 Consequences 2 (Entry 1/Access 1)

Ask learners to complete the sentences. Again, collect and redistribute the papers. This time the information should be easier to access because it is written in full sentences. Point out the upper case letters and full stops.

 4.6.3 Postcard template (Entry 1 and 2/Access 1 and 2)

Use this template for learners to compose their own postcards. Ensure learners plan and proofread their work.

Activity 7 letters, invitations and messages

 4.7.1 Letters and invitations/4.7.2 Replies (Entry 2/ Access 2)

These activity sheets can be used together. Cut out the responses on Activity Sheet 4.7.2 (blank spaces are left for individual responses from the learners).

Ask learners to select an invitation to reply to. Read through the choices of replies with learners. Ask them to select a number of appropriate responses to the invitation and arrange them into a short letter. Learners can then copy the message by hand or word-process it.

Differentiation

Limit the number of choices of reply for less confident learners.

Show more confident learners how to set out their reply as a letter.

Extension

 4.7.3 Telephone message (Entry 2/Access 2)

Spend some time role-playing taking a telephone message. Ask learners to explain the message before writing it down. Ensure learners understand what each part of the message sheet is for. If necessary, ask learners to write each piece of information on a sticky note and place it in the correct place on the message pad before copying it down. Be aware that listening and writing at the same time is an advanced skill that will require lots of practice.

4.2.1 Make a list

You are getting ready to go on holiday. Choose three things to put on your list.

Decide if you want to use:

numbers: 1 2 3
bullet points: • • •
or nothing at all.

Things to do before I go on holiday

take the dog to the kennels	pack a suitcase
get a passport	buy suntan lotion
cancel the papers	water the plants

4.4.1 Bicycle for sale

Write your own 'for sale' notice.

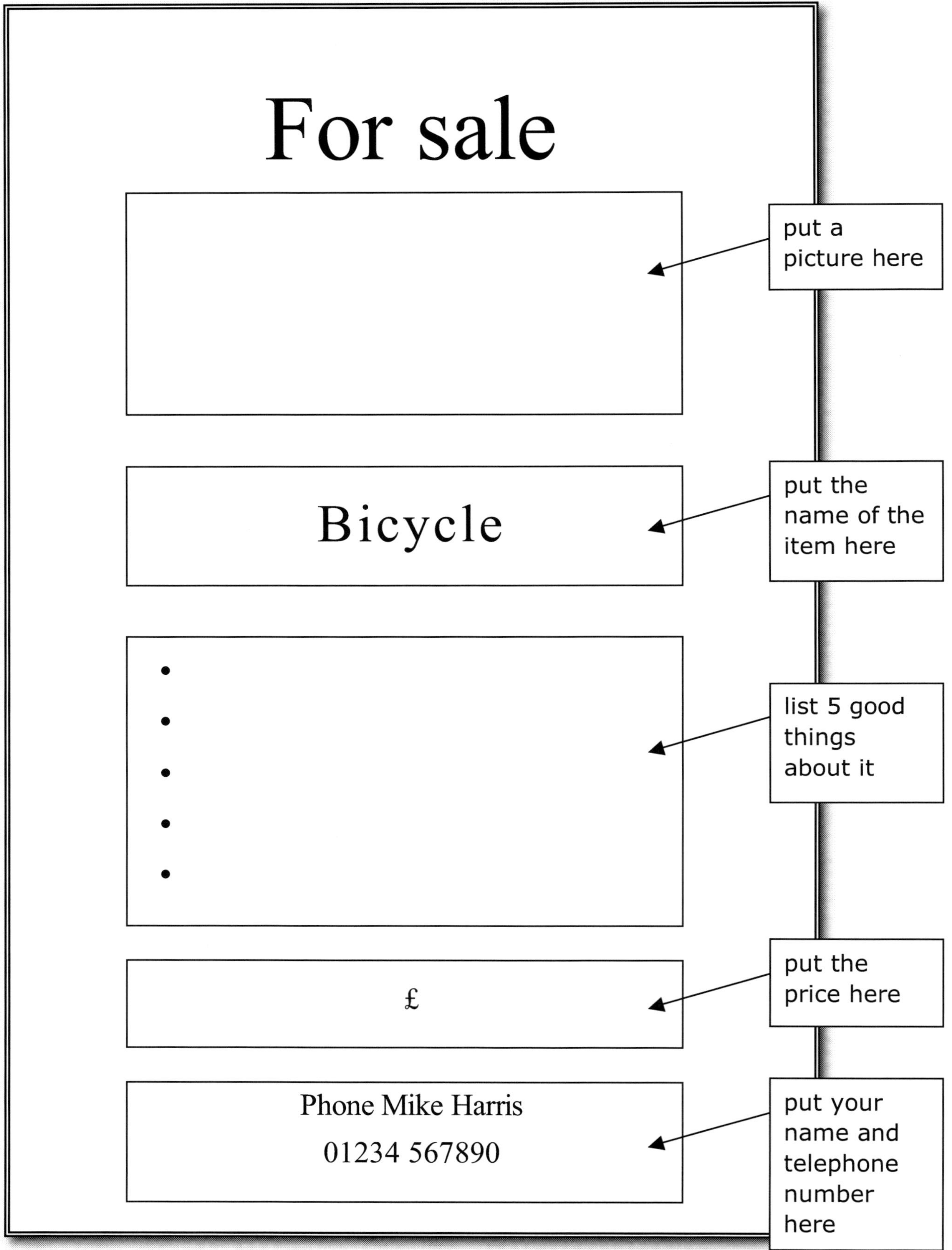

4.4.2 Internet advert

Plan an advert for a website.

Photo of sale item

Description of sale item:

4.5.1 Birthday wordsearch

Find 12 words to do with birthdays.

Cross off each word as you find it.

happy	returns	with	of
birthday	to	lots	best
many	from	love	wishes

b	e	s	t	m	h	m	a	n	y
i	l	c	n	w	a	w	t	s	u
r	b	d	e	i	p	i	f	v	l
t	k	a	j	s	p	s	w	x	o
h	m	d	p	h	y	h	r	c	t
d	e	l	r	e	t	u	r	n	s
a	t	o	i	s	s	s	g	h	k
y	a	v	o	h	b	i	j	l	n
f	z	e	p	q	f	r	o	m	y
g	q	s	w	i	t	h	f	o	r

4.5.2 Birthday words

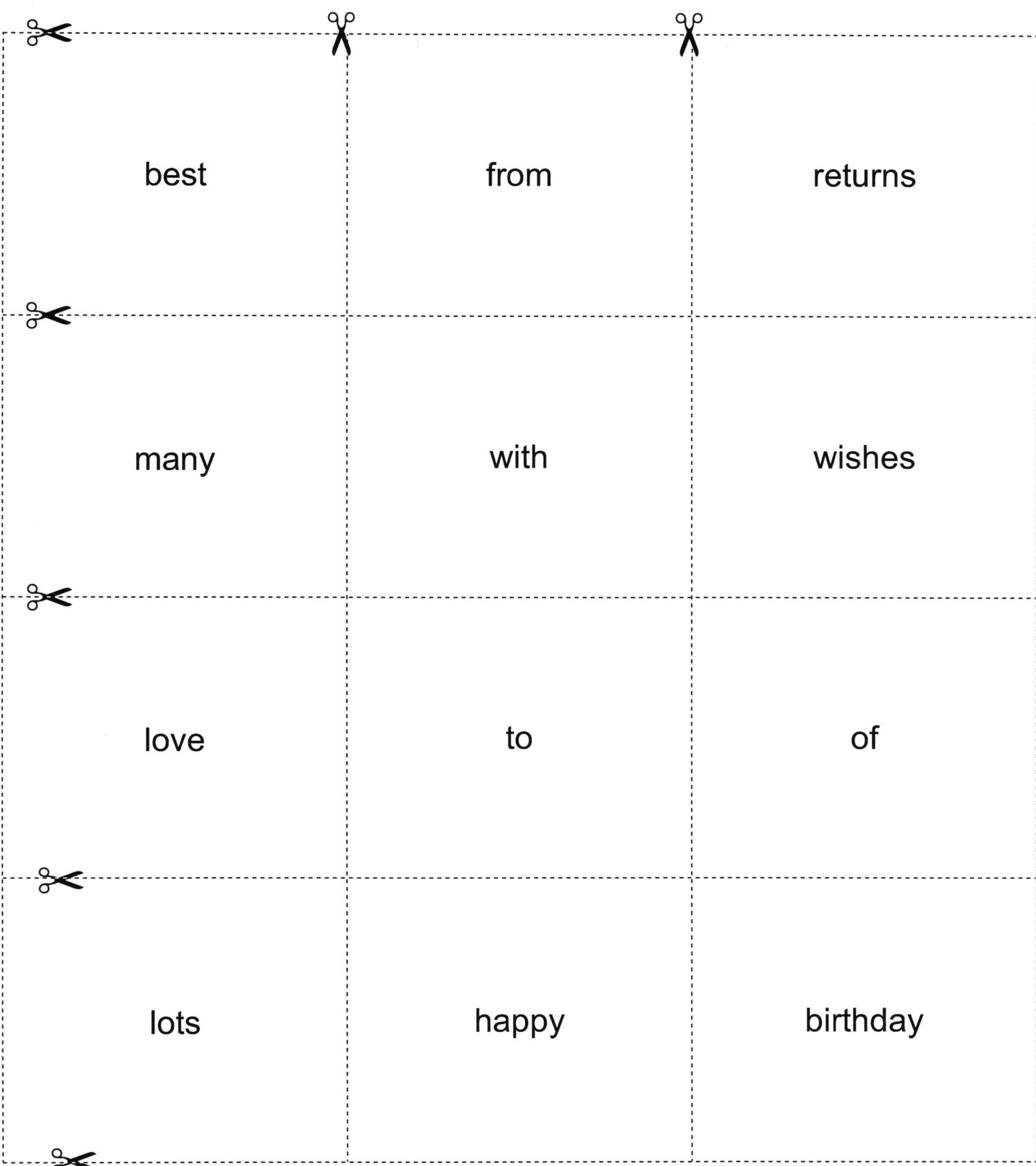

Note to tutor: can also be used with Activity Sheet 4.5.3.

4.5.3 Birthday bingo

Caller words

happy	birthday	from	to
many	returns	of	with
best	lots	wishes	love

Player cards

of	happy
many	returns

returns	to
birthday	best

many	wishes
love	best

from	with
lots	wishes

Note to tutor: this Activity Sheet can also be used in conjunction with the Bingo generator on the CD.

4.5.4 Birthday 'look, say, cover, write, check'

Cover each word, then write it and check. Repeat until it is spelt correctly.

Word	Write	Write	Write	Write	Write
happy					
birthday					
many					
returns					
to					
from					
with					
lots					
love					
of					
best					
wishes					

4.5.5 Birthday words missing letters

Fill in the missing letters.

Then write the words.

Happy Birthday

_appy _irthday

H_ppy B_rthday

Happ_ Birthda_

Ha_ _y Bir_ _day

_ _ _ _ _ _ _ _ _ _ _ _ _ _

Best Wishes

_est _ishes

B_ st W _ shes

Bes _ Wishe_

B _ _ t Wi _ _ es

_ _ _ _ _ _ _ _ _ _

With Love

_ith _ove

Wit_ Lov_

W_th L_ve

Wi_ _ Lo_ _

_ _ _ _ _ _ _ _

Many Happy Returns

_any _appy _eturns

Man_ Happ_ Return_

M_ny H_ppy R_turns

M_ _y Ha_ _y Ret_ _ns

_ _ _ _ _ _ _ _ _ _ _ _ _ _ _ _

4.6.1 Consequences

Write your answer in the space provided, then fold the sheet over and pass it on.

fold

fold

fold

fold

Note to tutor: ask learners to write the answers to your questions in the spaces provided before folding the section over and passing it on.

4.6.2 Consequences 2

Complete the sentences, then fold the sheet over and pass it on.

My name is______________________________________.

fold

Last year I went on holiday to__________________________________.

fold

The best thing about it was__________________________________

____.

fold

The worst thing about it was__________________________________

____.

fold

Next year I will go to____________________________________.

Note to tutor: ask learners to write the answers to your questions in the spaces provided before folding the section over and passing it on.

4.6.3 Postcard template

Write your own postcard. Don't forget to address it.

Stamp

To

View over the bay

4.7.1 Letters and invitations

Select an invitation then write your reply.

Mr and Mrs A G Richards

request the pleasure of your company at the marriage of their daughter

Laura
to
Mr James Whittick

at 2 o'clock on Saturday June 10th

at

St Peter's Church and afterwards

at

The Bull Hotel

We're having a party!
on
Saturday 31st December
24 Bridge Road
Hightown
8 till late
Bring a bottle
New Year Party!
Raj and Lee
RSVP

Georgia King was born on August 15th weighing 7lb 8oz.

Parents and baby are doing well!

Newtown School
Annual Family BBQ
on the school field
Friday 21st June
6pm

£2.50 a head
Fun for all the family
Parents v Pupils Rounders Match
Please let us know how many of your family will be coming

RSVP
The Head Teacher
Newtown School

Bring chairs and blankets

4.7.2 Replies

Thank you for your letter.
Thank you for the invitation.
I would like to come to the wedding.
I would love to come to the party.
I am sorry but I will not be able to come.
Congratulations on the birth of your baby.
Lots of love
I am looking forward to being there.
Dear
Six of us will be coming to the BBQ.
It sounds great fun.

Note to tutor: for use in conjunction with Activity Sheet 4.7.1.

4.7.3 Telephone message

Write each piece of information in the correct place on the message pad below.

Telephone message

Message for:
While you were out you were called by:
Telephone number:
Message: Please call ☐ Will call back later ☐ Other:
Time:
Date:
Received by:

Theme 5

Everyday information

Introduction

Many of us are faced with a barrage of information every day in the form of junk mail, fliers, television listings, newspapers or recipes. This information may be written as prose, tables or lists.

This theme looks at the format of some of this information and suggests strategies that learners can use to make sense of it, accessing information that is important to them. The intention is that simple, everyday information is used for these activities rather than simplified text. In this way learners use text that has meaning for them and are enabled to access information that is important to them. It is closely linked to Theme 6 Everyday reading, which looks in more depth at reading strategies.

Learning outcomes	Adult Literacy Curriculum references	ALAN Curriculum Framework for Scotland
To be able to read and understand text in different formats	Rt/E1.1 Rt/E1.2 Rt/E2.1 Rt/E2.3 Rs/E2.2 Rs/E2.3 Rs/E2.4	A1/A2 • Using strategies for reading unfamiliar words • Using pictures and graphic clues • Using layouts and headings • Reading for particular purposes
To be able to understand the key features of tables, charts and diagrams, lists and text		
To be able to use different techniques to aid understanding		

Links

Theme 1 What is it all about?; Theme 6 Everyday reading.

Key words

letter, capital letters, sentence, table, text, title, word.

Activity notes

Activity 1 Introducing the theme

Using a range of examples, such as take-away menus, newspaper articles, timetables or shopping lists, prompt learners to talk about what they read and how they do it.

- Did you read anything at breakfast, on your way to work or on your way here?
- Is it necessary to read everything you see?
- Is it necessary to read every word on each item?
- Are some things easier to read than others?

Other resources

A selection of texts in as many different formats as possible, e.g. magazine articles, newspaper cuttings, fliers, adverts, junk mail, shopping lists, bills, bank statements, packaging and recipes.

Look at the ways in which everyday information might be arranged. Show an example such as a holiday brochure or information leaflet on a whiteboard or flip chart and demonstrate how information can be arranged in a table, as a diagram, as prose or as a list. Stress that most information is a mixture of all these formats.

Conduct an information race with the whole group. Ask learners to find a particular type of text from those available. Stress that there is no need to read the text at this stage and that they are sorting by type not content. As each example is found, briefly discuss its properties. Use the language of texts (see 'Key words'). If appropriate, limit the texts to those concerned with work, home or leisure.

- What is this text about? How do you know?
- Is there an illustration or image? If so, what does this tell you?
- What about the layout/format? How easy is it to read?
- How is the information arranged? Is it in sentences? Is it a table? Is there a diagram? Can you spot a title? Are there any headings?

In pairs or small groups, ask learners to sort a pile of texts into sets of a similar sort, e.g. all those with an illustration, all those with a symbol, all those with a title. Encourage learners to discuss the texts and use the language of texts to do so. Emphasise that there are no right and wrong answers. Talk about the reasons for their choices, reinforcing the language used.

Ask learners to challenge each other to find a text of a particular format.

Differentiation

Give learners fewer texts to choose from and a reduced range of formats. Allow time to reinforce the language used to describe formats. Provide plenty of examples.

Suggest that some learners may start to use the title, headings and other features to extract information from chosen texts.

Other resources

Recycling information for the local area, highlighter pens, newspaper articles of relevance to the learners.

Activity 2 Using key words to find information

This activity shows how the same information can be presented in different ways and practises looking for headings, key words and sentences to extract information.

P Presentation 5 Reduce, reuse, recycle Entry 1 and 2/ Access 1 and 2)

Hold a discussion about recycling.

- What do learners recycle?
- How do they do it?
- What is the local council's policy?
- What colours are the recycling containers?

- What goes in them?
- Where is non-recycled rubbish put?

Talk about landfill sites. Allow time for discussion and exploration around each slide. Write key words on to the presentation as they occur in the discussion.

Slide 1

Talk about the image. What is it about? (*recycling*) What does it show? What message does it convey? Discuss the slide's title. What is the key word? (*recycle*) Explain that the key word helps you to decide whether the information is of interest to you and whether you need to read more.

Slide 2

Talk about the list. Read through each item, pointing at each word in turn so that learners can follow. Which word tells you what the list is about? (*recycle*).

Slide 3

Talk about the chart. What tells you what the chart is about? (the title). Is there a key word in the title? (*recycling*). Discuss briefly the other features.

Slide 4

Talk about the table. What tells you what the table is about? (the title). Is there a key word in the title? (*recycling*). Discuss briefly the other features. Is the information the same or different to the previous slide?

Slide 5

Talk about the text. Read through it, pointing at each word in turn so that learners can follow. What tells you what it is about? (the title). Is there a key word in the title? (*recycling*). Discuss briefly the other sentences. Is the information the same as or different from the previous slide?

Summarise the key points about the different types of text you have looked at. Ask learners to suggest ideas and add them to the slides. For example:

- the same information can be formatted in many different ways
- there are often titles and headings that tell you about the rest of the information
- there are often key words that tell you what the information is about.

Print appropriate screens from the presentation. Assist learners in highlighting the words *recycle* and *recycling*. Ask learners to point out the titles.

Encourage learners to add information about recycling in their area using a variety of formats.

 5.2.2 Newspaper article (Entry 1 and 2/Access 1 and 2)

Use this activity sheet to assist learners with looking for key words. Read through the newspaper article with the learners. Point out the features as demonstrated in Presentation 5. Ask learners to point out the headline. Remind learners that this gives an overview of what is in the article and a clue about the content. Ask learners to highlight the key words (*recycle* and *recycling*). Hold a question and answer session to check understanding.

 5.2.3 Recycling survey (Entry 2/Access 2)

Ask learners to circle and write the answers to the questions on this activity sheet. Stress the need to use key words and headings to find the information they need. The bold words in the questions will give learners clues on where to look.

A 5.2.4 Health and safety notice/5.2.5 What is the poster about? (Entry 2/Access 2)

- Use these two activity sheets together to help learners understand health and safety notices.
- Read through the poster together, picking out tricky vocabulary and check for understanding.
- Read through the statements on 5.2.5 to fill in the missing words from the poster.

Activity 3 Using sentences and punctuation to find information

 5.3.1 Sentences (Entry 2/Access 2)

Use this activity sheet to help learners make sense of text by using sentences. Remind them that sentences begin with a capital letter and end with a full stop, exclamation mark or question mark and make complete sense in between. Using full stops and capital case letters is a way of cutting the text into smaller chunks.

Ask learners to point out and highlight the sentences in the activity. After copying the sentences, encourage learners to read them to check for sense and understanding. Other texts can be treated in the same way.

There is additional work on charts and tables in the *Sure Skills Numeracy Tutor Support Pack*.

Confident learners can select other relevant newspaper articles, highlighting key words or matching headlines to find articles giving the same story.

 5.3.2 Newspaper report (Entry 2/Access 2)

Read through the newspaper report together before asking learners to highlight the punctuation.

 5.3.3 What is the report about? (Entry 2/Access 2)

Ask learners to read the newspaper report on Activity Sheet 5.3.2 before answering the questions on the sheet.

Activity 4 Using a range of skills to find information

A 5.4.1 Recycling leaflet (1)/5.4.2 Recycling leaflet (2) (Entry 1 and 2/Access 1 and 2)

These two activity sheets show different parts of a leaflet on recycling. Each section uses a different format to present information. There are titles and headings, a list, a table and some text.

Read through the information with the learners. Some learners may prefer to tackle it as a paired reading activity. Talk about each page.

- Where are the headings?
- What are the key words?
- How is the information presented?
- How can you find the information you need?

Draw out the different techniques for finding information covered so far.

A 5.4.3 Everything you need to know about recycling (Entry 2/Access 2)

This activity sheet is a comprehension exercise that can be used to aid learners in extracting information from the leaflet in Activity Sheets 5.4.1 and 5.4.2. Ask the questions orally first. Support learners to use the cues, read the text and use the different formats. Learners might prefer to work in pairs or small groups. The next activity deals with tables in more detail.

Differentiation

Cover the parts of the leaflet not applicable at the time for learners who may have difficulty focusing on one area.

Entry 1 learners can use the activities but complete them orally.

Extension

Extend the activities to include up-to-date local information familiar to your learners. Make sure that each source is thoroughly explored before learners have to compare information from a combination of sources.

Activity 5 Find what you need in tables

In this activity learners use titles and headings to find the information they need in tables.

Other resources

Local bus and train timetables, rulers, cards, L-shaped cards.

5.5.1 Bus timetable/5.5.2 What time is the bus? (Entry 1 and 2/Access 1 and 2)

- For this activity, the emphasis is on extracting information from a table and not on telling the time, so support learners with this aspect of the exercise. If appropriate customise the activity to reflect local names that are more familiar to learners.
- Discuss learners' experiences of public transport and timetables and any difficulties they may have encountered.
- Using sheet 5.5.1 ask questions that will enable learners to use headings, rows and columns to find the information they need. For example:
    - Demonstrate how to track across rows and down columns.
    - I'm meeting a friend at the swimming pool at 12 o'clock. What time is the bus from Castlefields?
    - I start work at 9 o'clock in the High Street. What's the latest bus I can get from Market Street to arrive on time?
- Pick out the use of bold and large text

In pairs, ask learners to support each other to find the information required to solve the problems on this activity sheet.

Learners can draw horizontal and vertical lines on Activity Sheet 5.5.1 if it helps them to find the time they need.

Differentiation

Learners who require further consolidation of reading tables may like to use these activity sheets:

5.5.3 Work rota (Entry 1 and 2/Access 1 and 2)

5.5.4 Cooking temperatures (Entry 2/Access 2)

Extension

Set the learners a task to find some local timetables and plan a journey from home to college, a football match or a holiday destination. They can then plan the return journey.

Learners familiar with the Internet can search for online timetables using www.rail.co.uk or http://timetables.showbus.co.uk.

5.2.2 Newspaper article

Highlight the key words in this newspaper article.

Haytown tops league for recycling

'Our recycling policy is one of the best in the country', says council leader

Haytown is one of the best towns in England when it comes to recycling. Only five other towns are better.

The people of Haytown have increased what is recycled every year since 2006.

Last year, 80 per cent of glass, 80 per cent of paper and 50 per cent of cans were recycled.

'We have to thank the people of Haytown,' said the council leader. 'Thanks to them we have made a big difference to the amount of rubbish going into landfill sites in the county.

'I hope next year will be even better,' he added.

5.2.3 Recycling survey

Using the information in the newspaper article and chart, answer the questions below.

Haytown tops league for recycling

'Our recycling policy is one of the best in the country', says council leader

Haytown is one of the best towns in England when it comes to recycling. Only five other towns are better.

The people of Haytown have increased what is recycled every year since 2006.

Last year, 80 per cent of glass, 80 per cent of paper and 50 per cent of cans were recycled.

'We have to thank the people of Haytown,' said the council leader. 'Thanks to them we have made a big difference to the amount of rubbish going into landfill sites in the county.

'I hope next year will be even better,' he added.

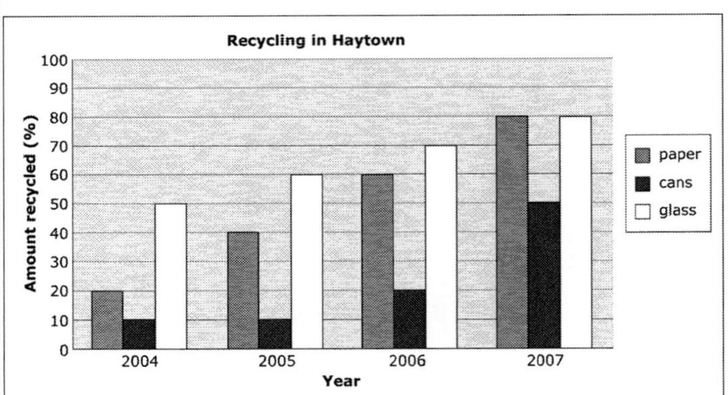

1 Can you give me a **list** of things you can recycle in Haytown?

1.

2.

3.

2 How much **glass** was recycled in **2006**?

60 per cent

70 per cent

80 per cent

3 How many **cans** were recycled in **2006**?

40 per cent

50 per cent

60 per cent

4 Is it true that Haytown is one of the best towns for recycling?

Yes

No

5 The council leader of Haytown is a man.

Yes

No

5.2.4 Health and safety notice

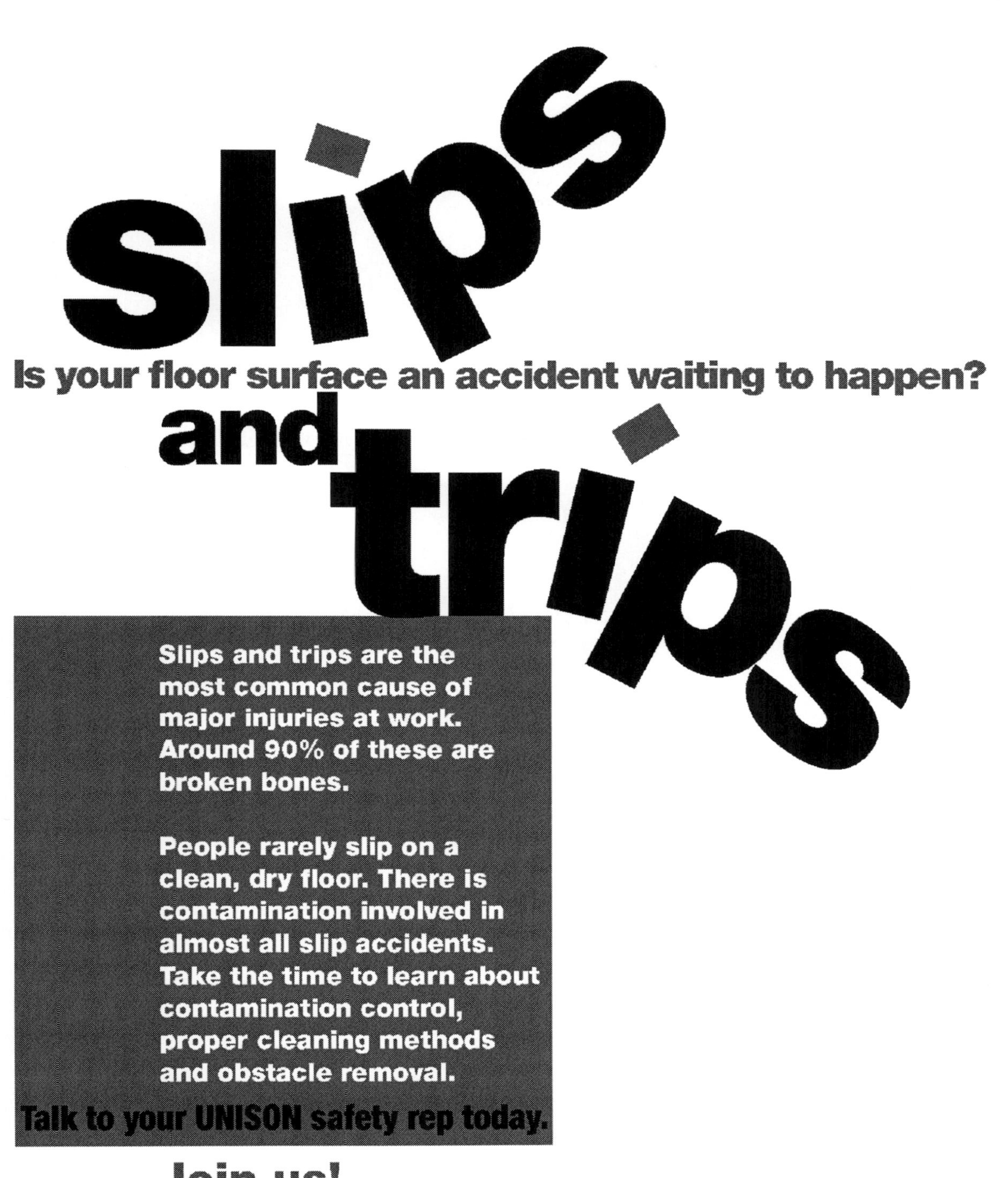

slips
Is your floor surface an accident waiting to happen?
and
trips
Slips and trips are the most common cause of major injuries at work. Around 90% of these are broken bones.
People rarely slip on a clean, dry floor. There is contamination involved in almost all slip accidents. Take the time to learn about contamination control, proper cleaning methods and obstacle removal.
Talk to your UNISON safety rep today.

Join us!

UNISON–Your friend at work

For general information about UNISON call **0845 355 0845** Textphone **0800 0 967 968** or visit our website **www.unison.org.uk**

UNISON Organising for Health & Safety

Designed and produced by UNISON Communications.
Published and printed by UNISON, 1 Mabledon Place, London WC1H 9AJ www.unison.org.uk
CU/October2005/15152/Stock number 2451

Note for tutor: for use with Activity Sheet 5.2.5.

5.2.5 What is the poster about?

Use this with Activity Sheet 5.2.4.

This is a poster about ____________________
and ____________________ .
Is your ____________________ surface an
accident waiting to happen?
Slips and trips are the most common cause
of major ____________________ at work.
Around 90% of these are
____________________ bones.
People rarely slip on a ____________________ ,
____________________ floor.
There is ____________________ involved in
almost all slip accidents.
Take the time to learn about contamination control, proper
____________________ methods and ____________________ removal.

5.3.1 Sentences

Find the sentences.

Mark the full stops at the end of the sentences.

Mark the capital letters at the beginning of the sentences.

Copy the sentences.

Read what you have written.

Every year we get better at recycling. In 2004, only 10 per cent of cans were recycled in Haytown. Last year 50 per cent of cans were recycled.

1. E
2. I
3. L

Haytown is one of the best towns in England when it comes to recycling. Only five other towns are better.

1.
2.

Putting our household waste into landfill sites uses up our scarce land resources. It is also expensive and it causes pollution.

1.
2.

5.3.2 Newspaper report

Find the sentences in this notice.

Highlight the full stops at the end of the sentences.

Highlight the capital letters at the beginning of the sentences.

Highlight the key words in each sentence.

Find out about any word you do not recognise.

Read the sentences.

Explain what you have read to a partner.

Sixty jobs to go at factory

Sixty jobs are to go at a Haytown factory less than a year after it opened.

Union officials today said that The Box Factory on Hay Road Industrial Estate will close on Friday.

Workers will get no redundancy pay because they have been working at the factory for such a short time.

The firm blamed a change in the way companies package their products for the loss of business.

A spokesman said, 'Packaging is wasteful. People do not want so much packaging on the things they buy these days.'

The company is also closing a factory in Yorkshire.

5.3.3 What is the report about?

Read the sentences and answer the questions.

Sixty jobs are to go at a Haytown factory less than a year after it opened.

1. How many jobs are going? ____________________

2. How long has the factory been open? ____________________

Union officials today said that The Box Factory on Hay Road Industrial Estate will close on Friday.

1. What is the factory called? ____________________

2. When will the factory close? ____________________

Workers will get no redundancy pay because they have been working at the factory for such a short time.

1. Will the workers get redundancy pay? ____________________

2. Why? ____________________

____

The firm blamed a change in the way companies package their products for the loss of business.

1. Why has the firm lost business? ____________________

____

A spokesman said, 'Packaging is wasteful. People do not want so much packaging on the things they buy these days.'

1. Why do people want less packaging on the things they buy? ____________________

____

5.4.1 Recycling leaflet (1)

Reduce **Reuse** **Recycle**

Putting our household waste into landfill sites uses up our scarce land resources.

It is also expensive and it causes pollution.

Haytown County Council wants to help you to cut down on the amount of rubbish that goes into landfill sites in our county.

Collection timetable: January and February

	blue box	red box	green wheeled bin	black wheeled bin
January				
Wed 3rd	✓		✓	
Wed 10th		✓		✓
Wed 17th	✓		✓	
Wed 24th		✓		✓
Wed 31st	✓		✓	
February				
Wed 7th	✓		✓	
Wed 14th		✓		✓
Wed 21st	✓		✓	
Wed 28th		✓		✓

Your collection day is **Wednesday**.

 Make sure your containers are on the roadside by 0700.

5.4.2 Recycling leaflet (2)

Here is what **we** will do.

- ☐ Give every household:
  - ☐ a blue box
  - ☐ a red box
  - ☐ a green wheeled bin
  - ☐ a black wheeled bin.
- ☐ Collect and recycle your household rubbish.
- ☐ Continue to provide Waste Recycling Centres ☎ 01234 567890 for details.

Here is what **you** can do.

- ☐ Make sure you recycle as much of your household waste as possible.
- ☐ Use the correct bins for your recycled waste.
- ☐ Put out the containers on the correct day.
- ☐ Compost vegetable waste at home – discounted compost bins available ☎ 01234 567890 for details.

What goes in the container?		
Container	**Yes** please ✓	**No** thank you ×
blue box	✓ newspapers ✓ magazines ✓ junk mail ✓ clothing and shoes	× cardboard × telephone directories
red box	✓ bottles ✓ glass ✓ cans ✓ plastic bottles	× mirrors × light bulbs
green wheeled bin	✓garden waste (grass cuttings, weeds, hedge clippings) ✓ cardboard	× kitchen waste × soil × ash
black wheeled bin	✓ non-recyclable household rubbish ✓ food waste (non-compostable) ✓ ash	× glass × aluminium × paper × garden waste

5.4.3 Everything you need to know about recycling

Read the recycling information to find the answers to these questions.

Use this with Activity Sheets 5.4.1 and 5.4.2.

What is the **collection** day?
What **time** are the containers collected?
What goes in the **black wheeled bin**?
What goes in the **blue box**?
I just broke a **mirror**. Can I put it in the **red box**?
What goes out on the same day as the **green wheeled bin**?
Where can I get a **compost bin** from?

5.5.1 Bus timetable

Find the information you need in the timetable below.

21 Castlefields Estate to High Street

Monday to Friday							
Castlefields Estate	07.22	08.10	09.22	10.10	11.22	12.10	13.22
Long Road	07.30	08.18	09.30	10.18	11.30	12.18	13.30
Market Street	07.35	08.23	09.35	10.23	11.35	12.23	13.35
Swimming Pool	07.46	08.34	09.46	10.34	11.46	12.34	13.46
High Street	07.52	08.40	09.52	10.40	11.52	12.40	13.52

Note to tutor: for use with Activity Sheet 5.5.2.

5.5.2 What time is the bus?

Use this with Activity Sheet 5.5.1.

Find out which bus each person needs to catch.

I live on the **Castlefields Estate**.

I am meeting a friend to go shopping.

She will be in the **High Street** at 11 o'clock.

What time is the bus?

I live in **Long Road**.

I am meeting a friend to go to the **Swimming Pool**.

He will be there at 2 o'clock.

What time is the bus?

I live on **Long Road**.

I work in the **High Street**.

I start work at 8 o'clock.

What time is the bus?

I live on the **Castlefields Estate**.

I have an appointment at the dentist.

The dentist is in **Market Street**.

The appointment is at 12 o'clock.

What time is the bus?

5.5.3 Work rota

Merrytimes Nursery Staff Rota					
w/c 5th August	**Mon**	**Tues**	**Wed**	**Thur**	**Fri**
Aisha	7.30-3.30	7.30-3.30	7.30-3.30	7.30-3.30	7.30-3.30
Bartec	sick	sick	sick	sick	sick
Fatima	10.30-6.30	10.30-6.30	10.30-6.30	10.30-6.30	10.30-6.30
Mary	holiday	holiday	holiday	holiday	holiday
Mike	9.30-5.30	9.30-5.30	9.30-5.30	9.30-5.30	9.30-5.30
Sue M	10.30-6.30	10.30-6.30	10.30-6.30	10.30-6.30	10.30-6.30
Sue S	11.00-3.00	11.00-3.00	11.00-3.00	11.00-3.00	11.00-3.00
Viran	11.00-3.00	11.00-3.00	11.00-3.00	11.00-3.00	11.00-3.00

Who is on **holiday** this week?

Who is **sick** this week?

Who is starting work at **7.30** on **Monday** this week?

Who is starting work at **9.30** on **Wednesday** this week?

Who is starting work at **11.00** on **Friday** this week?

Who is starting work at **10.30** on **Thursday** this week?

Who is starting work at **7.30** on **Tuesday** this week?

5.5.4 Cooking temperatures

Cooking poultry in your fan oven		
THOROUGHLY THAW FROZEN POULTRY BEFORE COOKING		
Food	**Temperature**	**Approximate cooking time**
Chicken	150ºC	20–25 mins per 500g +20–25 mins
	190ºC	15–20 mins per 500g +15–20 mins
Turkey	150ºC	20–25 mins per 500g +20–25 mins
	190ºC	15–20 mins per 500g +15–20 mins
Stuffed poultry	200ºC 160ºC	20 mins, then for remainder of time
Prepacked poultry (fresh and frozen)		Follow cooking times on packet

Circle the answers 'Yes', 'No' or 'Maybe'.

1. Are these cooking times for use with a **fan oven**? **Yes** **No** **Maybe**
2. Can you cook **frozen poultry** in a fan oven? **Yes** **No** **Maybe**
3. Are **turkey** and **chicken** both **poultry**? **Yes** **No** **Maybe**
4. Can you cook **chicken** at **160ºC**? **Yes** **No** **Maybe**
5. Can you cook **turkey** at **160ºC**? **Yes** **No** **Maybe**
6. If you cook **turkey** at **190ºC** do you cook it for 20–25 mins per 500g? **Yes** **No** **Maybe**
7. If you cook **chicken** at **150ºC** do you cook it for 15–20 mins per 500g? **Yes** **No** **Maybe**

Theme 6

Everyday reading

Introduction

Theme 5 Everyday information deals largely with how to access information presented in different formats. This theme looks at extracting and understanding that information so that it can be used in daily life.

As there is so much written material available to us, we all have to make choices about what we want or need to read. In this theme, learners can use key words to decide whether a text is of interest to them. There are also activities to allow them to support detailed reading.

Learning outcomes	Adult Literacy Curriculum references	ALAN Curriculum Framework for Scotland
To be able to read and understand short narratives and text that have personal significance	Rt/E1.1 Rt/E2.1 Rt/E2.3 Rs/E2.2 Rs/E2.3 Rs/E2.4	• Use strategies for reading unfamiliar words • Using pictures and graphic cues • Reading for particular purposes • Reading critically

Links

Theme 5 Everyday information.

Key words

exclamation mark, full stop, letter, line, question mark, sentence, upper case letter, word.

Activity notes

Activity 1 Introducing the theme

 **6.1.1 Missing dog (Entry 1 and 2/Access 1 and 2)**

This activity enables learners to practise getting the gist of a text before reading it in detail. This activity sheet is also incorporated into the following presentation, so you could annotate this file with the learners' responses.

Display the activity sheet on a whiteboard or enlarge a copy for the whole group to share. Ask learners to make suggestions about the content. Discuss the features that give clues to the type of text it is such as the heading, format and font.

Before they read it, ask learners to guess what the text might say. Write up key words as they are suggested by the learners: *dog*, *lost*, *missing*, *find*, *information*, *reward*.

Other resources

Texts of interest to the learners, e.g. short local newspaper articles, workplace documents, sports centre information, home appliance instructions and posters.

Read through the text expressively. Emphasise the intonation suggested by the punctuation. Ensure understanding of the text and discuss any unknown vocabulary. Add to the key word list as required.

Read the first sentence again: 'We have lost our pet dog Scruffy.' Discuss how this sums up what the reader is about to read. Point out that it is an indication of the theme of the text. Theme sentences can be used to help readers decide whether the paragraph is of interest to them. They are usually at the beginning of a paragraph.

P Presentation 6 Have you seen our dog? (Entry 1 and 2/ Access 1 and 2)

Each slide follows a similar pattern. On each slide, a word is missing, which you should encourage learners to work out using clues on the slide to help them. The illustrations, context and punctuation will all help.

Involve learners in the presentation by asking them to suggest words that would fit, annotating the slides with their ideas before typing the 'correct' answer into the gap.

Slide 1

Set the scene by talking about the sorts of notices and signs that learners might have seen in shop windows. This one is a plea for help – a family has lost a pet.

Slide 2

This slide is a copy of Activity Sheet 6.1.1, which you can annotate.

Slide 3

Read the text on screen. What is the missing word? Click to bring up the word. Point out the upper case letter. Point out the exclamation mark. Ask for further examples of when this might be used in writing. Add to the slide any suggestions such as *Help*! *Come here at once*! *That's fantastic*! *Oh no*! *That's excellent*! Read them out expressively and encourage learners to join in.

Slide 4

Read the text on the slide. What is the missing word? Click to bring up the word. How do learners know? (from the illustration) Point out the upper case letter. Point out the full stop. What is it for? Ask for examples of sentences where a full stop is used at the end and add them to the slide. Read the suggestions expressively and encourage learners to join in.

Slide 5

Read the text on the slide. What is the missing word? Click to bring up the word. How do learners know? Point out the upper case letter. Point out the question mark. What is it for? Ask for examples of questions and add them to the slide. Read the suggestions expressively and encourage learners to join in.

Slide 6

Read the text on the slide. Point out the upper case letter. Point out the full stop. What is the missing word? Click to bring up the word. Add suggestions to the slide, e.g. *contact*, *ring*, *phone*. Read the sentence out with each of the suggestions in place of the line. Which ones make sense? Point out that they are all good guesses and make sense in this context. Learners are able to make sense of the text even though the word they select may not be precisely what was chosen by the writer.

 **6.1.2 Where is our dog? (Entry 1 and 2/Access 1 and 2)**

Use this activity sheet for learners to complete the sentences by supplying the missing words. Encourage learners to read the text aloud as expressively as possible.

Ask learners to think about what they have just read. In pairs, ask them to explain to a partner what the poster is about.

Differentiation

Less confident learners can be given a list of missing words to cross off as they use them in the text.

Pair less confident learners to work together on the text.

Pair a confident learner to act as a scribe for a less confident learner.

In pairs, ask learners to read out alternate sentences. This allows them to practise stopping at a full stop, question mark or exclamation mark.

Some learners may confuse a sentence with a line of text. Ask them to highlight the punctuation marks in the text and then read the text through, stopping briefly at each punctuation mark to consider what they have just read.

If appropriate, read each line of text as if it were a sentence (i.e. not a question or exclamation). Ask learners if they can make sense of the text when read this way.

Extension

Provide posters or short newspaper articles of local interest. Ask learners to:

- read the headline, title or theme sentence and ask themselves what the text is going to be about
- pick out any key words from the text
- highlight the punctuation
- read the text, trying to make a guess at unfamiliar words and checking for sense as they go
- ask themselves what they have just read and go back to anything they are unsure of.

Use a variety of texts and ask pairs of learners to highlight the first sentence of each text, read it and decide between themselves what the rest of the text is about. They can then read the text together before deciding whether they were correct.

Other resources

Notebook, small cards, highlighter pens.

Activity 2 Key words

Key words are the words in a sentence that tell the reader what the sentence is about. They help the reader get the gist of a text.

 **6.2.1 Wedding day (Entry 1 and 2/Access 1 and 2)**

Use this activity sheet to help learners identify key words. Focus on the first article for E1/A1 learners and the second article for E2/A2 learners.

Ask learners about what strategies they use for finding out what a piece of text is about. Acknowledge the value of these if success is achieved. Stress that it is not always necessary to read the complete text – if you want to know what is on television at 9 o'clock there is no need to read all the programmes that are on that day.

Show learners an enlarged copy of this activity sheet. Ask them what they think the text is about. What sorts of things might they find out from reading the text? List suggestions for key words on the whiteboard or flip chart.

Use a highlighter pen on the enlarged copy of the text to highlight the key words suggested by the learners.

Summarise the text using the key words: 'So this is about a couple who got married in a registry office...'

Ask learners to highlight key words on their own copy of the activity sheet.

In pairs, ask learners to explain to a partner what the text is about.

Differentiation

Use a tracking exercise to encourage learners to read from left to right and top to bottom of the page.

Write the key words on cards for learners to have to hand while reading the text.

Reinforce the use of key words with further practice using other activity sheets in this support pack. Alternatively, use extracts of interest supplied by the learners.

Ensure learners have a small notebook in which they can write any personal key words for further use.

Extension

The following activity sheets give opportunities to practise reading skills in various settings and contexts. For each text discuss what it might be about, assist learners in highlighting the key words and then using them to summarise the text.

- A 6.2.2 The day of the wedding (Entry 2/Access 2)
- A 6.2.3 Anti-bullying sign (Entry 1/Access 1)
- A 6.2.4 Anti-bullying policy (Entry 2/Access 2)
- A 6.2.5 Be safe on your bike (Entry 1/Access 1)
- A 6.2.6 Safe cycling (Entry 2/Access 2)

Activity 3 Reading for detail

Discuss why learners would read something in detail, e.g. an employment contract, an insurance schedule, instructions about how to operate machinery and need to completely understand what they have read. Ask for examples from the learners' lives.

Use Activity Sheet 6.2.1 Wedding day again. Remind learners about what they thought they were going to find out from the extract the last time they looked at it. Read through the description of the wedding fluently and with expression. Ask learners to follow on their own copy. Does it say what they expected?

Discuss the sentences. How do they help the reader make sense of what they read? Read through the text again one sentence at a time.

Write up the following embolded key words, which learners should look for in their own versions. Then ask them the questions one at a time. As learners find each key word, encourage them to read the whole sentence that the key word is in and to find the answer to the question. This is not a test of memory but a test of reading.

- What kind of **car** did the bride and groom use?
- What was the **bride**'s name?
- What was the **groom**'s name?
- How many **bridesmaids** were there?
- How many **pageboys** were there?
- Where was the **ceremony** held?
- Where was the **reception** held?
- Where did the couple go on **honeymoon**?
- Where will the couple **live**?

Read through the whole text once more, again with the learners following. Did they find out what they expected to?

Address any other issues learners may have.

Talk about strategies for finding out about unknown words, e.g. asking a friend or colleague, looking at the first letter, sounding it out, reading on past the word and guessing the word from the sense of the sentence, looking at its shape, thinking about similar words.

Extension

Use any of the following activity sheets in a similar way depending on the interests and abilities of your learners:

- **A** 6.2.2 The day of the wedding

  Here, learners are asked to decide whether the statements about Activity Sheet 6.2.2. The day of the wedding are true or false or whether there is no evidence. The learners will need to infer some answers.
- **A** 6.2.3 Anti-bullying sign
- **A** 6.2.4 Anti-bullying policy
- **A** 6.2.5 Be safe on your bike
- **A** 6.2.6 Safe cycling

Make sure the learners get the gist before reading in detail. Ask questions to guide them towards key information and to check understanding.

Activity 4 Understanding what you have read

This activity comprises a selection of comprehension exercises to check understanding. They can be adapted for use with different texts.

A 6.4.1 Hospital appointment/6.4.2 Mr. Morgan's questions (Entry 1 and 2/Access 1 and 2)

Use Activity Sheet 6.4.1 to set the scene for Activity Sheet 6.4.2. Point out to learners that as this is a hospital appointment card it is important to read it in detail so that they can answer the questions fully.

Go through the stages of:

- deciding what the text is about
- looking for key words to get the gist
- reading in detail.

Ask the questions on Activity Sheet 6.4.2 orally before asking learners to complete the sheet.

Differentiation

For learners who have difficulty writing, go through the questions orally and copy the answers they give on sticky notes. Ask them to match the answers with the questions.

Cut the questions and the appointment card up and ask the learners to match the questions with the part of the card that contains the answer.

Extension

Repeat the activity in different contexts using the following activity sheets:

Reading at home

- A 6.4.3 Flooding in Shrewsbury (Entry 1 & 2/Access 1 & 2)

Reading at home

- A 6.4.4 Could you apply for this job? (Entry 1/Access 1)
- A 6.4.5 Stress at work (Entry 2/Access 2)

6.1.1 Missing dog

Please help!

We have lost our pet dog Scruffy. Have you seen him? He is black with a white flash on his chest and white tipped feet. He is wearing a faded red collar with a leather lead attached.

He was last seen outside Somerfield supermarket on Saturday 15 April at 14.30.

Please help us to find him. He is a well-loved family pet. The children are missing him. We can offer a small reward for any information.

Have you seen him?

Please contact us on one of these numbers.

01234 567890
07970 987654

Thank you.

Note to tutor: use this sheet to support reading for gist, before reading in detail.

6.1.2 Where is our dog?

Can you work out the missing words? Fill in the gaps.

MISSING

Please _____!

We have lost our pet dog ___________. Have you ___________ him? He is ___________ with a white flash on his chest and white tipped feet. He is wearing a faded red ___________ with a leather lead attached.

He was last ___________ outside Somerfield supermarket on Saturday 15 April at 14.30.

Please help us to ___________ him. He is a well-loved family pet. The children are missing him. We can offer a small ___________ for any information.

Have you seen him?

Please ___________ us on one of these numbers.

01234 567890
07970 987654

Thank you.

6.2.1 Wedding day

A

A cream Rolls Royce car helped bride Lisa Roberts and groom Juan Lopez start married life in style. The bride was accompanied by seven bridesmaids and three pageboys.

The ceremony was at Haybridge Registry Office. It was followed by a reception at the Haven Hotel. The couple went on honeymoon to Spain. They will live in Haybridge.

B

Joanna Richards, eldest daughter of Rosemary and William Richards of Woodland Road, Haybridge, has married Peter Priestley, second son of Roy and Ann Priestley of Hightrees Avenue.

The ceremony was at Haybridge Castle and the bride was given away by her father. She wore an ivory satin dress and carried ivory roses.

Kelly Kowalczyk and Sarah Priestley were bridesmaids and Ali Koul was best man.

A reception was held at Haybridge Castle for 80 guests and the couple went on honeymoon to Hawaii.

The couple will make their home in Wales.

Note to tutor: use A with E1/A1 learners and B with E2/A2 learners.

6.2.2 The day of the wedding

Answer these questions.

1.	Joanna Richards has got an older sister.	True	False	Not sure
2.	Joanna Richards has got a younger sister.	True	False	Not sure
3.	Peter Priestley has got an older brother.	True	False	Not sure
4.	Peter Priestley has got an older sister.	True	False	Not sure
5.	There were two bridesmaids.	True	False	Not sure
6.	The bridesmaids wore ivory satin dresses.	True	False	Not sure
7.	There were 80 people at the reception after the wedding.	True	False	Not sure
8.	Joanna Richards is now called Joanna Priestley.	True	False	Not sure
9.	Ali Koul made a funny speech.	True	False	Not sure
10.	When they get back from Hawaii the couple will be living in Wales.	True	False	Not sure

Note to tutor: for use with Activity Sheet 6.2.1 Part B.

6.2.3 Anti-bullying sign

☺ We want to make our factory a happy ☺
place to work
You can help us.
Are you being bullied?
Do you know somebody else who is
being bullied?
Do you know a bully?
Speak to your line manager in confidence or
ring 01234 567890 for a chat.
Remember!
Bullying is everyone's business.
You do not have to put up with it.

6.2.4 Anti-bullying policy

Anti-bullying policy

Bullying is everyone's business.

Bullying is when someone deliberately hurts another person or makes them feel unhappy. This may happen over and over again. People can be bullied for any reason. Bullying at work is not allowed. No one should have to deal with it on their own.

Everyone has the right to be protected from physical, verbal and indirect bullying.

- **Physical bullying**:
  hitting; kicking; spitting; slapping; demanding money
- **Verbal bullying**:
  threats; name calling; insults; racist, sexist, homophobic or sexual remarks
- **Indirect bullying**:
  deliberately ignoring; spreading gossip; graffiti; damaging property; offensive or abusive emails, text messages or posts on websites

We want everyone to feel confident about reporting bullying whenever and wherever it happens, and to get the help they need to feel safe again. We will work with and support both the bullied and the bullies.

If you are being bullied or know about someone else who is being bullied, you can speak to your line manager in confidence. 01234 567890 is a confidential helpline. You can use it to report a bully or to speak to someone about bullying.

Remember, bullying is everyone's business.

6.2.5 Be safe on your bike

Highlight the key words and use them to summarise the information.

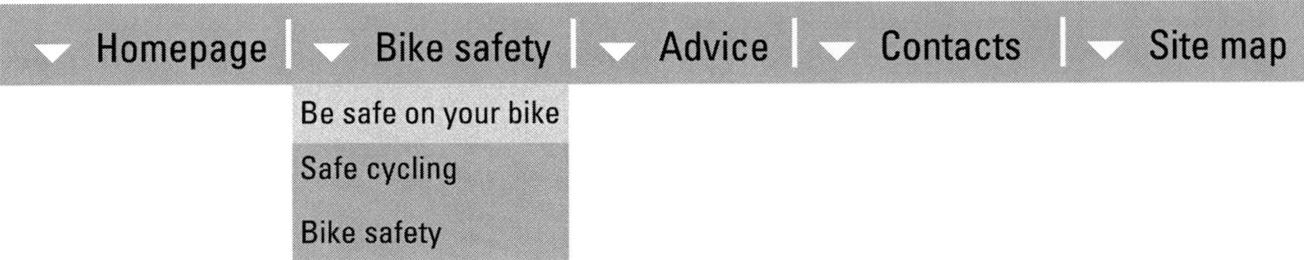

Be safe on your bike

You can make cycling safe and enjoyable if you follow some simple rules.

- Clean your bike at least once a month. As you clean it, you can look out for problems.
- Always keep tyres pumped up hard. Carry a pump and puncture kit at all times.
- Check that the brake blocks are not worn down.
- Make sure the mudguards do not rattle.
- Check the batteries on your lights before cycling at night.
- Look at your pedals to make sure they are not broken or loose.

6.2.6 Safe cycling

Highlight the key words and use them to summarise the information.

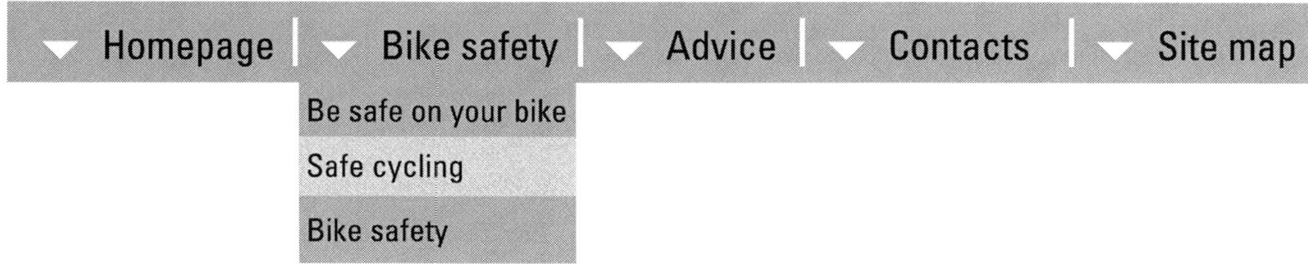

Safe cycling

A few simple rules will make your cycling fun and enjoyable.

Clothing

Do not wear baggy clothing that might get caught in the chain or wheel spokes. Wear something bright so that you can be seen by other road users. If the weather is cold, wear gloves so that you can use the brakes properly. Shoes with stiff soles will not slip on the pedals.

Follow the Highway Code

Do not jump red lights. Do not ride on pavements. Do not ride the wrong way down one-way streets.

Make sure you can be seen

Wear bright clothing. Always use your lights after dark or in bad weather.

Think ahead

Show drivers what you plan to do. Always look and signal before you start, stop or turn. Make eye contact with drivers so that you are sure they have seen you.

Wear a helmet

Check that your helmet fits correctly and that the straps are securely fastened.

6.4.1 Hospital appointment

Royal Hayshire Hospital

OUT-PATIENT APPOINTMENT

Dear Mr Morgan,

An appointment has been made for you to see: *Mr D Khan*

On: *Friday 2nd September*

At: *11.30 a.m.*

Please report to reception on arrival.

Please bring this card with you on the day and a note of all medicines you may be taking.

If this is your first appointment, please bring a urine sample.

To arrange ambulance transport to the hospital, please ring 01234 987654.

If you cannot keep this appointment, please phone the appointments secretary at the hospital on 01234 567890 as soon as possible. Your appointment can be offered to someone else and we can offer you an alternative appointment.

6.4.2 Mr Morgan's questions

Use this with Activity Sheet 6.4.1.

Mr Morgan has not been to the hospital before.

He has some questions about his appointment.

Fill in the answers to his questions.

Which hospital do I have to go to?
Which doctor will I see?
What time is my appointment?
I am on holiday on 2nd September. What should I do?
What do I have to do when I arrive at the hospital?
What do I have to take with me?
1.
2.
3.
What should I do if I need transport to the hospital?

6.4.3 Flooding in Shrewsbury

Circle the word that fits best. The first one has been done for you.

Flooding hits Shrewsbury

Fishing shop sells out of boots/rods

Can you believe it? Despite the floods, customers are finding their way to the **door/roof** of one Shrewsbury fishing shop. Don Bradman, owner of The Angling Centre in Old Street, said he had sold **out/in** of angler's waders.

'We do not normally sell many pairs but on Monday they started going really **slowly/quickly**. We have sold **more/less** than 20 pairs this week already,' he said.

The shop is just metres away from the **worst/best** flooding in Shrewsbury. Despite road diversions people wanting to keep **dry/wet** during the floods were still making their way to the shop.

A **new/old** delivery of waders was expected today. Mr Richards did not think stocks would last very **long/short**.

Choose the word that makes sense.

Despite the floods, customers are finding their way to the **door/roof** of one Shrewsbury fishing shop.

Don Bradman, owner of The Angling Centre in Old Street, said he had sold **out/in** of angler's waders.

'We do not normally sell many pairs but on Monday they started going really **quickly/slowly**.

We have sold **more/less** than 20 pairs this week already,' he said.

The shop is just metres away from the **worst/best** flooding in Shrewsbury.

Despite road diversions people wanting to keep **dry/wet** during the floods were still making their way to the shop.

A **new/old** delivery of waders was expected today.

Mr Richards did not think stocks would last very **long/short**.

6.4.4 Could you apply for this job?

Answer the questions.

Do you have the right skills?
Yes No Maybe

Can you work full-time?
Yes No Maybe

Will the company train you?
Yes No Maybe

Are you hard-working?

Are you a people person?

Did you answer yes to both questions?

You may be just the person we are looking for!

We are a new company with offices in your area.

We are looking for customer service staff to work either full-time or part-time.

Full training will be given.

If you are interested, call Judy Hardcastle to arrange an interview.

01234 567890

[HARMONY LEISURE]

BECAUSE YOU CARE, WE CARE.

Do you work hard?
Yes No Maybe

Do you get on with people?
Yes No Maybe

Did you answer yes to both questions?
Yes No

6.4.5 Stress at work

Read the notice.

STRESS AT WORK
A guide for employees

Stress is not an illness but it can make you ill. If your work is making you feel stressed you should take steps to tackle it.

How can you tell if someone is stressed?
Everyone reacts to stress in a different way. People can have panic attacks, mood swings, changes in sleep patterns or changes in eating habits.

What can you do at work?
You can talk to your colleagues and to your employer about how you are feeling. Speak to your doctor if you are worried about your health.

What can you do at home?
- ❖ You can try to keep yourself healthy. This means eating healthy food, stopping smoking and cutting down on alcohol.
- ❖ You can exercise more. Exercise gives you more energy.
- ❖ You can learn to relax. This might help you cope with pressure.
- ❖ Do not bottle things up. Talk to family and friends about how you are feeling. They can support and encourage you.

Remember
Stress is not a weakness and you do not have to suffer.

Complete the sentences using these words.

feeling	talk	not	should	healthy	exercise	different

Tackling stress at work

A guide for employees

Stress is __________ an illness but it can harm your health.

If your work is making you feel stressed you __________ take steps to tackle it.

Everyone reacts to stress in a __________ way.

At work you can __________ to your colleagues and to your employer about how you are feeling.

At home you can try to keep yourself __________.

You can __________ more. Exercise gives you more energy.

Do not bottle things up. Talk to family and friends about how you are __________ . They can support and encourage you.

Theme 7

Using the alphabet

Introduction

Learners need to learn the alphabet in both upper and lower case in order to read and write accurately. This theme is concerned with the alphabet as a means of reference and concentrates on the names of letters and not the sounds used to build words.

Adult learners use alphabetical order primarily to locate information they need, such as in an index, street directory, telephone directory or dictionary.

Many learners may be familiar with the alphabet through the use of mobile phones and computer keyboards and this point should be raised when teaching the alphabet.

The activities in this theme allow learners to recognise upper and lower case letters and to use alphabetical order to locate information. It is important to establish the language that you will use to describe these letters – upper case or capital letters – early on in the session depending on your learners' history of learning in this theme.

Learning outcomes	Adult Literacy Curriculum references	ALAN Curriculum Framework for Scotland
To be able to recognise the letters of the alphabet in both upper and lower case	Rt/E2.2 Rt/E2.3 Rw/E1.3 Rw/E2.4 Rw/E2.5	• Using alphabetical order • Matching letters and sounds
To be able to understand the idea of alphabetical order		
To be able to find information in an alphabetical list		
To be able to use initial letters to find words in an alphabetical list		
To be able to use letters to put words into an alphabetical list		

Links

Theme 8 Filling in forms; Theme 2 Signs and symbols.

Key words

alphabet, alphabetical order, capital letters, first letter, letters, lower case, next, second letter, upper case.

Activity notes

Other resources

A selection of alphabetical lists, e.g. catalogues, street indexes, atlases, telephone directories, Yellow Pages, books with indexes.

Activity 1 Introducing the theme

Familiarise learners with the alphabet in both upper and lower case as well as with places where the alphabet and alphabetical order are often used.

Check learners' understanding of the word 'alphabet'. Discuss their experiences of using the alphabet, both orally and in reading and writing.

- Where is the alphabet seen, written or displayed?
- Do they send text messages?
- Can they alter the font on their mobile phones so that messages can be created in upper case only/lower case only/sentence case?
- What about car number plates or postcodes?

Write the alphabet on the whiteboard or flip chart and point out that the letters of the alphabet come in a particular order. Recite the names of the letters together. Ask if any learners have any tips for remembering the order. Acknowledge good ideas and reassure learners who do not yet know the order that they will be practising this throughout the unit.

Demonstrate that the same letter can have different shapes depending on what it is being used for. Ask learners how upper case letters might be used in writing, giving examples such as 'I', the first letter of a name, month or day, for filling in forms or writing postcodes. Repeat the exercise with lower case letters, giving examples such as for writing the rest of a name, month or day or for writing a brief note. Use some everyday texts such as TV guides or newspapers to highlight this point.

Briefly show how alphabetical order is used in everyday situations or ask learners to brainstorm ways that it is used, e.g. in dictionaries, address books.

Differentiation

Explain how using different fonts can change how some letters look, such as '**a**' and 'a', '**g**' and 'g'. Learners could research different fonts on the computer or in everyday texts. Learners could create a display of the same letter written in different fonts for the whole alphabet.

Other resources

Newspapers and magazines, felt-tip pens.

Activity 2 Recognising the letters of the alphabet

Familiarise learners with the letters of the alphabet in both upper and lower case and encourage them to say the names of the letters.

Using pages from magazines and newspapers, ask learners to circle all the upper case letters they can find and to name them.

Ask learners to look at brand names and logos. Where are upper and lower case letters used?

7.2.1 Upper case and lower case letters (Entry 1/ Access 1)

Try the following ways of using this activity sheet. You can adapt the font size and type on the customisable version on the CD.

- Cut up several copies of the upper case letters and distribute them around the room. Ask learners to find an A. Write it on the whiteboard or flip chart so that they know what letter they are looking for. Repeat the exercise with the lower case letters, adjusting the quantity of letters according to the ability of the learners.
- Give learners a card each and ask them to find its partner. This can be done using upper/lower case letters.
- Ask learners to match upper and lower case letters.
- Use the cards as a pelmanism or snap game.

7.2.2 Writing the alphabet (Entry 1/Access 1)

Use the letters individually or in groups as appropriate for your learners.

Differentiation

It may take some learners some time to learn the names of the letters. It is important to practise little and often using a variety of methods, giving them a chance to consolidate their learning before moving on. Take the alphabet one letter at a time, building it into groups and finally the whole alphabet. Encourage learners to speak, read and write the alphabet and engage with it as interactively as possible.

Encourage learners to develop their own strategies for remembering the letters such as associating each upper case letter with the name of a friend or relative.

Extension

Ask learners to type the alphabet as a text message on their mobile phones and send it to a fellow learner.

Encourage confident learners to write their personal details in lower case with appropriate upper case letters and in upper case letters throughout. At first they may require a prompt card of their own details but in time they should be able to write from memory.

Ask learners to type the alphabet using a keyboard, by selecting the 'Change Case' function from the Format drop-down menu to change the text to upper or lower case. Invite them to experiment with different fonts.

7.2.3 Car number plates (Entry 1 and 2/Access 1 and 2)

Use this activity sheet to help learners see the correlation between upper and lower case letters.

 7.2.4 Postcodes (Entry 1 and 2/Access 1 and 2)

Use this activity sheet to help learners consolidate their understanding of the correlation between upper and lower case letters.

Differentiation

For less confident learners, work through the activity sheets together or give them small parts of the sheets to work on at a time.

More confident learners might like to collect some car registration numbers or items with postcodes on them and trace them to the area from where they originated.

Other resources

A selection of everyday items that can be arranged in alphabetical order, examples of text where alphabetical order is used, such as an address book, a filing cabinet, a dictionary and an index, alphabet cards.

Activity 3 Alphabetical order

The activities below give suggestions for putting the whole alphabet in order and ordering items into alphabetical order. Use them as required until learners are secure in their knowledge of the alphabet.

- Ask learners if they can say, read and write the alphabet in order? Reinforce suggested methods of learning it – singing works for some people, repeating sections aloud for others, using 'look, cover, say' for others. Establishing a physical sense of position is a strong memory aid for some learners. Encourage them to sort letter cards physically.
- Ask learners to arrange themselves in alphabetical order by first name initial. Repeat the exercise with surname initials. Mention what happens when two or more words begin with the same letter.
- Play a game of 'My grandmother went to market', in which each item begins with the next letter of the alphabet. Keep a crib sheet up on the whiteboard to support learners.
- Choose a theme such as makes of car and ask learners in turn to think of one that begins with each letter of the alphabet (Alfa Romeo, Bentley, Chrysler, etc.) Repeat the exercise with girls' names, dogs or whatever is appropriate.
- Give each learner a card and ask the group to arrange themselves in alphabetical order. Ask learners to say, as quickly as they can, the letter that comes before the letter they are holding and the letter that comes after it.
- Use the cards to play 'follow me'. Scatter alphabet cards on the floor and ask learners to stand on the initial letter of their first names. Repeat the exercise using the initial letter of their surnames.

Differentiation

At first, some learners may need to tackle the alphabet one section at a time. To build confidence, you may need to encourage plenty of practice in saying, writing and sorting the alphabet over a period of time.

It may help learners to associate a letter of the alphabet with the name of a friend or an item from their personal vocabulary list.

Encourage learners to make their own prompt card. This may at first contain the whole alphabet but in time be reduced to the parts of the alphabet the learner finds tricky.

Extension

Ask learners who are confident with alphabetical order to use the computer to type some of their personal key words from their vocabulary list in alphabetical order by first letter. They can use the 'Sort' function from the Table drop-down menu to check if they are correct.

Encourage more confident learners to complete the activity using the second letter to decide on the order in which the words should be sorted.

7.3.1 Missing letters (Entry 2/Access 2)

Ask learners to use this activity sheet to complete the alphabet.

Activity 4 Letters on the keyboard

This activity looks at the way upper and lower case letters are formed on a keyboard. Demonstrate how to use a computer keyboard with a group of learners, before they practise individually.

- Talk about learners' experience of using computers, keyboards and typing – have any of them used a keyboard before? What sorts of documents need typing? What sorts can be written by hand?
- Explain that a typical computer keyboard does not have the letters arranged in alphabetical order. The letters on the keyboard appear in upper case. Point to each letter and say it in turn. Ask learners to join in if appropriate.
- Point out the difference between upper case letters on the keyboard and lower case letters on the screen. Explain the use of the Caps Lock key to create upper and lower case letters.
- Say the alphabet in sections as the letters appear on the screen. Encourage learners to join in.
- Demonstrate the use of the Shift key to form upper case letters. Explain how some words are made of a mixture of upper and lower case letters.

Other resources

Computer keyboards.

A 7.4.1 Signs: upper and lower case (Entry 1 and 2/ Access 1 and 2)

Cut out the signs on this activity sheet and ask learners to match the words on the signs. The signs could be made into cards and used as a snap or pelmanism game.

Extension

Ask learners to type out the alphabet in order in upper and lower case. Then ask them to use the 'Change Case' function from the Format drop-down menu to alter what they have written.

Ask learners to type words from their personal dictionary that require both upper and lower case letters. Then invite them to use the 'Sort' function from the Table drop-down menu to arrange the words into alphabetical order.

Ask learners to copy the words on the signs on Activity Sheet 7.4.1. They can then use the 'Sort' function to arrange them into alphabetical order.

Ask learners to use a mobile phone to send and receive text messages in upper and lower case.

Other resources

Dictionaries, atlases, street finders, telephone directories, catalogues.

Activity 5 Find the word you want

This activity looks at the way alphabetical order can be used to retrieve information.

Ask learners to consider why some things are arranged in alphabetical order. Make sure they can see the importance and value of speed and accuracy when using the alphabet to sort and find information. Use appropriate scenarios such as: what would happen if their notes got mixed up with someone else's at the hospital? How quickly could they find an important phone number?

 **7.5.1 Company manual (Entry 1 and 2/Access 1 and 2)**

Explain how to find a particular word from an alphabetical list. Explain the context and the purpose of a company manual if necessary.

Go through the following points.

- Ask learners to look at the first letter of the word they want to find so that they can decide where to begin looking. Say that it is not always necessary to start at the beginning of a list.
- Ask them to use a finger, strip of card or ruler to keep their place.
- Ask them to cover the text that is not useful to minimise distraction.
- When they are roughly in the right place, learners should look carefully at the word they want to find from the list and, if necessary, keep looking back at it to be sure they are looking for the right word.
- When the correct word is found, learners should use their finger, card or ruler to help their eyes to track across to the page number.

Ask learners to find other items from the list. Write these words on a whiteboard or flip chart for learners to see.

The following activity sheets can be used to practise alphabetical order in different contexts.

- A 7.5.2 Yellow Pages (Entry 1 and 2/Access 1 and 2)

  Use this activity sheet to repeat finding words from an alphabetical list using the Yellow Pages.

- **A** 7.5.3 Using an address book (Entry 1 and 2/Access 1 and 2)

  Use this activity sheet to repeat these activities using an address book.

- **A** 7.5.4 Street directory (Entry 2/Access 2)

  The following activity is suitable for E2/A2 learners. Entries are sorted by the second letter so are appropriate for more confident learners.

- **A** 7.5.5 Catalogue (Entry 2/Access 2)

Differentiation

When using real dictionaries, atlases and phone books, learners will need to practise opening the book at about the right page. This means using their knowledge of the alphabet to decide whether to start looking at the beginning, the middle or the end of the book.

Extension

Encourage learners to use real catalogues, phone books and street atlases to find information relevant to them.

Ask learners to find the meaning of a selection of words using a simplified dictionary.

Encourage learners to begin an address book for an email account.

7.2.1 Upper case and lower case letters

A	B	C	D	E
F	G	H	I	J
K	L	M	N	O
P	Q	R	S	T
U	V	W	X	Y
Z				

a	b	c	d	e
f	g	h	i	j
k	l	m	n	o
p	q	r	s	t
u	v	w	x	y
z				

7.2.2 Writing the alphabet

Write the alphabet over these letters. Say each letter as you write it.

A	B	C	D	E
F	G	H	I	J
K	L	M	N	O
P	Q	R	S	T
U	V	W	X	Y
Z				

a	b	c	d	e
f	g	h	i	j
k	l	m	n	o
p	q	r	s	t
u	v	w	x	y
z				

7.2.3 Car number plates

Change these number plates to capital letters. The first one is done for you.

Number plate	Capital letters
p l 0 2 f h b	P L 0 2 F H B
y 4 5 6 r e p	4 5 6
r s 5 7 w a v	5 7
x 9 8 7 c u x	9 8 7
t p 0 4 y t d	0 4
g h 5 1 s u z	5 1
h z 0 8 b m r	0 8
p n 5 3 j o c	5 3
k f 5 8 p e d	5 8
m g 0 6 l o m	0 6
b d 5 6 l m n	5 6

7.2.4 Postcodes

Write these postcodes in upper case letters.

ah1 8qx	1 8
bj2 9ry	2 9
ck3 1sz	3 1
dl4 2te	4 2
em5 3ua	5 3
fn6 4vg	6 4

7.3.1 Missing letters

Fill in the missing letters.

A		C	D	E

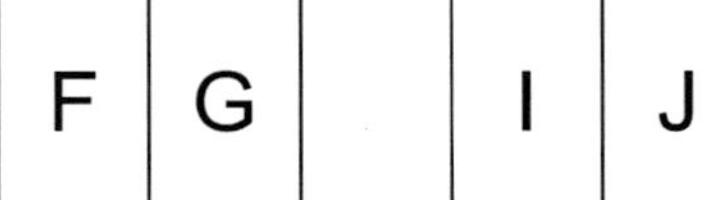

F	G		I	J

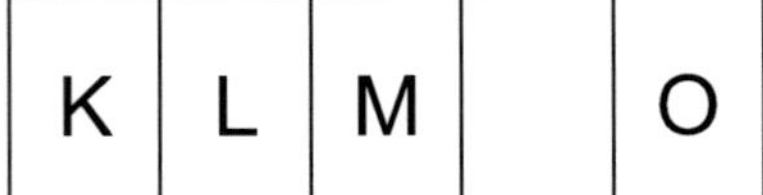

K	L	M		O

P	Q	R	S	

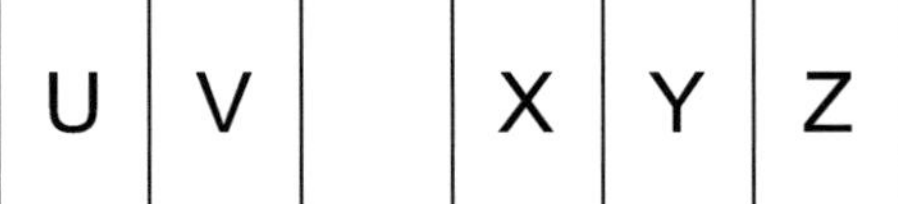

U	V		X	Y	Z

a		c	d	e

f	g		i	j

k	l	m		o

p	q	r	s	

u	v		x	y	z

a	b	c		e

f	g	h		j

k		m	n	o

p		r	s	t

u	v	w	x		z

7.4.1 Signs: upper and lower case

NO SMOKING

no smoking

PUSH

push

PULL

pull

EXIT

exit

NO PARKING

no parking

IN

in

OUT

out

TOILETS

toilets

7.5.1 Company manual

Proffit and Co

Company manual

Index

On what page would you find information about:

1) Fire drills _____

2) Pensions _____

3) Taking holidays _____

4) Safety issues _____

7.5.2 Yellow Pages

PLAYGROUPS	**969**
See also: Adventure and activity centres	34
Childminders	57
Crèches	66
Day nurseries	369
Nursery schools	882

RESTAURANTS	**1035**
See also: Banqueting suites	29
Cafés	163
Fish and chip shops	526
Takeaway food	1168
Wedding food and drink	1266

Carl wants to find a fish and chip shop near where he lives. Which page should he look on?

He should look on page _____.

Emma wants to find a childminder near where she lives. What page should she look on?

She should look on page _____.

7.5.3 Using an address book

Where should you put these names and addresses?

Circle the letters on the address book.

Mr Z Ali
Upper Road
Westhampton
Boreshire
WS1 5TH

Miss F Lee
The Cottage
Kington
Lowshire
KZ2 5SH

A B C D E F G H I J K L M N O P Q R S T U V W X Y Z

Mrs S Smith
25 Woodlands Road
Hightown
Lostshire
HT5 9OQ

7.5.4 Street directory

Haddon Road – Kilner Street		
Haddon Road	3D	**62**
Hemlock Way	1K	**93**
High Street	8J	**44**
Holland Close	5B	**85**
Hull Grove	8E	**21**

Sambrook Road – Tynley Close		
Sambrook Road	8C	**32**
Scott Street	4A	**80**
Sermon Lane	2B	**21**
Short Close	5D	**99**
Sidney Gardens	6E	**12**
Snowdon Hill	5F	**48**
South Way	6G	**55**
Spring Avenue	3B	**11**
Stanley Row	2A	**61**
Sussex Place	1F	**77**

Bill lives in Holland Close. Which page shows a map of where Holland Close is?

Holland Close is on page _____.

Barbara's friend lives in South Way. Which page shows a map of where South Way is?

South Way is on page _____.

7.5.5 Catalogue

Index

Jim wants to buy a shed. Which page should he look on?

He should look on page ______.

Pat wants to buy a television. Which page should she look on?

She should look on page ______.

Theme 8

Filling in forms

Introduction

Filling in forms is an activity encountered by learners of all levels. It is generally not an everyday activity and can be perceived to be a daunting task, particularly if performed in front of others. For these reasons it is important for learners to feel confident about their skills, to establish useful strategies and to recap at frequent intervals.

The successful completion of a form relies on accurate spelling of personal information as well as confidence in reading the instructions and headings on the form. The activities in this theme practise both reading and writing aspects of form filling. They should be selected as appropriate to the learner.

Learning outcomes	Adult Literacy Curriculum references	ALAN Curriculum Framework for Scotland
To be able to read and understand words on a form To be able to spell personal key words and familiar common words correctly To be able to write using both upper and lower case letters To be able to produce legible text	Ww/E1.1 Ww/E1.2 Ww/E2.1 Ww/E2.3 Ww/E2.4 Rw/E2.1	A1/A2 • Using layouts and headings • Reading symbols and sight words • Using spelling strategies • Handwriting

Links

Theme 6 Everyday reading; Theme 7 Using the alphabet.

Key words

address, age, application, block letters, capitals, complete, date, date of birth, email, first name, form, initials, Miss, Mr, Mrs, Ms, name, no., postcode, print, signature, surname, telephone number, tick, title, town.

Other resources

A selection of forms relevant to the life experiences of the learners.

Activity notes

Activity 1 Introducing the theme

Discuss learners' experiences of form filling. When have they been asked to fill in a form? What does a form look like? What are forms used for? What sorts of thing do they have to write on forms? Have available a selection of different forms for learners to investigate.

 **8.1.1 Enrolment form (Entry 1 and 2/Access 1 and 2)**

Use this activity sheet to highlight and discuss the common features of forms: headings, spaces to write in, instructions, where it is not necessary to write. Discuss dilemmas learners face when filling in forms. Where does each piece of information go? What happens if you make a mistake?

 **8.1.2 The golden ticket (Entry 1 and 2/Access 1 and 2)**

Use this activity sheet to discuss forms in general and to illustrate the amount of room some forms leave for inserting information. Discuss the 'small print' some forms contain. Do learners have strategies for reading this, such as asking a friend, seeking advice from the Citizens Advice Bureau for important forms, using their own reading strategies as suggested in Theme 6? Discuss the consequences of not reading the small print (in this case the phone call could cost £9.00).

Other resources

A selection of forms.

Activity 2 Reading a form

The first thing to do when faced with a form is to read it through to see what information and equipment are required, e.g. national insurance number, name and address of a referee, black pen. There are often several instructions on a form. These tell the writer how to complete it. Use a selection of forms and ask learners in pairs or small groups to highlight all the instructions. Compare the results of different groups. Write common instructions on the whiteboard or flip chart and read them through with the group, discussing what each one means.

A 8.2.1 Instructions on forms (Entry 1 and 2/Access 1 and 2)

Use this activity sheet to practise reading and recognising these instructions. Select a phrase from the sheet and read it with the learners. Discuss what it means. Offer alternative meanings for difficult words such as *delete* and *appropriate*. Cut out the one-word cards and distribute them to learners. Each learner decides whether he or she has a word from a phrase. If so, he or she matches it to the phrase card. When the phrase is complete, learners read it out. A new phrase is then selected. Blank cards have been provided for you to add any phrases or words that will be useful to your learners.

Differentiation

To make the game easier, use the cards containing only lower case letters. A mixture of upper and lower case makes the game more difficult.

If several sets of cards are made, word or phrase cards can be used as a snap, matching or pelmanism game. Vary the difficulty using upper case or lower case letters.

Extension

Ask learners to find and highlight the words or phrases on real forms. Ask them to tell a partner what they would have to do in each case.

Activity 3 Reading words on forms

Apart from instructions there are lots of other words to read on forms. These words indicate what information is required.

 8.3.1 Words on forms (Entry 1 and 2/Access 1 and 2)

Show learners a few cards at a time and read them out. Ask them if any of the words on the cards have the same or similar meaning. Put the suggested cards into pairs. There may be several combinations of pairs. Put these together into larger piles. Read out the cards from each pile. Ask learners to read the words too.

Ask learners to collect pairs of words or phrases that mean the same or similar things.

Deal each learner four cards and put the spare cards in a stack in the middle of the table. Turn one card face up. Learners can choose to pick an unseen card from the pack or to take the displayed card before they discard a card of their own onto the visible pile. The winner is the first one to have the most pairs of similar words or phrases.

Differentiation

For learners who have difficulty, reduce the number of cards. Restrict the words to the most familiar and commonly used. Use the blank cards for any other words which learners might be familiar with.

Make sure learners become familiar with the words by using the cards for games of snap, bingo or pelmanism.

Deal out one card to each learner. Ask them to call out the word or words on it when you display a card with a similar meaning to the one they are holding.

Ask learners to match the words on the cards with the words on an actual form.

Extension

Once learners have become familiar with the cards, extend the game so that learners have to collect sets of four similar cards.

To increase the difficulty, customise the cards to include only upper case letters.

 8.3.2 Where does it go? (Entry 1 and 2/Access 1 and 2)

Use this activity sheet in combination with an actual form for learners to match the information with the correct space on the form.

Go through the sheet with the learners, asking 'What is this?' for every item. As answers are given, e.g. 'an address', 'a date of birth', ask learners to point out where on the form this information should be entered.

Other resources

A selection of forms.

Ask less confident learners (E1/A1) to match the cards with the items on the form.

Ask learners to add significant words to a personal dictionary.

Other resources

A selection of forms, sticky notes, small cards.

Activity 4 Writing personal details

Remind learners that personal details such as name and address are commonly required on forms, and must be legible and spelt correctly. Discuss the implications of incorrect spelling/illegibility, e.g. you might not get the items you ordered from a catalogue if your details cannot be read.

Use Activity Sheet 8.1.1 or 8.1.2 and ask learners to think about what personal information they would need to write on the form. Ask them to point out where the name should be written, where the space for the address is, and so on.

8.4.1 Personal details (Entry 1 and 2/Access 1 and 2)

Use this sheet to ensure learners always spell their personal details correctly when filling in forms, as an aide-mémoire for their own details. Ensure learners write down their details correctly. Some learners may wish to complete one copy of the sheet in upper case letters and another in lower case with capitals used only at the beginning of proper nouns.

Differentiation

Encourage learners to experiment with different methods of learning to spell their personal details. For example:

- Using 'look, say, cover, write, check'
- looking at the whole word and trying to remember the shape of it
- teaching his or her hand to write the word
- saying each letter as the word is written down
- breaking up the word into easy-to-remember sections
- mispronouncing the word to accentuate difficult parts
- concentrating on difficult parts of the word.

A

8.4.2 Learn to spell some personal details (Entry 1 and 2/ Access 1 and 2)

Use this activity sheet to help learners learn to spell a word.

Prepare further exercises to help learners spell their own details. For example:

- filling the gaps, e.g. J__ne
- copying the word, folding over the paper, writing the word again, checking and writing it again
- for occasional words, mnemonics can be useful. Learners will remember better the word they need to spell if they make up the mnemonic themselves.

Suggest learners concentrate on getting one word at a time right before moving on to another. Suggest they set a realistic targets of learning a certain number of words in a week.

Extension

Suggest ways learners can practise spelling by:

- using odd moments in their day to repeat the letters in a word in their heads
- copying a word on a scrap of paper while waiting for the kettle to boil
- checking a word they think they can remember by writing it and checking it during the adverts in a television programme.

Allow learners to practise writing their details as small as possible. Let them practise writing their details in all upper case and then in lower case letters with capital letters in appropriate places.

Ask learners to practise writing the required personal information on sticky notes or small cards and matching each item with the correct heading before copying it in ink on the form.

Repeat the form-filling activity in different contexts using the activity sheets below. Stress that reading the form, gathering the information required, writing 'in rough' before attempting the final version and then reading the form again to check for errors are all part of the process aimed at completing the form as well as possible.

In each case, go through reading the form first, considering the information required. Allow learners to practise before completing each form. Discuss any words that may not be familiar, e.g. ZIP on Activity Sheet 8.4.3.

A 8.4.3 Computer form (Entry 1 and 2/Access 1 and 2)
A 8.4.4 Sell your car (Entry 1 and 2/Access 1 and 2)
A 8.4.5 Join the club (Entry 1 and 2/Access 1 and 2)
A 8.4.6 Order form (Entry 1 and 2/Access 1 and 2)
A 8.4.7 Job application form (Entry 1 and 2/Access 1 and 2)

Differentiation

Some learners may prefer to write lightly in pencil before committing themselves to writing in ink.

Some learners may prefer to photocopy the necessary form, fill it in and copy everything onto the final form when they are satisfied they have everything correct.

8.1.1 Enrolment form

Hayshire College

Enrolment form 2008/9

This form will be photocopied. Use black ink only.

Mr / Mrs/ Miss / Ms (delete as appropriate)

First name ....

Surname ....

Address ....

....

....

.... Postcode ....

DOB ....

Home phone no. ....

Mobile no. ....

Email address ....

For office use only

Course no.	*Start date*	*Title*	*Fee*

Concessionary Instalments

8.1.2 The golden ticket

GOLDEN TICKET

This ticket entitles you to claim an award.

£250 cash ***Free groceries for a year***

Weekend break for four ***Digital camera***

You have found a golden ticket!

To claim your award: ***Phone 01234 567890****

Complete the form below. ***Send it to Claims Department GT, King's Road, Hayshire.***

Mr ☐ Mrs ☐ Miss ☐ Ms ☐ (tick)

First name ....

Surname ....

House no./ House name ....

Address ....

....

Postcode ....

DOB (you must be over 18 to enter) ....

Home phone no. ....

Award claimed ....

Date ....

* Calls cost £1.50/min and will last no longer than 6 mins. The cost of calls from mobiles may vary. See envelope for full rules.

8.2.1 Instructions on forms

Delete where appropriate	Delete	DELETE
Delete where necessary	where	WHERE
Use block letters	appropriate	APPROPRIATE
Use capital letters	necessary	NECESSARY
Print in black ink	Use	USE
Use black pen	block	BLOCK
Tick the right box	letters	LETTERS
Use ink only	capital	CAPITAL
Complete in ink	Print	PRINT
Do not write below this line	black	BLACK
DELETE WHERE APPROPRIATE	pen	PEN
DELETE WHERE NECESSARY	Tick	TICK
USE BLOCK LETTERS	ink	INK
USE CAPITAL LETTERS	only	ONLY
PRINT IN BLACK INK	in	IN
USE BLACK PEN	ink	INK
TICK THE RIGHT BOX	Do	DO
USE INK ONLY	not	NOT
COMPLETE IN INK	write	WRITE
DO NOT WRITE BELOW THIS LINE	below	BELOW
	this	THIS
	line	LINE

8.3.1 Words on forms

Name	Surname	First name	Signature
Family name	Initials	Other names	Maiden name
Name at birth	Previous names		
City	Country	Email	email address
Address	Postcode	Town	County
Date of birth	DOB	Age	Age last birthday
DD/MM/YYYY	Date		
Married	Single	Divorced	Widowed
Telephone number	Tel no.	Mobile	Daytime phone no.
Mr	Mrs	Miss	Ms
Title	Other title		
Male	Female		
Occupation	Previous employer		
Nationality	Place of birth		

8.3.2 Where does it go?

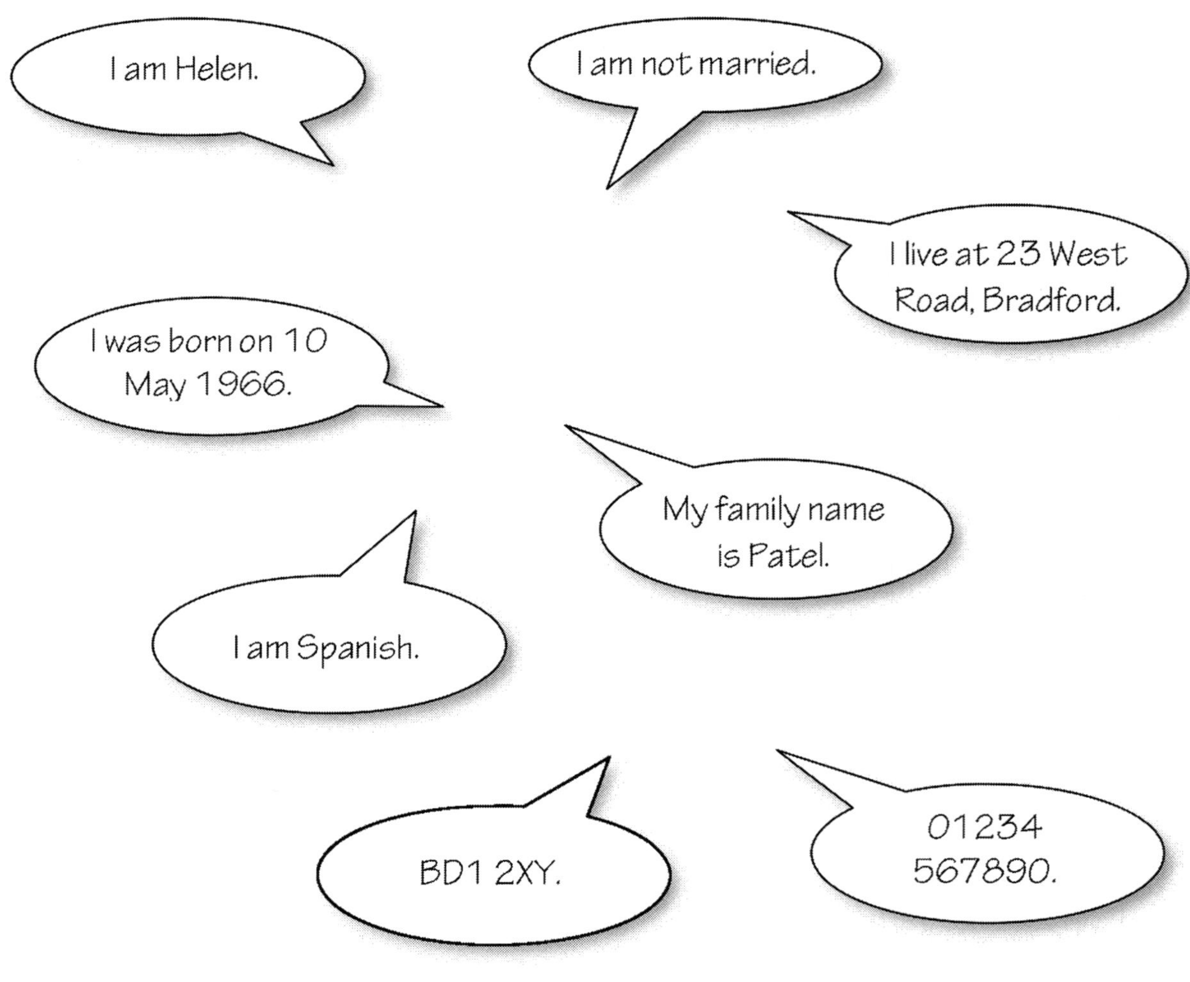
I am Helen.
I am not married.
I live at 23 West Road, Bradford.
I was born on 10 May 1966.
My family name is Patel.
I am Spanish.
BD1 2XY.
01234 567890.

FAMILY NAME	TELEPHONE NUMBER
FORENAME	DATE OF BIRTH
MARITAL STATUS	ADDRESS
POSTCODE	NATIONALITY

8.4.1 Personal details

TITLE: ....

FIRST NAME: ....

FAMILY NAME: ....

DATE OF BIRTH: ....

ADDRESS: ....

....

....

....

....

POSTCODE: ....

TELEPHONE NUMBER: ....

NATIONALITY: ....

8.4.2 Learn to spell some personal details

Write the word you want to learn here: ______________________

Look at the word.

Fold over the paper to the first dotted line.

Write the word.

Unfold the paper to check your attempt.

Do it again by folding the paper again until you can write the word without looking.

Try it again tomorrow.

1st try
2nd try
3rd try
4th try
5th try
Final try

8.4.3 Computer form

Tell us about yourself

Title: Mr

First name: *

Surname: *

Address 1: *

Address 2:

Address 3:

City/Town: *

County/State: *

Postcode/ZIP: *

Country: *

Email address:

Telephone number:

* required fields:

8.4.4 Sell your car

SELL YOUR CAR FOR JUST £10

Use YOUR local paper to sell your car

Fill in your details.

Print one word per box.

Name ________________________________

Address ________________________________

Daytime tel no. ________________________________

I enclose £ ______________ cheque/postal order made payable to My Local Paper Ltd

Or debit my credit card account Card No.

Expiry date ______________________

Send to: My Local Paper Ltd, Haybridge, Hayshire HA4 7TG

8.4.5 Join the club

New Member Application Form

NAME AND HOME ADDRESS DETAILS

HOUSE NUMBER

POSTCODE

ADDRESS

TITLE ✓

Mr Mrs Miss Ms

INITIALS

SURNAME

TELEPHONE NO.

DATE OF BIRTH

Your name and address will be added to a mailing list to receive details of exclusive offers. If you prefer not to receive these offers please tick this box ☐

FOR OFFICE USE ONLY

MEMBERSHIP NUMBER

8.4.6 Order form

Make difficult cleaning tasks easy!

Multi-purpose steam cleaner only

This powerful, multi-purpose steam cleaner removes dirt, grime and grease.

Kills bacteria without the use of chemicals.

It can be used for cleaning windows, bathrooms, upholstery, garden furniture and cars.

Just fill with tap water, turn on and wait for steam to appear.

The selection of attachments makes difficult cleaning tasks easy.

To order your multi-purpose steam cleaner, complete the form without delay. Send to:

Multi-purpose Steam Cleaner Offer
PO Box 123
The Warehouse
Haybridge
Hayshire
HA2 0EA

Title (delete where applicable)	Mr Mrs Miss Ms Other
First name	
Surname	
Billing address	
Delivery address (if different from above)	
Postcode	
Telephone number	
Credit card number	

Please allow 10 days for delivery. Enquiries to 0800 123 4567.

8.4.7 Job application form

APPLICATION FOR EMPLOYMENT

All application forms are confidential.

PLEASE PRINT. USE BLACK INK ONLY.

Application for the post of __|__|__|__|__|__|__|__|__|__| Post No. __|__|__|__|

PART A: YOUR DETAILS

Title __|__|__|__|__|__|__|__|__|

Full name __|__|__|__|__|__|__|__|__|__|__|__|__|__|__|__|__|__|__|__|__|__|

Address __|__|__|__|__|__|__|__|__|__|__|__|__|__|__|__|__|__|__|__|__|__|

__|__|__|__|__|__|__|__|__|__|__|__|__|__|__|__|__|__|__|__|__|__|__|__|__|

__|__|__|__|__|__|__|__|__|__|__|__|__|__|__|__|__|__|__|__|__|__|__|__|__|

Contact details:

Work __|__|__|__|__|__|__|__|__|

Home __|__|__|__|__|__|__|__|__|

Mobile __|__|__|__|__|__|__|__|__|

Email address __|__|__|__|__|__|__|__|__|__|__|__|__|__|__|__|__|__|

What is your preferred method of contact? __|__|__|__|__|__|__|__|__|__|

Are you employed at the moment? ☐ Yes ☐ No

If yes:

What is your current salary? __|__|__|__|__|__|__|__|__|__|

What is your notice period? __|__|__|__|__|__|__|__|__|__|

Do you have a driving licence? ☐ Yes ☐ No

If yes, please tick type of licence, e.g. HGV, provisional, full, other

Do you own a car? ☐ Yes ☐ No

*Please note that this company operates a strict **no-smoking** policy*

Theme 9

Writing about yourself

Links

Theme 8 Filling in forms.

Key words

accident, full stop, incident, insurance, sentence, upper case letter.

Introduction

This theme gives learners the opportunity to think about their skills, likes, dislikes and personal qualities and to practise writing this information in simple sentences which are recorded in a personal portfolio for later use. More confident learners have the opportunity to expand these sentences and use conjunctions and adjectives. These sentences can then be used in a variety of formats in forms, letters and on screen.

This theme presents many opportunities for speaking and listening as learners investigate their personal qualities.

Learning outcomes	Adult Literacy Curriculum references	ALAN Curriculum Framework for Scotland
To be able to write in complete sentences	Ws/E1.1 Ws/E1.2 Ws/E1.3 Ws/E2.1 Ws/E2.2 Ws/E2.3 Ws/E2.4	A1/A2 • Using sequencing and links to make meanings clear • Using language to express oneself • Using appropriate sentence length and complexity
To be able to use a capital letter for I and proper nouns		
To be able to use end-of-sentence punctuation correctly		
To be able to use adjectives		
To be able to use conjunctions		

Activity notes

Activity 1 Introducing the theme

Discuss reasons for talking clearly about ourselves: job interviews, dating, friendship.

Decide on a theme such as hobbies, home, work, television, pets or food and model asking some questions about the theme with a learner as your partner. Tell learners that their aim is to find out as much as they can about other's likes and dislikes on the theme.

Remind learners of the types of questions they might ask, for example, if football is the theme: What team do you support? Who is your favourite player? Did you see the match on Saturday? What is your favourite player of all time? Who would be in your dream team? Do you know the offside rule? Why do you dislike football?

In pairs, ask one learner to ask his or her partner about the theme for a few minutes. After a few minutes, ask learners to report back to the rest of the group on what their partner said.

Repeat the process with the same or a different theme. This time roles are reversed. The activity can be repeated over a number of sessions as learners build their confidence.

When learners are at ease with the process, decide on a new theme. This time, as learners report back, write key words on the whiteboard or flip chart. Model arranging these key words into a short, oral narrative, e.g. 'Beth supports Manchester United. She watches all their home games. She likes Wayne Rooney.' Write sentences on the whiteboard or flip chart.

Ask Beth how she would change the sentences to talk about herself. If necessary, model a few sentences about yourself, e.g. 'I support Liverpool. I do not like Everton. I like Steven Gerrard.' Change these sentences on the whiteboard so that they start with capital I. Discuss how we talk about ourselves. Write up the words *I*, *my* and *me*.

Remind learners what they have been talking about over the last few sessions. Select a new theme. Ask a confident learner to say one thing about themselves and the theme in a sentence that starts with I or My. Do the same thing with the rest of the group.

Differentiation

This section might take several weeks as learners build their confidence.

Extension

 **9.1.1 Theme cards (Entry 1 and 2/Access 1 and 2)**

Ask learners to select a card at random and say one thing about themselves associated with the card.

Activity 2 Writing simple sentences

In this activity learners begin to build a portfolio of personal information written in sentences that can be transferred later into relevant forms or letters.

Demonstrate the types of scenario where personal information is required in sentences, e.g. Internet social networking sites such as Facebook and My Space, CVs, application forms.

Explain that each learner is going to make a portfolio of useful information that can be used when completing application forms, letters and other items that require them to write about themselves. Hand out empty portfolios.

If possible, ask the group to photograph each member so that everyone has a photograph of themselves to put into their portfolios.

Other resources

A digital camera, small notebook or paper, examples of forms where personal information is needed.

Conduct a short discussion about personal appearance. Ask when learners might need to describe themselves, e.g. in a letter, on a social networking website, for a dating agency.

Model describing your own personal appearance. In pairs, ask learners to describe themselves to a partner. The role of the partner is to check the details are correct.

Play a game of 'Who am I describing?' Describe a learner and ask others to guess who it is. Ask for volunteers to describe another learner in a similar way. Write appropriate adjectives on the whiteboard or flip chart.

A 9.2.1 Personal appearance (Entry 1 and 2/Access 1 and 2)

Display the adjectives already discussed as well as those from the activity sheet. Ask learners to select suitable words from the cards to describe themselves and complete the sentences. Point out the upper case letter that starts the first word of each sentence and the full stop at the end.

Sentences can be copied into personal portfolios. Ask learners to read the sentences in their portfolios to check for sense and accuracy.

Differentiation

Limit the number of adjectives to be used. Make sure learners record these in a personal word bank.

Present each sentence one at a time and allow learners to place the correct adjective card in position before copying the whole sentence into their personal portfolios.

Ask learners to dictate any additional sentences that they feel are relevant for their own portfolio. Ask each learner to use the words in these sentences to build a personal vocabulary. This personal vocabulary can be kept on individual cards or in a small notebook and can be used by learners to create further sentences.

More confident learners will be able to complete some sentences for themselves using words from their personal word bank.

Extension

Cut sentences into individual words and ask learners to rearrange them in the correct order. Include the word beginning with a capital letter and the word that comes before the full stop.

Activity 3 Using conjunctions

Recap the sentences that learners have written about themselves. Suggest ways of making the sentences more interesting by combining sentences using conjunctions, such as: *as*, *and*, *but*.

Use the whiteboard to demonstrate how two sentences can be joined using a conjunction. Use examples from learners' experiences. Take two sentences and insert different conjunctions between them. Read the extended sentence aloud and ask learners to check for sense. Include some conjunctions that do not make sense, e.g. 'I always buy brown bread *or* I prefer peanuts.'

 **9.3.1 Joining sentences (Entry 2/Access 2)**

Cut the sentences and conjunction words into individual cards and copy multiple sets onto card.

Give each learner a set of conjunction cards and two sentences. Ask learners to find as many conjunctions as possible that could join their two sentences in a way that makes sense. After a few minutes ask learners to read out their new sentences. Repeat as many times as necessary with two new sentences.

Ask learners to decide what is wrong now that they have joined two sentences and made one. Try to elicit the response that only one capital letter and one full stop is needed in the new sentence.

Guide learners towards writing their compound sentences using correct punctuation.

Ask learners to select two random sentence cards and try to join them with as many conjunctions as possible. Discuss the different meanings they create.

When learners are comfortable joining sentences from the activity sheets, ask them to join two sentences from their own portfolio.

Cut sentences into individual words or sections and ask learners to sort the words or sections with a suitable conjunction to create a longer sentence.

Extension

 **9.3.2 Personal information (Entry 1/Access 1)**

Learners at E1/A1 can use a card from Part A to start writing a sentence about themselves. Point out the upper case letter that starts the first word of each sentence and the full stop at the end. Ask learners to copy the sentences into their portfolio, finishing the sentences with their own information from Activity Sheet 8.4.1. To reinforce the idea that a sentence must make sense, read each one aloud in a natural voice. Ask questions such as 'Does what I have just said make complete sense?' Ask learners to read each sentence.

The sentences in Part B can be used as required or more appropriate sentences can be substituted.

Activity 4 Writing more about yourself

In this activity learners begin to think about their hobbies, experience and personal qualities in preparation for completing a CV or personal statement.

Other resources

Whiteboard or flip chart.

9.4.1 Writing about your hobbies (Entry 1 and 2/Access 1 and 2)

Conduct a discussion with the group about hobbies. Write titles of hobbies on the whiteboard or flip chart. If learners need prompts, use this activity sheet cut into individual cards. Steer the discussion towards how hobbies can prepare employees for future employment. Ask learners to think about the things they do in their spare time that might be useful to them at work, e.g. using a computer, practical skills, working as part of a team.

Ask each learner to complete the sentences on the activity sheet. When they are happy with them, they can add them to their personal portfolio.

Ensure learners add relevant words to a personal dictionary or word bank.

The following activities can be used to provide more practice in different contexts.

Make sure that each activity is preceded by plenty of discussion and that extra ideas and relevant vocabulary are added to the activity sheets and each learner's personal dictionary. Make sure sentences are copied correctly into the personal portfolio and that learners check the sentences for sense and accuracy.

A 9.4.2 What else do you do? (Entry 1 and 2/Access 1 and 2)

A 9.4.3 What are you like? (Entry 1 and 2/Access 1 and 2)

A 9.4.4 What have you done? (Entry 1 and 2/Access 1 and 2)

A 9.4.5 Social networking website (Entry 1 and 2/Access 1 and 2)

Differentiation

More able learners can use a conjunction to join two sentences together.

Extension

Encourage able learners to write sentences about their hobbies, social life, qualities and experience that would be suitable to add to a CV or personal statement.

Other resources

Suitable job adverts from a local newspaper.

Activity 5 Other kinds of writing

In this activity learners can start to think about using the information collected in their personal portfolio in situations such as a formal letter or an incident report form. In each case, the information required needs to be planned carefully, checked over and copied legibly. Customise the scenarios to the needs of your learners.

 **9.5.1 Formal letter (Entry 1 and 2/Access 1 and 2)**

Discuss circumstances when a formal letter is needed, e.g. applying for a job or writing a complaint. Stress that there is no need to start each letter from scratch. Once the format is decided, the details can be altered for the particular circumstances.

Show learners the letter on this activity sheet. Customise the letter to suit the interests of your learners. Read it aloud with learners following the words.

Discuss the position of the address, the date, etc. and the reasons why each part of the letter is needed.

9.5.2 Formal letter writing plan (Entry 2/Access 2)

Give learners a copy of this activity sheet. Read it through to reiterate the points. Ask learners to cut the letter into its component parts and reassemble it.

Differentiation

Learners can substitute their own address to create a template for a letter to keep in their portfolio of information.

Provide job advertisements for learners to use as if they were applying for actual jobs.

Extension

Assist learners to create an onscreen template that they can use when applying for jobs.

9.5.3 Incident report form (Entry 2/Access 2)

Discuss the reasons for completing incident or accident forms. Ask learners to relate any incidents or accidents they might have had or know about.

Display this activity sheet on a whiteboard and discuss it in detail. What information is required in each section?

9.5.4 Incident report form cards (Entry 2/Access 2)

Distribute the cards on this activity sheet or use other relevant scenarios.

In pairs, ask learners to give an account of the incident described on the card as if the incident happened to them. Then get them to swap roles.

Repeat this activity until the learners are comfortable with the idea of reporting an incident.

Ask learners to complete the information for a form on Post-It notes and to put each piece of information into the correct position before copying it into the form.

Differentiation

Reassure learners that all the information they require is on the cards. There is no need to start each form from scratch, just substitute the relevant parts.

Create a cloze exercise where the parts of the sentences that stay the same are available with blanks for new information.

Extension

Repeat the exercise using actual forms.

Learners familiar with the Internet will find forms to print off and complete.

9.1.1 Theme cards

My job	My house	My family
My childhood	My school days	My favourite holiday
My pets	The best job I ever had	The best day I ever had
Where I live	What I like to eat	How I keep fit
What I look like	My habits	Where I was born
My worst day ever	My hobbies	What I like to watch on television
My favourite film	My favourite book	My neighbourhood
My best friend	My favourite album	The funniest thing I ever did
The worst job I ever had	My best quality	My worst quality
What I am good at	How I relax	My ambition
What makes me happy	What makes me angry	What makes me sad

9.2.1 Personal appearance

What do you look like?

Choose from the words below to complete the sentences.

My face

My face is ____________________.

I have ____________________ eyes.

I have ____________________ hair.

I have ____________________ lips.

I have a ____________________ nose.

I have ____________________ teeth.

My body

I am ____________________.

I ____________________.

I ____________________.

attractive	beautiful
big	black
blonde	blue
brown	curly
dark	even
fair	full
good-looking	green
grey	handsome
long	lovely
narrow	plump
red	rosy
round	short
slim	small
straight	tall
white	pretty

9.3.1 Joining sentences

I always buy brown bread.	I prefer peanuts.
I always eat breakfast.	It sets me up for the day.
I have to take a packed lunch.	I get up early to make it.
I like to cook food.	I buy it at the supermarket.
I like to eat crisps.	I do not eat them every day.
I like to eat out in restaurants.	I really like curry.
I never drink coffee.	It makes me feel ill.
I should eat more fruit.	I want to stay healthy.
My favourite snack is chocolate.	I eat it every day.
My favourite takeaway is pizza.	I eat it most Saturdays.

---

because	as	and
although	or	but
when	so	if

9.3.2 Personal information

Use these cards to help you begin the sentences you need for some of your personal information.

Part A

My name is
I live in
My postcode is
My date of birth is
My telephone number is

Part B

I have	brothers called
I have	sisters called
I have	children called
I have	pets called

9.4.1 Writing about your hobbies

Choose a hobby to finish these sentences.

I enjoy ____.

I like it because ______________________________________.

____.

fishing	gardening
aerobics	cycling
playing football	dancing
playing darts	running
painting	swimming
car maintenance	photography
knitting	scrapbooking
computer games	cookery
reading	jigsaw puzzles
keeping pets	DIY

9.4.2 What else do you do?

What else do you do?

Choose an activity to complete the sentences.

In my spare time I belong to ____.

I enjoy it because ____.

____.

a choir	a quiz team
a PTA	a football team
a youth club	a band
a tenants' association	a swimming club
a drama group	a church group
an angling club	a chess club
a Scout group	an adult education class
a local committee	the Territorial Army
the St John Ambulance	a hockey team
a golf club	an environmental group

9.4.3 What are you like?

Complete the sentences.

I think I am ______________________________.

I could be more ______________________________.

active	calm
efficient	experienced
funny	hard-working
lively	organised
patient	positive
professional	qualified
reliable	resourceful
sensible	serious
tolerant	helpful

9.4.4 What have you done?

Think about your life experiences.

Complete the sentences.

In my life I have ____.

This has helped me to ____.

____.

arranged parties
been on a committee
brought up children
done work experience
looked after a car
looked after a flat
looked after a motorbike
looked after household equipment
managed a household budget
operated DIY tools
raised funds

9.4.5 Social networking website

Profile edit **Friends** ▼ **Networks** ▼ **Inbox** ▼ home account logout

▼ **My profile**

Personal

About me:

Activities I enjoy:

Hobbies:

Favourite music:

Favourite books:

Favourite television shows:

9.5.1 Formal letter

10 Woodland Road
Billbrook
Hayshire
HA4 5TG

10 December 2008

The Manager
Hayshire Care Home
Hayshire
HA9 7TC

Dear Sir/Madam

I wish to apply for the job of care assistant that was advertised in the *Hayshire Times* this week.

I have worked in care homes for many years before I had my children. I now want to return to work and this seems a very interesting job.

I have enclosed a copy of my CV with this letter. I hope you will get in touch with me at the above address.

Yours faithfully

Shona Mehta

SHONA MEHTA

9.5.2 Formal letter writing plan

Write your address here so that the person you are writing to knows where to send a reply.

Write the date here.

Write the name and address of the person you are writing to here.

Write the name of the person you are writing to here. If you do not know the name, write Dear Sir/Madam.

Write what you want to say here.

If you know the name of the person you are writing to, write Yours sincerely. If you do not know the name of the person you are writing to, write Yours faithfully.

Put your signature here.

Print your name here.

9.5.3 Incident report form

INCIDENT REPORT FORM

Details of incident

Date of incident	Time of incident	Place of incident
Give full particulars of injury (e.g. cut, burn, fracture) and part of body		
What were you doing at the time of the incident?		
Describe how the incident occurred.		

9.5.4 Incident report form cards

It is 29 August at 4 p.m.

You are working in a supermarket.

You are in the fruit and vegetable department.

You are filling the shelves.

You slip on a grape that has dropped on the floor.

You twist your ankle.

You have to go to A&E.

It is 2 May at 7.30 a.m.

You are cleaning some offices.

You are in the corridor.

You are mopping the floor.

You slip on the wet floor.

You fall on your arm.

You have to go to A&E.

It is 21 March at 11.15 a.m.

You are working in a care home.

You are looking after Mr French.

You are helping to lift him into bed.

You strain your back.

You have to see your GP about it.

It is 15 November at 2.30 p.m.

You are working in a hair salon.

Mrs Banks is your client.

She is having a cut and blow dry.

You snip your finger as you are cutting her hair.

You have to see the first-aid officer in the salon.

Theme 10

Sure Skills
literacy

Reading instructions

Introduction

This theme looks at the key features of written instructions: imperatives and direct language; sequenced, often numbered steps; words indicating order; positive and negative language. The examples given could be adapted to your learners' needs.

Recognising the typical features of written instructions at work can help learners to follow them carefully and play their part in maintaining a safe working environment. At home, reading instructions accurately can mean the difference between success and failure in many scenarios such as cooking and DIY.

As a means of introducing the theme and throughout the various activities, some emphasis is also given to verbal instructions.

Learning outcomes	Adult Literacy Curriculum references	ALAN Curriculum Framework for Scotland
To be able to understand the key features of instructions	Rt/E2.1 Rt/E2.2 Rs/E2.1 Rs/E2.4	A1/A2 • Reading instructions using layout and headings to navigate a text
To be able to understand linking words and adverbials		

Activity notes

Activity 1 Introducing the theme

This activity concentrates on speaking and listening to instructions as learners become familiar with the language used in instructions.

Ask if any learners have experience of satellite navigation systems. Discuss the way instructions to the driver are worded.

Construct a maze of tables in the room. Blindfold a volunteer. Give the volunteer clear instructions to navigate the maze using as much instructional vocabulary as possible, e.g. 'First take two steps forward. Now turn right. Take three steps straight ahead. Next turn left.'

For comparison, repeat the activity using more conversational language, e.g. 'Deepak, would you mind taking two steps forward when you are ready?'

Links

Theme 11 Labels.

Key words

after, after a while, always, before, during, finally, first, if, last, meanwhile, never, next, then, when.

Other resources

A selection of instructions in different formats.

Discuss with learners which instructions were easiest to follow. Why is this?

Ask learners to take turns to navigate a partner through the maze, making their instructions as clear as possible.

Repeat the activity in different scenarios. Navigate from the teaching room to the canteen, from the canteen to the library, etc.

Model giving some instructions for learners to draw what you describe. Use the language of instructions, e.g. 'First draw a..., then draw a...' Start simply to ensure success and gradually increase the difficulty.

A 10.1.1 Instructions for drawing (Entry 1 and 2/Access 1 and 2)

In pairs, ask learners to sit back to back. One learner has a picture on a card and tells their partner what to draw. This activity sheet contains some examples but learners could come up with their own ideas. Success is measured by the similarity of the two drawings at the end of the exercise.

Discuss the difficulties learners encountered. Were the instructions given in the right order? Which words give clues about the order in which things should be done? Begin a list of suggestions on the whiteboard or flip chart for display throughout the theme.

Discuss scenarios when written instructions are used, e.g. recipes, putting together flat-pack furniture, fire drills. Show examples of each and go through the following points:

- How do we know what the instructions are for? Look at titles, statements of purpose, e.g. 'Planting your bulbs', 'Assembly instructions'.
- Why do some instructions have pictures?
- What difference do the words make? Show examples where words add detail to the instructions.
- Is the order in which we do things important? How do we know what to do first? Point out words on the whiteboard. Talk about numbered instructions.

Ask learners to sort the available instructions. Can they pick out any features, e.g. a clear title, numbering, direct language.

Give each learner a set of instructions. Ask them to point out the features as you name them.

In pairs and small groups, ask learners to cut up a set of instructions and begin to make a group display of:

- titles
- instructions with numbers
- instructions that are pictures only
- sequencing words (*first*, *next*)
- imperative verbs (***cut*** *the meat*, ***break*** *the eggs*, ***put*** *the bulb on the compost*).

These displays can be added to throughout the theme as learners become more confident with the subject.

Differentiation

Learners at E1/A1 will need to spend time concentrating on one aspect of the instructions. Some of the above activities could be used to summarise the theme rather than to introduce it.

Activity 2 What is it all about?

This activity looks at titles and statements of purpose.

Using a selection of different instructions, cut out titles and statements of purpose from the rest of the instructions and ask learners to match the pieces.

Discuss what gives us clues about which part goes with which. Expect a variety of answers. Stress that learners are using their existing knowledge of text to perform the task.

Differentiation

Ask learners to look through a magazine or newspaper and mark all the instructions they can find. They can then highlight the titles/statements of purpose, e.g. entering competitions, completing lifestyle quizzes, sending off for goods on offer.

What do learners do when they come across a word they do not understand? Suggest some tactics, e.g. ask a friend or colleague, read to the end of the sentence and go back to try to make sense, sound out the word.

Suggest learners rephrase the sentence with the new word in it into their own words to try to explain it to a friend or colleague. This tactic can be applied to reading and understanding the instructions as well as the title. Give the learners examples of this technique and model using it.

Other resources

A selection of instructions in different formats, some using pictures, some numbered, some using words alone.

Activity 3 Getting things in the right order

This activity uses familiar household tasks such as making a cup of tea to help learners concentrate on the language used to ensure instructions are performed in the correct order. Substitute more familiar scenarios if appropriate.

A 10.3.1 How to make a cup of tea (Entry 1 and 2/ Access 1 and 2)

Use this activity sheet for learners to use pictures in order to describe to a partner how to make a cup of tea. This activity sheet can also be cut up and rearranged into the correct order.

A 10.3.2 Getting things in the right order cards (Entry 1 and 2/Access 1 and 2)

A selection of cards from this activity sheet can be used to number the order chosen by learners for the instructions on Activity Sheet

10.3,1 or as prompt words to aid them when they verbalise the instructions.

A 10.3.3 Getting things in the right order wordsearch (Entry 1 and 2/Access 1 and 2)

This activity sheet can be used by learners to assist them in memorising words used to indicate the order of instructions. Ask learners to look at a word that they want to search for from the list and try to remember the first letter or groups of letters in it. Then they track left to right across the wordsearch and top to bottom to locate the letter or whole word. Ask learners to spell out the letters in each word as they find it to try to commit it to memory. They can also copy useful words into their personal word bank.

Differentiation

Learners will need lots of opportunity to give verbal instructions. Provide scenarios with which they are familiar and encourage them to practise as often as possible.

Extension

These activity sheets can be used to arrange instructions in the right sequence.

A 10.3.4 How to plant a hyacinth (Entry 1 and 2/Access 1 and 2)

A 10.3.5 Using a cashpoint machine (Entry 1 and 2/Access 1 and 2)

More confident learners may wish to create their own instructions and try them out on colleagues.

Other resources

The ingredients to make a smoothie, a blender, the ingredients to make a sandwich, a piece of string.

Activity 4 Reading things in the right order

In this activity learners are asked to read instructions.

P Presentation 10 Making a smoothie (Entry 1 and 2/Access 1 and 2)

Slide 1

This presentation shows how to make a smoothie. If possible, watch the presentation and then follow the instructions to actually make the smoothie.

Slides 2–4

Read the instructions and accentuate the words 'first', 'next' and 'then'.

Slides 5–6

Point out that sometimes there is more than one instruction in a sentence. Read the instructions and accentuate the word 'and'.

Look at slides 3 and 4 again. Could these instructions be put together? How?

A 10.4.1 How to make a sandwich (Entry 1 and 2/ Access 1 and 2)

Read the instructions on this activity sheet in stages with the learners. Discuss the language used. Ask learners to highlight the words that tell them the order in which to perform the instructions. If possible, allow learners to make the sandwich from the instructions before completing the activity sheet. If appropriate, substitute this activity with one that is very familiar to your learners, e.g. boiling an egg, making a bowl of cereal.

A 10.4.2 How to tie a reef knot (Entry 1 and 2/Access 1 and 2)

Learners can extend this activity sheet by learning how to tie other knots and teaching others how to tie them.

This activity sheet can be cut up and used to put the words into the correct order, to number the instructions in the correct order or to test the chosen order by explaining the instructions to a partner.

A 10.4.3 Credit card procedure (Entry 1 and 2/Access 1 and 2)

Learners can use this activity sheet to role-play using a credit card machine. The speech bubbles can be put in order as well as the numbered items.

Activity 5 Command words

This activity looks at how imperatives are used in instructions. Set the scene for each scenario and emphasise the fact that the examples used are not all that needs to be done to keep everyone safe from fire. Useful information can be found at www.firekills.gov.uk/leaflets/index.htm.

Discuss learners' experience of fire and what can be done to prevent it.

 10.5.1 Fire safety (Entry 1 and 2/Access 1 and 2)

Ask learners to point out the words that tell them what to do if their clothes catch fire. How many things are there to do? Do they have to be done in the right order?

Brainstorm other command words (imperatives) that tell the reader what to do from written material in the room, e.g. ***Wash*** *your cup after use*, ***switch off*** *the lights*. Extend the discussion to computer commands (*print*, *open*, *close*) and/or verbal commands (*sit down*, *stand up*).

Sometimes negative instructions are necessary (*do not switch off at the wall*, *never smoke near naked flames*). Give learners some positive and negative instructions.

Other resources

Highlighter pens, simple dictionary or thesaurus, workplace procedures and instructions, e.g. how to operate machinery, first-aid procedures, resuscitation instructions.

A 10.5.2 What to do in a fire (Entry 1 and 2/Access 1 and 2)

Display this activity sheet on a whiteboard. Read it through with the learners. Ask them to pick out the command words and highlight them. Are there any negative commands? Highlight them in a different colour.

Differentiation

Learners can work in pairs or small groups, using the most appropriate activity sheet.

A 10.5.3 What to do in a fire questions (Entry 1 and 2/Access 1 and 2)

More able learners can complete this activity sheet whereas learners at E1/A1 can complete it orally.

A 10.5.4 Fire action (Entry 1 and 2/Access 1 and 2)

Ask learners to answer the questions on this activity sheet by circling their choices. Use the sheet orally with E1/A1 learners.

A 10.5.5 How to plant a hyacinth words (Entry 1 and 2/Access 1 and 2)

Further practice can be obtained by asking learners to use this activity sheet.

Differentiation

Institute a game of 'Call My Bluff' to assist learners to guess the meaning of words which they do not immediately know. Give learners three alternative words to try in place of the one they are having trouble with and ask them to try each one in its place and decide which makes sense.

10.1.1 Instructions for drawing

Describe the drawings below to your partner and compare the two drawings.

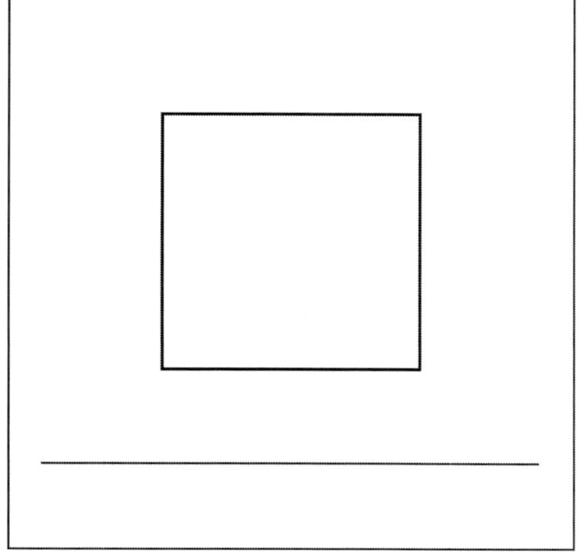

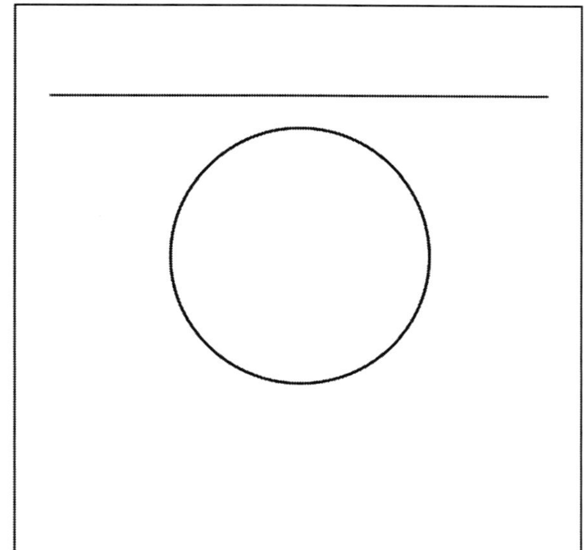

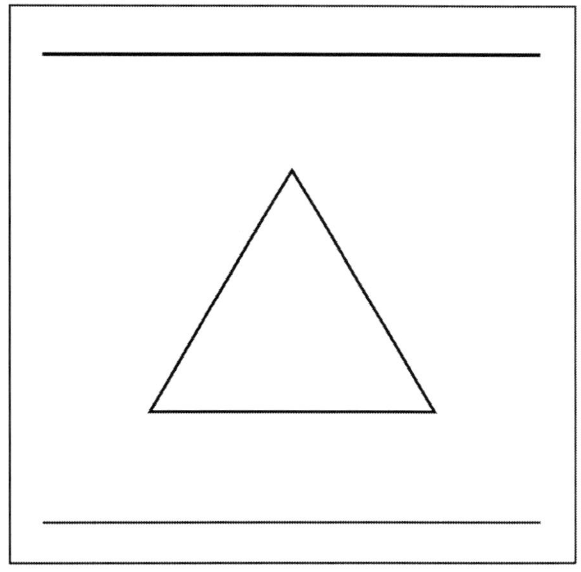

10.3.1 How to make a cup of tea

Rearrange these pictures into the correct order.

a)

b)

c)

d)

e)

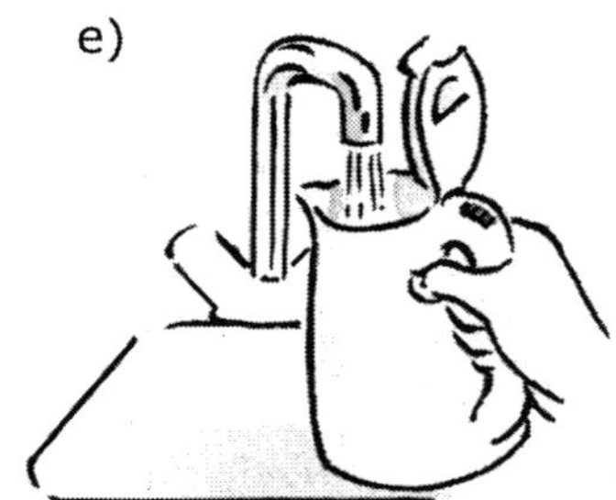

f)

g)

h)

10.3.2 Getting things in the right order cards

first	1
second	2
third	3
fourth	4
fifth	5
sixth	6
seventh	7
eighth	8
ninth	9
tenth	10
first	first of all
second	next
third	then
last	finally
before	during
meanwhile	when
never	always
if	

Note for tutor: use this with Activity Sheet 10.3.1.

10.3.3 Getting things in the right order wordsearch

Find these words in the wordsearch.

Cross off each word as you find it.

next	then	first
second	finally	last
after	before	during
while	when	always
never	if	

a	l	w	a	y	s	n	l	a
w	s	d	a	f	t	e	r	b
h	e	g	r	i	e	v	r	e
i	c	y	m	r	o	e	g	f
l	o	l	a	s	t	r	m	o
e	n	e	x	t	h	e	n	r
g	d	u	r	i	n	g	e	e
w	h	e	n	f	e	i	l	a
e	f	i	n	a	l	l	y	n

10.3.4 How to plant a hyacinth

Rearrange the pictures into the correct order.

a)

b)

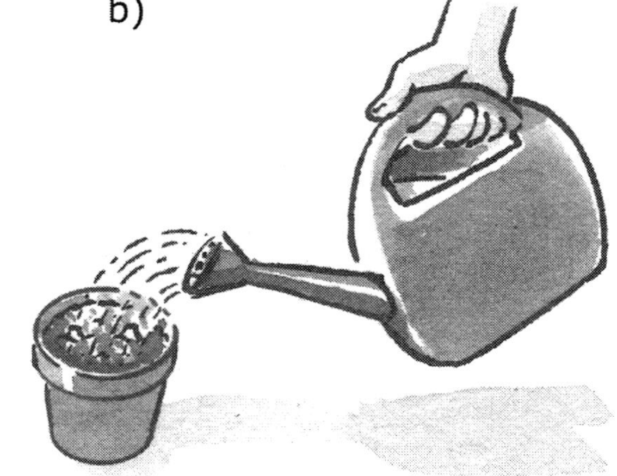

c)

d)

e)

f)

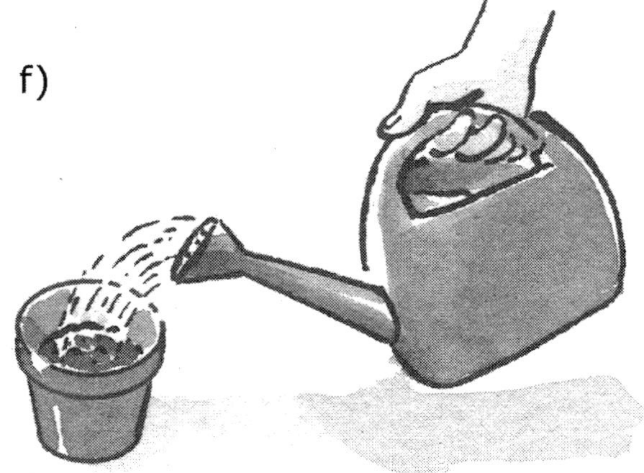

10.3.5 Using a cashpoint machine

Rearrange the pictures into the correct order.

a)

b)

c)

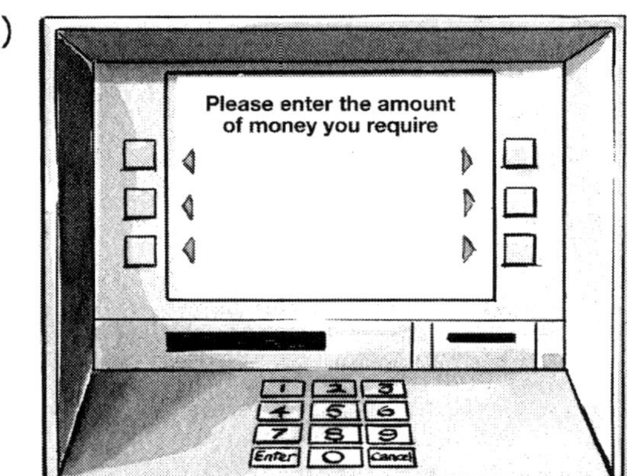

d)

e)

f)

g)

10.4.1 How to make a sandwich

Fill in the missing words.

Choose a word from the box at the bottom.

____________ gather the ingredients:

- two slices of bread
- low-fat spread
- a slice of ham
- a sliced tomato.

____________ spread the low-fat spread on the slices of bread.

____________ put the slice of ham on top of one slice of bread.

____________ put the sliced tomatoes on top of the ham.

____________ put the second slice of bread on top of the tomatoes.

____________ cut the sandwich in half.

Enjoy!

Finally	Next	After that	Then	Next	First

10.4.2 How to tie a reef knot

You will need two pieces of string.

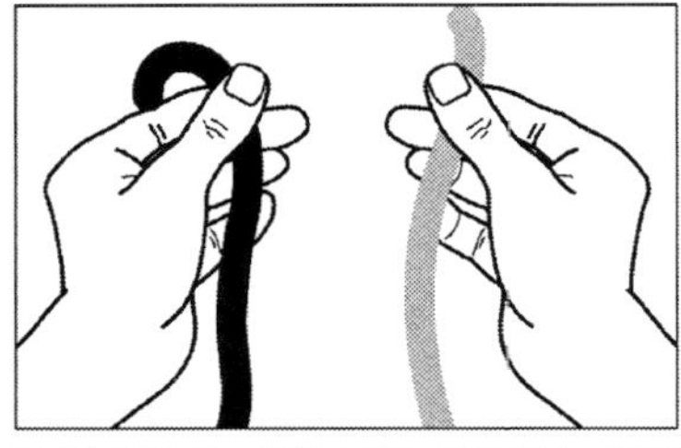

Hold one piece of string in each hand.

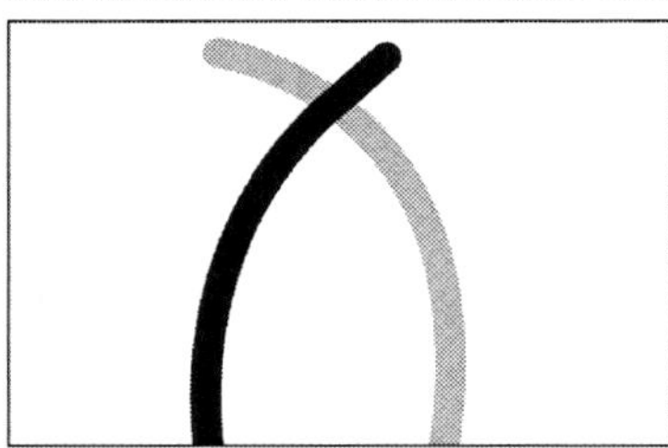

Twist the string in your left hand around the one in your right, first over...

...and then under, then over again.

Pull gently to tidy up.

Twist the string in your right hand around the one in your left, first over...

...and then under, then over again.

Pull gently to tidy up again.

10.4.3 Credit card procedure

1 Ask the customer to put their card into the slot on the machine.

2 Enter the amount in figures.

3 Press Enter.

4 Hand machine to customer.

5 Ask customer to:

- check amount is correct
- enter PIN
- press Enter
- hand machine back to you.

6 Press Enter to get a receipt for the till.

7 Press any button to get a receipt for the customer.

8 Hand the card and the receipt to the customer.

Please put your card into the slot on the machine.
Please could you check the amount is correct? Then enter your PIN and press Enter. Can I have the machine back please? Thank you.
Here are your card and receipt. Thank you.

10.5.1 Fire safety

If your clothes catch fire:

	**STOP** what you are doing immediately
	**DROP** to the floor
	**ROLL** over to put out the fire

10.5.2 What to do in a fire

Pick out the words telling you to do something and highlight them.

IN A FIRE

Immediately tell everyone.

Get out – do not waste time investigating or rescuing valuables.

Remember – use the stairs. Never use lifts in a fire.

Keep low where the air is clearer.

Call 999.

Never go back inside – wait outside for the Fire and Rescue Service.

IF THERE IS A FIRE… Get Out

Stay Out

and call

999

10.5.3 What to do in a fire questions

Use this with Activity Sheet 10.5.2

Answer the questions true, false or maybe.

Put a circle around the answers you choose.

If you find a fire where you live you should:

Tell everyone straight away	True	False	Maybe
Get out as quickly as possible	True	False	Maybe
Collect your valuables	True	False	Maybe
Collect your cat	True	False	Maybe
Use the stairs	True	False	Maybe
Use the lift	True	False	Maybe
Keep low	True	False	Maybe
Dial 999	True	False	Maybe
Go back inside	True	False	Maybe
Wait for the fire and rescue service	True	False	Maybe

10.5.4 Fire action

Use the fire action sign to help you answer the questions.

Put a circle around the answers you choose.

Fire action
Sound the alarm
Leave building by nearest available exit
Report to assembly point
Fire assembly point
Do not return to the building until authorised to do so
Do not use the lifts

1 How many times can you find the word 'fire'?

a) 1

b) 2

c) 3

2 What is another word for 'operate'?

a) push

b) cut

c) run

3 What is another word for 'exit'?

a) in

b) out

c) window

4 What is an assembly point?

a) a place for everyone to meet

b) a place to say prayers

c) a market place

5 How many things must you do?

a) 1

b) 2

c) 3

6 How many things must you **not** do?

a) 1

b) 2

c) 3

7 Write three words that tell you things you must do

____

____

8 Write down one thing you must **not** do.

____

____

10.5.5 How to plant a hyacinth words

Match the instructions to the pictures.

Half-fill the pot with compost

Water well

Place the bulbs on the compost, pointed side up

Add more compost around the bulbs

Water again

Put in a cool, dark place

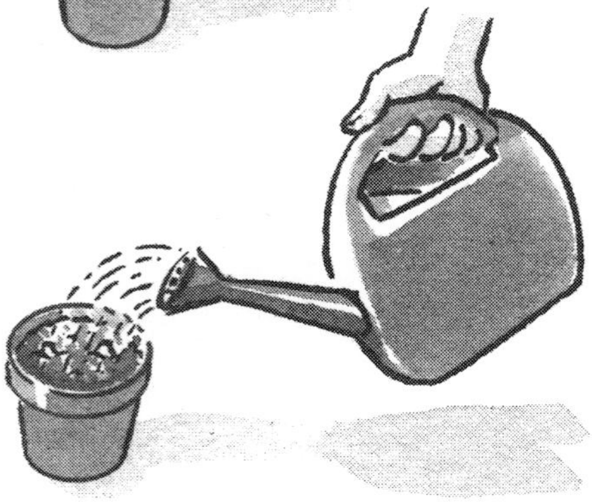

Theme 11

Labels

Introduction

At work, product labels often contain health and safety advice as well as instructions for use. At home, labels on clothes and food items also contain important information.

Labels are often printed in a small font with lots of different information vying for space. This can make labels difficult to read.

To make the information more accessible, this theme looks at the way labels are arranged and gives some practice in selecting what to read and what can be ignored. It also offers strategies for understanding difficult vocabulary.

Further information about food labelling can be found at www.foodstandards.gov.uk/multimedia/pdfs/foodlabels.pdf.

Learning outcomes	Adult Literacy Curriculum references	ALAN Curriculum Framework for Scotland
To recognise the key features of labels To understand graphical information on labels To recognise text features on labels To locate information on labels To begin to develop strategies for understanding the meaning of difficult words	Rt/E2.1 Rt/E2.4 Rs/E2.1 Rs/E2.3 Rs/E2.4 Rw/E2.3	A1/A2 • Recognising signs, symbols and social sign words • Reading for understanding

Activity notes

Activity 1 Introducing the theme

Show a variety of familiar product labels with the logos obscured to the learners. Can learners guess what the product might be?

Links

Theme 2 Signs and symbols; Theme 10 Reading instructions.

Key words

label, product, symbol.

Other resources

A selection of product labels and logos.

Discuss logos on product labels. What are they for? What do they tell you? Reveal the hidden logos or display some easily recognised ones.

Discuss what else is on a label. Find out what learners know already about labels by conducting a question-and-answer session:

- What are labels for?
- What kind of information do they contain?
- Do labels need to have certain information by law?
- Why do you need to know that information?
- How do you know where to look and what to look for?

Give some examples, such as someone with high blood pressure who has been advised to cut down on salt; someone using a cleaning product at work who would need to know how to dilute it; someone washing a jumper for the first time who would need to know what temperature water to use. Ask learners for further examples from their own experience.

A CD 11.1.1 Salt and vinegar crisps (Entry 1 and 2/ Access 1 and 2)

Display this activity sheet on a whiteboard. Acknowledge how difficult the text is. Why is it difficult? Ask for suggestions from learners, e.g. small text, difficult vocabulary, use of capital letters, mixture of numbers and letters.

Point out and discuss the key features of the packet:

- logo (remind learners of previous discussion)
- description of the product
- symbols – why are symbols used?
- ingredients – why do you need to know what is in a product? Ingredients have to be listed in order of quantity in the product, with the greatest first
- nutritional information – discuss the traffic light system
- details of the manufacturer – why might you need to know this?
- bar code – what is this for?

Read through all the text so that learners can follow. Take time for learners to decide the importance of each of the features and the relevance to their lives.

Cut the crisp packet into different sections. Which section is most important to learners? Which section would the learner not usually need to read? Ask learners to prioritise the importance of each section.

Discuss the symbols in more detail. Why are symbols used? How could learners find out what they mean? To add to their knowledge, ask them to collect symbols throughout this theme.

Discuss the text in more detail. Are there any words that learners are unfamiliar with? How could they find out what they mean? At this stage accept suggestions and add any you feel are relevant.

Differentiation

To avoid confusion, cover the sections of the label not under discussion.

Cut the label into sections and present learners with one section at a time.

Present learners with their own copy of the activity sheet to mark up or highlight as you discuss each section.

For Entry 2/A2 learners, use the following sheet:

 **11.1.2 Salt and vinegar crisps (Entry 2/Access 2)**

Extension

Use the following activities to give more practice in different contexts. All the sheets can be used as E1 and 2/A1 and 2.

11.1.3 Dogs' Dinner pet

 11.1.4 Dogs' Dinner pet food

 11.1.5 Red Square

 11.1.6 Red Square Cement

The exercises on Activity Sheets 11.1.1 and 11.1.2 can be reinforced for different scenarios using these activity sheets.

Activity 2 Words on labels

This activity looks at common phrases used on labels as well as discussing how the meaning of unknown words in text can be ascertained.

  **11.2.1 Words on labels (Entry 1 and 2/Access 1 and 2)**

Ensure learners recognise all the products. Give a few examples and then ask for suggestions of what might be written on each product's label.

Select five sentences or phrases from this sheet that contain words which learners are unlikely to recognise. Model the following methods of deciding on the meaning of unknown words:

- *Ask a colleague to explain*. Display a written phrase on the whiteboard and ask for suggestions about what it says. Acknowledge correct answers. If there are learners who are unfamiliar with one or more of the words, explain any difficult words and rephrase them. Ask learners to put the whole phrase into their own words to check for understanding.
- *Read to the end of the sentence.* Display another phrase, this time read from the beginning of the sentence, stopping at the difficult word, missing it out and reading on to the end of the sentence. Ask learners for suggestions for what the missing

Other resources

A selection of food, household and garden products with labels.

word might be. Rephrase the sentence and ask learners to do the same.

- *Use a dictionary*. Display another phrase. Look up the difficult word in a dictionary and substitute the given meaning for the word in the sentence to check for sense.
- *Use visual clues*. Display another phrase. Is the shape of the word familiar? Does it look like another word that you know? Model using visual clues to decide what a word might be. Try out potential meanings in the sentence.
- *Use phonic clues*. Display another phrase. Does the unknown word contain letters that can be sounded out? Model sounding a word out.

Distribute all the phrases from this activity sheet to learners individually or in pairs. Ask them to use the above techniques to read what their phrase says. Display a product. Learners with appropriate phrases should call out their phrase. Acknowledge correct answers. Display another product and continue until every learner has called out at least once. Reassign the phrases to different learners.

Distribute copies of this activity sheet. Ask learners to match the products with phrases and record their answers on the sheet.

Differentiation

For less confident learners limit the number of phrases to be used.

Extension

Learners within particular vocational areas might need to work on particular symbols found on work products, e.g. planting instructions in horticulture; precautions when using particular chemicals in cleaning, building or hairdressing; storage instructions for food.

A CD 11.2.2 More words on labels/11.2.3 More words on labels (Entry 1 and 2/Access 1 and 2)

These activity sheets can be used to investigate different words on labels.

Extend the activity to other words found in the text of labels.

Learners can add important words to their word bank.

Activity 3 Knowing where to look

P Presentation 11 Knowing where to look (Entry 1 and 2/Access 1 and 2)

This presentation looks at different fonts and colours on labels and how they can be used as an aid to reading the text. Learners with a good grasp of ICT will be able to use their skills to create a label.

Slide 1

Discuss the idea of buying a sandwich at lunchtime. How do learners choose which one to buy? Do they go for the healthy option? Or vegetarian? All this information is on the label.

Slide 2

Read the text and discuss the logo. What does the colour green suggest? What about the size? Why are the words 'Cheese and spring onion' written bigger and bolder than 'mayonnaise'? Why is 'white bread' slightly smaller?

Slide 3

Discuss the traffic lights wheel. How are the colours used? What does this symbol tell you about this sandwich?

Slide 4

Why is 'Keep refrigerated' written in upper case letters?

Slide 5

Why is the price and the use by date contained in a box?

Quickly run through the presentation again. Ask learners to summarise why different parts of the label are presented in different ways.

Show another label. Does it show the same information? Which parts do learners look at first and why? Which parts are important and why? Are there any parts they do not need to read?

Differentiation

Give E1/A1 learners a copy of slide 6 and ask them to talk about the different fonts and features.

Give learners the same information written in a simple font in a Microsoft Word document. Ask them to customise the information using different colours and fonts. Compare the results.

Extension

11.3.1 More words on labels questions (Entry 2/Access 2)

To help learners become more familiar with labels, ask them to complete this activity sheet. Ask learners at E1/A1 to answer the questions orally.

11.3.2 Design a label (Entry 1 and 2/Access 1 and 2)

In pairs or small groups, ask learners to invent a product.

Learners can use this activity sheet to help them create a label for their product either by hand or using ICT.

11.1.1 Salt and vinegar crisps

CRISPs 4U
Potato crisps with sea salt and vinegar
INGREDIENTS: potatoes, sunflower oil, sea salt, dried vinegar, potato maltodextrin, white sugar, citric acid.
Best before 25.08.2008
NUTRITIONAL INFORMATION
Typical Values Per 100g
Energy 1992kj/4767kcal
Protein 5.9g
Carbohydrates 56.8g
of which sugars 2.9g
Fat 25.0g
of which saturates 2.6g
Fibre 4.5g
Sodium 0.75g
Store in a cool, dry place away from bright lights.
Each 30g serving contains:
Calories 143 7%
Sugar 0.9% 1%
Fat 7.5% 11%
Saturates 0.8g 4%
Salt 0.6g 10%
Made in England by Crisps 4U,
Hayshire Industrial Est.
Hayshire HA1 2PC
www.crisps4u.co.uk
1 25002 74135 0
30g
Salt and Vinegar
CRISPs 4U
Suitable for vegans and coeliacs
Contains no artificial flavours or colours
Free from monosodium glutamate

11.1.2 Salt and vinegar crisps questions

Use this with Activity Sheet 11.1.1.

Put a circle around the answers you choose.

How much does the packet weigh?
1.5g 30g 60g
What colour is the packet?
blue red green
The crisps contain no artificial flavours.
true false
What is the main ingredient?
potatoes salt vinegar
Which country are the crisps made in?
France England USA
The crisps contain all the salt you need in one day.
true false

11.1.3 Dogs' Dinner pet food

Dogs'

Dinner

Original with
Chicken and
Sunflower Oil

Easily digestible

For strong teeth
and healthy coat

Benefits the
immune system

Dogs' Dinner

For adult dogs

Dogs' Dinner Original with chicken and sunflower oil is a highly palatable, tasty and complete pet food for adult dogs

Feeding Guide:

Size	Weight	Tins per day without mixer	Tins per day with mixer
Toy	Up to 5kg	Up to 1	Up to ½
Small	5kg–10kg	1–2	½–1
Medium	10kg–20kg	2–3	1–1½
Large	20kg–35kg	3–5	1½–2½

An individual dog's requirements may differ from this guide. Adjust the amount given to keep your dog in a lean, active condition. Lactating bitches may require up to four times as much food as their normal intake. Dogs' Dinner Original is suitable for weaned puppies and senior dogs.

Typical anaysis
Moisture 81% Protein 7% Oil 6% Ash 4% Fibre 1%
Vitamins A, D, E

Ingredients
Meat and animal derivatives (chicken 4% min), Vegetable Protein Extracts, Oils and Fats (sunflower oil 2% min), Minerals, Colour and Preservative. 400g

Produced in the EU for
Dogs' Dinner
www.dogsdinner.co.uk

If you are not entirely satisfied with this product, let us know on the Dogs' Dinner customer care line 01234 567898

Storage
Store unopened in a cool, dry place

Remember Fresh drinking water should always be available

RECYCLABLE STEEL

11.1.4 Dogs' Dinner pet food questions

Use this with Activity Sheet 11.1.3.

Marcus is talking to the owner of a pet shop.

Answer his questions.

How much does the dog food in this tin weigh?
What flavour is the meat in this tin?
What about if I give her mixer? How many tins then?
My dog weighs 6kg. How many tins should I give her every day with no mixer?
Is there anything else I should remember?
How much of this tin is moisture?

11.1.5 Red Square Cement

RED SQUARE CEMENT

When you need the best, choose RED SQUARE

For your concrete or mortar needs follow the mixing guide below

MIXING GUIDE

GENERAL PURPOSE CONCRETE:	1 Part Cement 2 Parts Sharp Sand 3 Parts Gravel
MORTAR:	1 Part Cement 4 Parts Sharp Sand

The amount of water will vary.
As a guide start with 10 litres per 25kg of cement.
Additional water may be added to achieve the correct consistency for the job.

Always mix cement on a clean, flat surface or in a clean cement mixer.
Mix dry ingredients before adding water.
Wash all tools thoroughly after use.

Health and safety Advice

Risk of serious damage to eyes.

Risk of damage to skin.

Always wear appropriate PPE.

Avoid breathing in dust.

If contact with skin or eyes occurs, rinse immediately with plenty of water.

If contact with eyes occurs, seek medical advice immediately.

Keep out of reach of children

IRRITANT

24-hour helpline 0800 123456

11.1.6 Red Square Cement questions

Use this with Activity Sheet 11.1.5.

Joseph has never used cement before. What does he need to be aware of?

Answer his questions.

When I am using cement there is a risk of serious damage to my ___________.
There is also a risk of damage to my ___________.
I should always wear appropriate ___________.
If contact with my skin or eyes occurs, I should rinse them immediately with plenty of ___________.
If contact with my eyes occurs, I should also seek ___________ advice immediately.
I should avoid breathing in ___________.
To make mortar I need to mix 1 part cement with ___________ parts sharp sand.

11.2.1 Words on labels

Match the words with the product.

There is more than one correct answer.

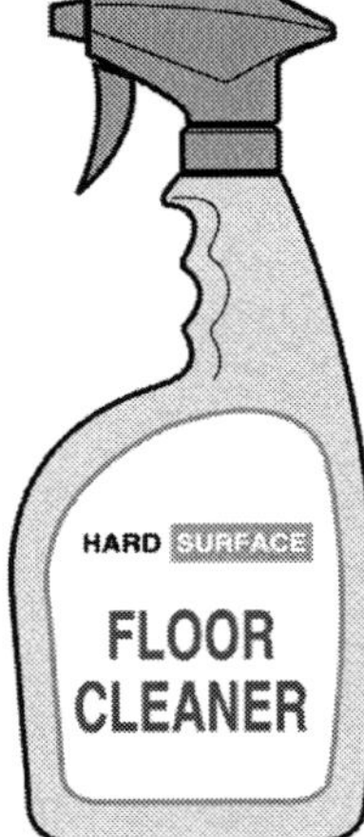

May contain nuts

Keep out of reach of children

Shake well before use

Wash hands after use

Use within 2 weeks of opening

Do not breathe spray

Once opened keep refrigerated and use within 3 days

Store in a cool, dry place

If splashed in eyes, rinse out with plenty of water

Do not use if safety button can be depressed before opening

Gluten-free

See cap for best before end date

Do not use on leather, suede or silk

11.2.2 More words on labels

Fran is going to buy a new fridge freezer. You can see the label from it below.

Put a circle around the answers you choose.

1. A is the letter that tells you that a fridge freezer is very energy efficient.	True	False	Maybe
2. G is the letter that tells you that a fridge freezer is not at all energy efficient.	True	False	Maybe
3. This is the most energy-efficient fridge freezer there is.	True	False	Maybe
4. This fridge freezer is very noisy.	True	False	Maybe
5. This fridge freezer uses a lot of power every year.	True	False	Maybe

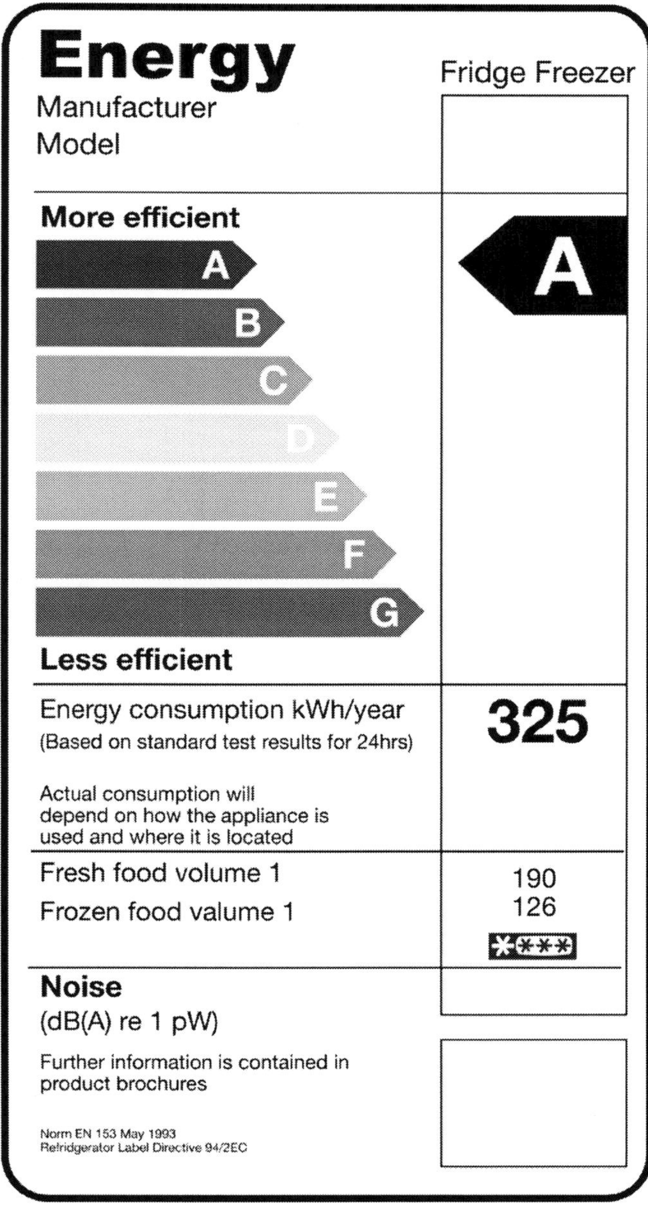

Energy
Fridge Freezer
Manufacturer
Model
More efficient
A
B
C
D
E
F
G
A
Less efficient
Energy consumption kWh/year
(Based on standard test results for 24hrs)
325
Actual consumption will depend on how the appliance is used and where it is located
Fresh food volume 1
Frozen food valume 1
190
126
Noise
(dB(A) re 1 pW)
Further information is contained in product brochures
Norm EN 153 May 1993
Refridgerator Label Directive 94/2EC

11.3.1 More words on labels questions

Marina is going to buy a new car. You can see the label from it below.

Put a circle around the answers you choose.

6. A is the letter that tells you that a car does not use much petrol.	True	False	Maybe
7. G is the letter that tells you that a car uses a lot of petrol.	True	False	Maybe
8. This car uses a lot of petrol.	True	False	Maybe
9. This car does not use much petrol.	True	False	Maybe
10. There is a car that uses less petrol.	True	False	Maybe

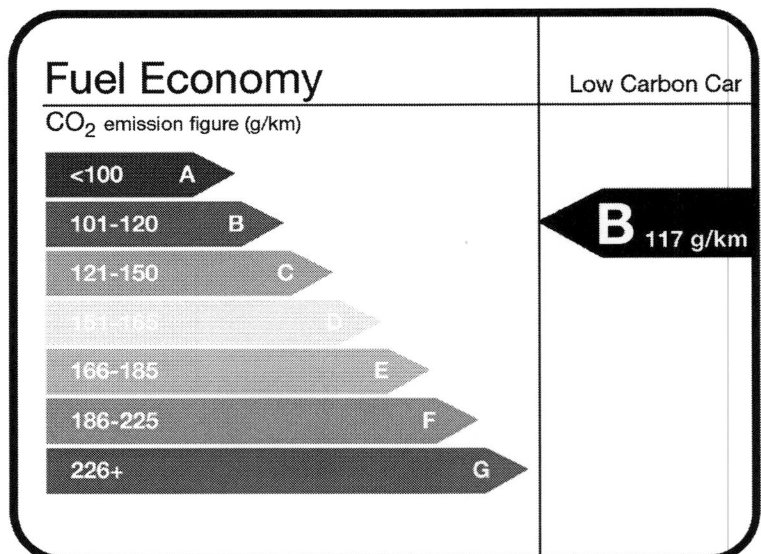

11.3.2 Design a label

Write the name of your product here	
Insert a picture of your product here	Write what your product is for here
Write what is in your product here	Write how to use your product here
Write any health and safety advice here